THE GLOBAL SHOPPER

THE GLOBAL SHOPPER

Richard McBrien

HEADLINE

First published in Great Britain in 1994
by HEADLINE BOOK PUBLISHING

10 9 8 7 6 5 4 3 2 1

ISBN 0-7472-7864-4

Typeset by Avon Dataset Ltd., Bidford-on-Avon

Printed and bound in Great Britain by
Mackays of Chatham PLC, Chatham, Kent

HEADLINE BOOK PUBLISHING
A division of Hodder Headline PLC
338 Euston Road
London NW1 3BH

Contents

v

Part 1
MAIL ORDER BASICS

1 Introduction

A few years ago ordering goods from overseas was considered exotic, glamorous and perhaps even a little foolhardy. Restricted to people living in remote areas or eccentric specialists seeking unusual equipment, it was the province of just a handful of firms. Today the market is crowded with companies from all over the world jostling for international custom.

There are several reasons for this rapid growth, from the popularity of the credit card – which has made complex currency transactions virtually invisible – through to the emergence of private courier companies and the development of global brands, such as Sony and Apple. In addition, as more and more people travel so they have become aware of what is available in other countries – both in terms of goods and prices.

It is a small step from there to continue to order from back home. With improved telecommunications an international call is no longer complex or even expensive. Currency exchange is handled by the credit card companies and most multi-national manufacturers now offer world-wide guarantees on their products regardless of where they were purchased. And of course with the advent of the Free Market in the EC, European consumers no longer have to pay duty on goods ordered from within the Community. All of this has come together to make international mail order both easy and popular.

However, until now there has been a major obstacle preventing this new form of shopping from truly taking off – a lack of information. While many people would like to order from overseas they simply do not know how to go about it or who to contact. It is precisely these problems which **The Global Shopper** addresses.

As a comprehensive guide to who is selling what world-wide it enables the consumer to make intelligent, informed decisions about where to buy goods. In addition, it provides a simple-to-follow procedure for ordering from overseas and gives clear advice on such things as international guarantees, safety regulations and consumer rights.

HOW THE BOOK IS ORGANIZED

The Global Shopper is divided into three sections. The first, Mail Order Basics, is a detailed discussion of procedures: ordering catalogues, ways of paying, dealing with Customs, how to complain and so on. This is followed by the Directory, a list of international companies who ship overseas, listed by product category. Finally, the Appendices contain reference material, such as rates of duty, cost of postage and insurance, international clothing sizes and useful addresses. In addition, at the end of the book there are two indexes, one by product, the other by company.

♦ **WARNING!** Before going any further it is as well to establish that not everything is worth importing from abroad. Some items are too heavy, others are incompatible, others still are simply cheaper at home.

And of course one always has to keep an eye on two things: the current exchange rate and the cost of duty and tax. It is vital to add up the TOTAL cost of the goods BEFORE parting with any money. The formula for doing this is given in the *Quick User's Guide*, below. Many people have jumped in, ordered items with their credit card and then been horrified by the final cost.

NOTE TO READERS OUTSIDE THE UK

The Global Shopper is intended to be used by readers all over the world. However, the bias IS towards consumers resident in the UK and European Community. Obviously the directory entries are applicable to virtually everywhere, although if you live in a particularly obscure part of the world it is best to check with individual suppliers before sending off any money.

2 Basic Procedures

Many people are put off ordering goods from overseas because they think it is complicated, costly and unreliable. Nothing could be further from the truth. Thanks to modern technology it is as easy to buy something from abroad as it is within your own country. However, you do have to be aware of how the system works and of potential pitfalls.

THE MAIL ORDER BUSINESS

International mail order houses operate like any other mail order companies, in fact most are large domestic suppliers who have simply expanded their market worldwide. The majority issue catalogues (usually in their own language and/or English) but some simply have a price list or ask customers to call for further information. These usually sell specialized items, such as antiques, or have such a large range of products and prices that a catalogue would be impractical.

Most catalogues are free but some companies do charge to send them abroad (in many cases the price is refundable on the first order). This is largely to deter the 'catalogue collector', who sends off for anything free but rarely orders. We would urge readers to avoid this temptation since it only increases costs for the suppliers who will in the end pass them on to the consumer.

ORDERING A CATALOGUE

Despite the name, most mail order catalogues are not requested by post. The phone or fax is preferable and seems to elicit a faster response. Payment should be made in local funds, usually by credit card (see *Methods of Payment*, below).

While many catalogues arrive with astonishing speed (for example, two days from the US to the UK), others, sent by Fourth Class Mail or as Printed Matter, can take up to six weeks. In addition, the process can be slowed down by the time of year you happen to place your order. Many companies issue several catalogues a year (commonly Winter, Spring, Summer and Autumn) and if you happen to hit the middle of one period you may have to wait until the new catalogue is ready.

ORDERING THE GOODS

Nearly all catalogues have simple-to-follow order forms but there are a number of tips worth noting.

- It is often better to call or fax your order since this gets a quicker response. It is also useful to speak to someone in case the price has changed, the item is no longer available and so on.

- If ordering over the phone, fill in the form as if you were mailing it. You can then read off the information in the correct order for the sales assistant to take down and thereby save phone time and eliminate errors.

  Remember to spell out unusual words (which may be the entire address) and assign words to any letters in post codes, i.e. SE22 would be S for sugar, E for Edward... The assistant may be entirely unfamiliar with your country's address format so indicate when to start a new line.

- If writing, make sure your address is clear. This may seem obvious but many stories of woe can be traced back to a jumbled address. If filling in an order form always write in capitals. Faxed handwriting can come out 'bitty' so be sure to write clearly in a bold, dark colour and never use pencil.

- Lay out your address in the correct way for YOUR country. Order forms tend to format addresses for the domestic market and can therefore wreak havoc with foreign addresses if you follow them slavishly. This is particularly true of postal codes, which can end up jumbled, in the wrong place or even missing altogether. It is therefore best to make absolutely clear how you want your address laid out, even if you have to place a label over the printed form and ignore the assigned boxes.

- Remember to put your country. It may seem obvious but is easy to forget.

- When ordering by credit card make each number clear – it is easy to confuse 0 with 9 and 7 with 1. Write 1s as straight lines and do not put a slash through the middle of a 7 as this can get confused with a 3. Write zeros as 0 not as Ø. Split up the credit card number into a series of digits rather than one long number which can be misread. And of course do not forget to include the expiry date of the card, written as a number not as a full date, e.g. 11/94 rather than November 94.

METHODS OF PAYMENT

There are now many ways to arrange international payment, most of them extremely simple.

Credit Cards

A credit card enables you to pay in your currency while suppliers get paid in theirs. The exchange itself is handled invisibly by the credit card company. This makes the whole transaction as simple as buying something down the road.

However, not all suppliers take cards. Companies in the US, UK and South East Asia are the best in this regard with the vast majority accepting credit card orders both by mail and over the phone. The picture is very different in continental Europe. Card ownership is more expensive here and therefore less widespread. In addition, mail order houses are not used to taking credit card payment over the phone – indeed many are horrified at the thought of doing so! This situation should improve as the Community becomes more unified but meanwhile other methods of payment may have to be used (see below).

Which cards to use

The two cards most widely accepted are Visa and Mastercard (also called Access in the UK and Eurocard in Europe). Diners Club and American Express are far less popular, even in America itself. This is because they can be more complicated and expensive for the merchant to process.

Ordering with a credit card

When ordering by credit card you need to supply the following information:

> the card number
> the expiry date
> the full name as on the card
> the billing address

Many suppliers will only send goods to the billing address of the card and indeed strictly speaking they are required to do so. However, sometimes they will accept sending items to a different address as long as they have both.

How it works

When you give your details, either in writing or over the telephone, the merchant makes a record of these in one of two ways. They can write out a voucher by hand, including your number, expiry date and address, and put 'Phone Order' where you would sign. Alternatively, they can enter just the number and expiry date into an electronic terminal.

The merchant then banks the order. In the case of an electronic terminal this can be done instantly down a phone line. With a voucher, it is usually physically banked at the end of the day. There is then some delay while the bank processes it.

The actual transaction occurs when the credit card company is informed of the order and this is the moment when the exchange of currency takes place. It can therefore be difficult to predict EXACTLY what the exchange rate will be, since the transaction may happen some time after you have given the details to the supplier.

Your card statement will show how much you paid but will not include the exchange rate. Instead it will look something like this:

11 Dec   Voucher for 7341.00 on 4 Dec from XXX   43.29

The first date is for the transaction (i.e. when the currency exchange was made) while the second is when the card was actually used. In this case there was a seven day gap.

The number after 'Voucher for' is the local currency (in this case 7,341 Spanish Pesetas) and the XXX the name of the supplier. Finally, there is the amount you have been charged in pounds (or whatever your own currency is). Only by dividing the two numbers can you work out the exchange rate used by the credit card company. Here it is $7341.00 \div 43.29 = 169.57$ Pesetas to the Pound.

Fraud

Some people are reluctant to give their credit card details over the phone – especially abroad – in case they get charged for items they never ordered. Certainly this is possible; after all, if someone has all your details they could ring up another supplier pretending to be you. However, it is most unlikely that a reputable supplier will misuse your card. They are carefully checked by the card issuing authorities and if there is any hint of fraud their merchant privileges are removed.

If there has been fraudulent use of a card, the supplier is responsible, not you. They will therefore have to reimburse the money in full and suffer the loss themselves.

To minimize fraud:

- Always check your credit card bill as soon as it arrives and BEFORE paying it.

- If you find an item which you have not authorised, contact the credit card company immediately and ask for 'proof of purchase'. You might like to settle the remainder of the bill along with a letter explaining why you are withholding the disputed amount.

The credit card company will now contact the supplier and ask for further information. It is the supplier's responsibility to prove that it was indeed a genuine order. They will need to produce either the original, signed voucher or, in the case of a phone order, your full name and address as well as details of what you ordered and when.

If they are unable to provide these you will not be charged. But remember NOT to pay the disputed amount before you question it – it is far more difficult to get it back once you have paid it.

Points to watch for

Although paying by credit card is very simple and efficient there are a couple of points to watch for.

- Does the mail order house add a fee for taking cards? All suppliers who accept credit cards have to pay a percentage to the credit card company, typically 4% of the transaction. Most simply absorb this as an overhead, but a number have taken to adding it as a fee, so there is one price by cheque and another by card. They may even add a further fee if the card originates outside the country. This is relatively rare but it is as well to ask up front rather than get an unpleasant shock later.

- Beware of credit card companies themselves charging for making a foreign currency transaction. Again, most do not but it is worth checking. In the UK the main companies, Access and Visa, do not currently charge. The position may be different in other countries.

Other Methods of Payment

Although credit cards are by far the easiest way to pay, some people may not have one or come across suppliers who do not take them. In either case you will have to choose another way of paying.

Sending a normal cheque from your own bank, in your local currency, is a waste of time. It is far too expensive and time consuming for the company to bank this and they will either return the cheque (if you are lucky) or simply throw it away and you will be left for weeks wondering what is going on. You therefore need to use special services to send money abroad.

Essentially these break down into systems which use your own bank and those which do not. None is ideal and all can be expensive. For example the minimum charge on a bank transfer would cover two years' fee for a UK credit card. They can also be slow, taking a minimum of four days (the so-called Express services) and a maximum of seven working days.

Security is not always guaranteed and if payments do get lost in the system the bank may have no legal obligation to reimburse you. It is therefore necessary to take out separate insurance.

Services available from banks

The following information refers mainly to the UK but is likely to be similar in other countries, although charges may vary. Most large banks will offer these services, although not all their branches may do so – check by phone first.

INTERNATIONAL MONEY TRANSFER

Here the money is transferred directly from your bank account to the supplier's. This can be done either by mail or telex.

Typical costs:	25p per £100
	Minimum charge £13
	Maximum £19
Security	Good but not guaranteed

BANK DRAFT

This is a cheque written out to the supplier in their own currency which you then send forward yourself.

Typical costs:	25p per £100
	Minimum charge £13
	Maximum charge £40
	Express £6 extra
Security	Relies on postal system. You can buy insurance from the Post Office for some but not all countries.

INTERNATIONAL MONEY ORDER

A cheque drawn in US $ for amounts up to $1,000. You then send it to the supplier yourself.

Typical cost:	£7
Security	Relies on postal system. You can buy insurance from the Post Office for some but not all countries.

EUROCHEQUE

The big four High Street banks – Midland, Lloyds, National Westminster and Barclays – all issue Eurocheques. In the rest of the EC they are available from large national banks. They operate in exactly the same way as a normal cheque book but can be written in European currencies. Suppliers cash them in the same way they would a domestic cheque while your account is debited in your own currency. It is perhaps the easiest and best way to pay European suppliers. Each bank has different rates, so it is worth shopping around.

Typical costs:	£7.50 – £9.00pa for card and cheque book Cost per cheque: 1.6% of amount Minimum charge 80p Maximum charge £3.50 (Some banks charge a fixed fee of £1.90 per cheque) Maximum payment per cheque £700
Security	Relies on postal system. You can buy insurance from the post office for some but not all countries

ACCOUNTS IN FOREIGN CURRENCIES

Most large banks will allow you to open an account in a foreign currency. However, there may be a minimum deposit as well as service charges. For a small number of transactions it is therefore not worth it.

Typical costs:	Minimum deposit $1,000–$3,000 (depending on bank) Service charge £60 pa
Other charges	(e.g. bank transfers) at above rates

You can also open 'off-shore' foreign currency accounts. These come with cheque books which can be used in the US and other countries. However, there are charges of around £50 per year and you have to watch the tax position carefully.

Other services

TIPANET

The Co-Op Bank in the UK offers its own system of money transfer to selected countries for a very reasonable fixed fee of £5. The money is transferred from the local branch to the Co-Op's international section where it is fed directly into the recipient country's clearing system.

One of the attractive features, apart from the cost, is that it is available for Canada as well as most European countries. The process takes from four to seven days, though if you are not a Co-Op customer they may wait to clear your cheque to them. You need the supplier's full bank details, i.e. name, sort code and account number.

Cost:	£5 per transfer, regardless of amount
Countries	Austria
	Belgium
	Canada
	France
	Germany
	UK
	Italy
Contact:	Any Co-Op bank. Call their head office for details of one in your area. (in UK 071 480 5171)

GIRO

The Girobank, which in the UK is run by the Post Office, offers another cheap way of sending money abroad, especially to Europe. There are two services for sending money to companies: cheque and Giro transfer.

The cheque method involves the Girobank writing out a cheque in a foreign currency which you forward to the supplier.

Giro transfer works by money being directly transferred from one Giro account to another. This may not seem useful but in fact many

---

European companies do use the Giro system and have accounts. The charge for Giro account holders is a very reasonable £5 (it costs nothing to set up an account).

Cost:	Cheque:	£15 fixed fee
	Giro Transfer:	£15 fixed fee
		£5 fixed fee for Giro account holders

COUNTRIES COVERED BY GIRO

Name	Cheque	Giro	Name	Cheque	Giro
Algeria	•		Luxembourg	•	•
Australia	•		Malaysia	•	
Austria	•	•	Malta	•	
Bahrain	•		Netherlands	•	•
Bangladesh	•		New Zealand	•	
Belgium	•	•	Norway	•	•
Canada	•		Oman	•	
Cyprus	•		Pakistan	•	
Denmark	•	•	Philippines	•	
Finland	•	•	Portugal	•	
France	•	•	Qatar	•	
Germany	•	•	Singapore	•	
Greece	•		South Africa	•	
Hong Kong	•		Spain	•	•
Iceland	•		Sweden	•	
India	•		Switzerland	•	•
Indonesia	•		Thailand	•	
Ireland	•		Turkey	•	
Italy	•	•	UK	•	•
Japan	•	•	USA	•	

Contact:
International Banking Branch, Girobank plc, Triad, Stanley Road, Bootle, L20 3LT, Tel: 051 933 3330
Or any Post Office

3 Delivery

There are two main ways goods are shipped from overseas, either via the normal mail or by a private carrier.

The mail is the cheapest and simply means your goods are packaged up and sent through the mail service of the country you have ordered from. You can elect to use either Air Mail or Surface Mail. The former is more expensive, at about twice the cost of Surface Mail, but of course has the advantage of speed.

Surface Mail goes by sea and takes a VERY long time, especially if it is from another continent. For example, a package from the US to the UK will take around twelve weeks. If you are not in a hurry this is fine but most people find the extra cost of Air Mail well worth it.

Printed Matter has its own set of rates which are much cheaper but the package has to be unsealed (i.e. only tied up with string), must genuinely only contain printed matter and, despite going Air Mail, can still take a rather long time (hence the delay in receiving some catalogues).

The quality and speed of postal systems varies from country to country. In Europe, statistics show that the UK is the most efficient, followed by Germany and France with Italy and Greece bringing up the rear. Here the service can be appalling and delays of several weeks are not uncommon.

Private carriers offer a similar service to Air Mail and have their own fleet of planes and vans. They are more expensive but have the advantage of being quicker, usually delivering packages from anywhere to anywhere within four or five days (US to UK in 48 hours). Typical companies are USP, Federal Express, DHL and TNT.

Private carriers offer an excellent service and if you are ordering something large, expensive and fragile – such as a computer or fax machine – then the extra cost is well worthwhile. For smaller, less valuable goods the mail is a perfectly good alternative.

Some people find that Customs tend to be more thorough with private carriers while packages in the ordinary mail sometimes slip through without attracting any duty. I have no personal evidence that this is true but it might be worth bearing in mind.

You can usually choose which method of shipping you want on the order form. Some American companies give you a number of options including 'Best Way' which means they use their discretion. However, it is preferable to choose yourself so that you can work out the exact charge before paying.

In most cases the supplier will add the cost of shipping to your original invoice but occasionally they supply goods COD. This is to be avoided since there is an extra charge for the service, of around 3%. (Consumers in Germany are very used to paying COD but will find nearly all international mail order companies prefer not to trade in this way.)

4 *Insurance*

While it is rare for goods to arrive broken or damaged it happens often enough to warrant taking out insurance. Most merchants will offer some kind of cover, either through the mail/courier company or with a policy of their own. Make sure this includes accidental damage, loss in transit and the expense of return postage if a repair is necessary. Also establish whether you are entitled to a full rebate or have to pay an excess yourself (i.e. the first x number of pounds).

To make claims easier, keep a copy of all correspondence, including any faxes. If the order was sent by phone then either tape it if you can or write down exactly what was said. Make sure to take the name of the person you are talking to, make a note of the time of the call and any reference number you are given.

5 Customs

Once the goods arrive you may have to pay tax on them. This is assessed by the Customs Authority as they enter the country – it is NOT calculated or paid for by the original supplier (in this usage 'country' also means the whole of the EC. See *The European Free Market*, below, for full details). In the UK and Europe there can be three taxes imposed:

> Import Tariff
> Excise Duty
> VAT

Other countries may have slightly different systems but the principle remains the same. Import Tariff is what we usually think of as Customs duty, i.e. it is a percentage of the value of the goods. Excise Duty is an additional tax which is only applicable to three types of goods: tobacco, alcohol and oil. VAT, or value added tax, is levied at a standard rate on most items.

In the case of the UK, your package first goes to HMS Customs & Excise. They work out how much is owed and add it to the package in the form of a sticker. The balance is then payable on delivery (i.e. to the postman). You can pay in cash or by cheque but credit cards are not accepted.

You therefore make two payments for any order: first to the supplier for the goods and postage and secondly to the deliverer for tax.*

---

*In some countries you may have to go down to a central depot and pay Customs direct.

IMPORT TARIFF

This is the first tax you may have to pay and is imposed by the government on foreign products. It varies from country to country and from item to item. In the EC it is only payable on goods which have been ordered from outside the Community. Goods from within the EC attract no tariff, only VAT. For a fuller discussion of this see *The European Free Market*, below.

While paying Import Tariff is very simple the way it is calculated is not. In Europe, Customs officials go through a complicated procedure to arrive at the final figure. Although it is not practical to reproduce the pages and pages of regulations here, it is as well to know the outline of the system so you can have some idea of how much you will have to pay and therefore what is and isn't worth importing. (For details of where to find the full regulations see *Further Information*, below).

Calculating Import Tariffs

The UK now shares a common Import Tariff policy with the rest of the EC. Every product is given a rating, expressed in percentage terms. For example, denim material is taxed at 10% while fax machines are rated 7.5%. There is a list of Duty Rates for specific items in the *Appendix III*, along with information on where to find a comprehensive listing for all products.

The system may seem simple enough but there is also the complication of what the tax is a percentage of.

Evaluation for Import Tariff

Each country has its own way of evaluating goods for Import Tariff but within the EC this has been harmonised. There is now an agreed procedure which provides six ways of working out the value of any item so tax may be levied on it. Officials work their way down the list only if the previous method cannot be applied. In other words they will try to use Method 1 but if it is not suitable they will move on to Method 2 and if that cannot be applied they move to Method 3 and so on. In the vast majority of mail order cases Method 1 will be sufficient.

Method 1: the transaction value of the imported goods; i.e. the amount you paid for the goods. This is included in the shipping documents and declared on the Customs form by the supplier. (For how Customs calculate foreign currency see below.)

Method 2: the transaction value of identical goods; i.e. goods which are the same in all respects including physical characteristics, quality and reputation. Here officials estimate what identical goods would be worth.

Method 3: the transaction value of similar goods; i.e. goods which have like characteristics and component materials which enable them to perform the same functions. If officials can't find identical goods to compare the price with they find ones that are similar.

Method 4: the deductive method, the value derived from the selling price of the imported goods or identical or similar goods in the EC. Self explanatory – and could be considerably more than by Method 1.

Method 5: the computed value, the value based on the built-up cost of the imported goods. That is, an estimation of how much the goods would have cost to make.

Method 6: the fall-back method, the value based on reasonable means constituent with valuation principles. Here officials just assign a value which they think reasonable.

Clearly the best bet is to have your goods valued by Method 1. This requires the supplier to identify the nature and cost of the goods on the Customs' declaration form. All reputable suppliers do this but it is nevertheless advisable to check that they will do so on your order.

The next step in calculating the correct tariff is for Customs to convert all values into the local currency (pounds sterling in the UK). The rate they do this at is published each month. In the UK this is available from the Customs Entry Processing Unit at your local Customs and Excise office (see phone book for address). Elsewhere contact your local Customs Authority.

Finally, the full amount due is printed on an invoice which is attached to the parcel in the form of a sticker.

EXCISE DUTY

Excise Duty is only imposed on three types of product: tobacco, alcohol and oil. The rates for these are complex, vary from product to product and are not harmonised across the EC (hence the difference in the price of wine in the UK and France). Remember that perfume counts as alcohol.

In general they are very high, usually over 50%. The result is that it is only worth importing such goods if you are after something rare or of high quality. The high duty rate wipes out much chance of a bargain.

VAT

The third form of tax is VAT (written TVA in some countries). This is only applicable to consumers living within the EC. Therefore if you are ordering European goods from elsewhere be certain to indicate that you should NOT be charged this tax. If you do find yourself paying it, it can be a lengthy and frustrating business to get your money back.

European consumers have to pay VAT on most goods, whether or not they originate from within the Community. If the goods are ordered from within the EC – i.e. from another EC state – then VAT is added by the supplier in the normal way and Customs are not involved. For full details of which country's VAT rate is applicable see *The European Free Market*, below.

If the goods are ordered from elsewhere, VAT is calculated and added by Customs in a similar way to the Import Tariff. One important difference is that VAT is assessed as a percentage of the TOTAL cost of the goods. That is, on the price of the product, the shipping charge AND any Import Tariff payable. All these are added together and VAT incurred on the total. When working out likely costs do not make the mistake of applying VAT just to the price of the goods alone. (See *Working Out the Total Cost*, below, for a formula to calculate the final figure.)

AVOIDING TAXES

There are only two legal ways not to pay tax in the UK: if the item is worth less than £7.00 or if it is a 'gift'. Gifts must be:

Worth less than £71 if from the EC and £36 from elsewhere
Have been sent by a private person to a private person
Must not have been paid for by you
Cannot be for regular use

These rules effectively wipe out anything ordered from a catalogue. Furthermore if the goods are either alcohol or tobacco then there is a limit to the quantity permitted: 50 cigarettes, 1 litre of wine, 1 litre of spirits and 50g of perfume.

However, although it may not be legal to avoid paying Import Tariffs or VAT, this hasn't stopped people trying. Some ask the supplier to lower the value of the goods on the Customs' declaration form. This is illegal and if the supplier agrees is proof you are dealing with a dodgy business.

Another trick people use is to have the goods sent to a contact in the country of origin who then re-packages them and fills in a new Customs form saying they were worth less, or even removes the invoice altogether and claims the goods are second-hand (though duty and VAT are both incurred on second-hand goods).

In general it is not worth trying to dodge the taxes. Customs Officers are not stupid and know every trick in the book. If they feel you are trying to cheat they have the right both to fine you and confiscate the goods.

While it may be impossible to avoid paying taxes it is quite often the case that one ends up not paying them nevertheless. This is because Customs do not check every package and goods do slip through with nothing to pay at all. It is a bit of a lottery, though some claim using the normal mail service, rather than a private courier, heightens the chances of items slipping through tax free.

WORKING OUT THE TOTAL COST

The total cost of any order will consist of six possible elements:

> Price of the goods
> Postage & Insurance
> Import Tariff
> Excise Duty (if tobacco, alcohol or oil)
> VAT (if in Europe)

The order these are added is important. VAT is assessed as a percentage of the total cost of the goods. That is, on the price of the product, the shipping charge and any duty payable. So if you bought something for $100 the calculation might look like this:

Goods	100.00
Shipping & Insurance	12.00
Duty @10%	11.20
TOTAL	123.20
VAT @17.5%	21.00*
Grand Total	**144.20**

In addition the Post Office sometimes tacks on a 'handling charge'. This is to assess the value of the goods for Customs purposes. Most packages, especially if they are properly documented, will not incur this charge, as it is only necessary on those parcels which have to be opened and then re-sealed.

♦ **WARNING!** As mentioned above, Customs & Excise include the cost of shipping in their calculations. If the accompanying documents do not show this they assess it using a standard value according to weight. This may seem an arcane point but can have dramatic effects. One reader ordered software from the US valued at $25 and was stunned to get a bill for £1.95 duty and £7.04 VAT, which would seem disproportionate to the original cost.

The explanation was that the invoice did not show the cost of the shipping so it was assessed by weight. The manuals that accompanied the software being rather heavy, the shipping costs as calculated by Customs came to more than the value of the goods and hence the high bill.

The moral is two-fold. First, make sure that shipping costs are clearly marked on the package. Secondly, beware ordering goods which are heavy in relation to their value.**

*VAT for EC countries only.
**My thanks to Mr Ian Gardner of Sutton Coldfield, UK for this point.

6   *Compatibility*

Although we live in an increasingly international marketplace goods do vary from country to country and are not always compatible. A television which works fine in the US, for example, would be useless in the UK and one from the UK would not work in France. It is therefore as well to be aware which products work where and how one can overcome compatibility problems.

The following suggestions assume that consumers are ordering FROM the UK; obviously the advice has to be adapted if you are resident elsewhere.

USA

Electrical Goods

American electrical appliances differ from UK ones in two main respects – the physical shape of the plug (flat two prong) and the power supply itself.

With plugs, the solution is simple – just cut off the US plug and attach a new one of your choice. If for some reason you want to keep the original (for example you intend to use it in America at a later date) then you will need an adapter. These are available from most travel shops and convert US to UK or European plugs, and vice versa. However, this is not a good permanent solution and anyway does NOT overcome the second problem – the difference in power supply.

The US uses a different voltage and cycle from the UK and Europe. In the UK we are on 240 volts at 50Hz, the US has 110v at 60Hz. The two systems are not compatible.

If you try to use an American rated appliance in the UK or Europe it will either run very fast or, if you are unlucky, burn out or even blow up. The other way round is less dramatic; appliances simply run more slowly.

Does this mean you cannot buy US electronics and appliances? Fortunately not. Nearly all electronic goods are made for the international market and have means of adjusting the volts/Hz requirement. This usually consists of a simple switch on the back. Other appliances – typically computers – make this adjustment automatically. They sense the power supply and adjust accordingly. Apple computers, for example, work this way.

However, occasionally – and particularly with products made for the internal US market – there is no means of altering the input requirement. In these cases your first move is to ask the supplier to fit a voltage regulator. This is a simple task and most merchants will undertake it. If this fails you will need a transformer.

Transformers

A US/UK transformer will convert 240v/50Hz to 110v/60Hz and usually comes with a UK plug on one end and a US socket on the other.

♦ **WARNING!** Simple travel plugs, the sort you take on holiday, will not do this! For the most part they do not contain a transformer but simply allow a British/European plug to fit a US socket. They assume that the appliance itself is adjustable.

Even those travel adapters which do contain transformers are not suitable for heavy loads. They may be fine for a small hair-dryer or shaver but that is all. They are not designed for major appliances.

The type of transformer needed is quite large and heavy (i.e. the size of a fat paperback). Douglas Electronic Industries Ltd make a series of suitable ones, which cost from around £11.00 (plus £2.00 postage) for the basic model suitable for most applications, through to their heavyweight model costing around £130 (£8.25 postage).

Douglas Electronic Industries Ltd
Eastfield Road
Louth
Lincolnshire
LN11 7AL
Tel: 0507 603643
Fax: 0507 600502

Readers in the US might like to try one of the suppliers listed in the directory, The Travellers Checklist.

Low voltage appliances

Many products run on low voltage and come with their own transformer. For example most answering machines run off 12v and have a transformer to step down the mains. The same goes for cordless and portable phones, some fax machines, computer accessories and most re-chargeable appliances (electric toothbrushes, screwdrivers, torches and so on).

There are two possible solutions. First, you could buy a large transformer to put between the mains and the supplied transformer. Alternatively – and this is a neater solution – buy a small transformer to replace the one provided. This steps down the mains to the voltage required directly. The plug that fits into the back of the appliance itself will be one of several standard sizes and most transformers come with a universal adapter.

Such devices are readily available in most electrical shops, such as Tandy in the UK, for under £5. However, be sure to check that the output is the same as the transformer supplied, both in terms of volts and amps. It is best to take the original along to the shop and seek advice.

EUROPE

Continental Europe uses a slightly different voltage than Britain, at 220v as opposed to the UK's 240v. However, the difference is marginal and will not affect the running of most appliances. There are plans to bring in a pan-European voltage of 230v and you may see a sticker indicating this on some equipment already.

However, the plug problem still remains – there is no standard plug in Europe. Again, it is simply a matter of cutting off the supplied plug and attaching your own, or alternatively using an adapter (although these may not stand up to repeated use).

PRODUCT COMPATIBILITY

Batteries

Most battery sizes are now universal. If in any doubt ask for the size and check in your local shop.

Cameras & Film

No compatibility problems.

CDs & Audio Cassettes

CDs and cassettes are the same the world over and there will be no compatibility problems. This goes for DAT and Digital tapes as well as ordinary compact cassettes.

Clothing

Clothing and shoe sizes are different in the US, Europe and the UK. See *Appendix IV* for a comprehensive conversion table.

Computers

Again, computers are international and there are no special problems apart from the power supply difference.

Computer Software

Computer software attracts no duty (just VAT) and therefore offers some of the best bargains to be had. While on the whole it is completely compatible (after all it is made for a computer which is the same everywhere) there are a couple of points to watch out for.

US word processing packages or spreadsheets may not have a £ sign (or signs for other European currencies either). Spell-checking programmes from the States use American spelling (color instead of colour and so on). Some come with an additional British dictionary while others may need extra modules.

Most software now comes with some kind of telephone hotline support – a number you can call if you get stuck. In the US these are often toll-free 1-800 numbers. These do not work from outside the country (but see under *Telephone Tips* below for ways of accessing them from outside the US). Some do operate international toll-free numbers, otherwise be sure to get their normal, paying number.

It is also worth checking to see if they have a hotline in your own country (many do) and whether you are eligible to use this even though you bought the product in America. If you are in continental Europe some companies may have hotlines in the UK only, but this is still cheaper than calling the States.

Fax Machines

Fax machines are internationally compatible. The only differences will be the working voltage and the plug which fits into the phone line. Treat this as you would a phone (see below, *Telephones*).

Stationery

While European paper sizes are standard (A3, A4, A5 etc.), American sizes are different. Where we have A4, they have a smaller sheet, about eight and a half by eleven inches. The same goes for envelopes and computer listing paper. This can be important when ordering a computer printer which takes sheets or has a feeder tray – be sure to ask whether it comes with an A4 tray or can be adapted to take this size of paper (the majority can).

Telephones

Telephones divide into two types, pulse and tone (sometimes known as MF). Pulse phones are the old-fashioned variety and are silent when you dial. Tone phones make beeping sounds as you press the digits. All rotary phones (i.e. where you put your finger in a dial rather than press buttons) are pulse. Most, but not all push button phones are tone.

The majority of Western European countries are now switching over to using tone phones. This requires digital exchanges which can then connect calls much faster as well as provide a host of other services. All of the US and Canada work on the tone system. The UK is now mostly converted as are Germany and France.

The compatibility of telephones depends on which system is operating in your country. Tone phones are the same the world over but pulse phones are not. You therefore need to establish which system your telephone company is using before ordering a phone from abroad – simply ring them up and ask. If it is tone, go ahead; if pulse think again.

Having said this, there are two other factors to take into account: regulations and the plug. Some countries license telephone handsets. That is, they will not allow equipment which has not been approved by the phone company to be connected to the system. For example, in the UK British Telecom only allows customers to use certain phones. These are indicated by a sticker on the appliance – a green circle with the word 'Approved' written across it. Other equipment carries a red triangle which forbids it to be connected to the BT network.

However, this is a bureaucratic rather than practical technicality. In fact any tone phone will work perfectly well on the UK system. The same goes for other European countries. While we would not want to encourage people to break the law, it is an accepted fact that many people have unapproved telephones operating on the network (after all, many shops in the UK sell them, so someone must be buying them).

The second problem is the plug. Each country has its own style of phone plug (i.e. the piece of plastic on the end of the lead which then plugs into the wall socket). There are a number of ways round this.

The easiest is to buy an adapter – one end fits into your wall socket, the other has a slot for the plug the phone came with. In the UK these cost about £4.00 from good phone or electrical shops. If you have trouble locating one locally try: Harp Electronics, 237 Tottenham Court Road, London W1. Tel: 071 436 0022. They also sell adapters for European countries.

In the UK, the High Street chain Tandy sells a replacement lead, with a US plug on one end and a UK plug on the other. The item name is: Replacement Modular Line Cord, 431A plug to RJ11 plug and is made by Archer.

The second solution is to do the same as you would with a mains lead – i.e. simply cut off the old plug and replace it with one that fits your system. Spare plugs can be bought from most telephone shops who will also fit them for you. This shouldn't cost more than a few pounds.

As far as the electronics of the phone are concerned there will be no problem at all. However, if you wish to use additional exchange services, such as Call Waiting or Diversion, you may find that on American and Japanese phones the R button is replaced by a Flash button. This should work in the same way, though I have heard reports of difficulties with this feature.

Some cordless telephones are illegal in the UK, depending on what frequencies they operate and their range. For further details on this see *Appendix III*, below.

♦ **WARNING!** Call Identifiers are all the rage in the US at the moment, either as separate standing units or built into phones. These display the number of the caller on an LCD screen before you pick up the receiver. You can thus either ignore the call if you do not want to speak to that person or baffle them by calling them by name before they have a chance to speak.

These do not work in all countries. They require the phone company to send a pulse down the line containing the caller's number. In the UK BT intends to introduce the service in 1994/5. It is not yet clear whether machines made to US specifications will also work in the UK.

TV & Video

Television may be the universal medium but it is NOT universally compatible. There are several competing TV systems and they are mutually exclusive. This is also true of videos – despite the fact that the format (e.g. VHS or 8mm) may be the same. This is because of the difference in the way the images are recorded.

The result is that if you buy a TV or camcorder in the US it will not work in the UK. In the case of the TV it will not receive broadcast pictures and the camcorder will not play back on a UK TV. However, it will still record and you could display its pictures on an American (and therefore compatible) TV.

For historical reasons countries have adopted different TV systems. The following table details which country uses which.

World TV systems

PAL (also PAL 1)
Hong Kong
Ireland
South Africa
UK

PAL B/PAL G
Afghanistan
Australia
Austria
Belgium
Canary Islands
Denmark
Finland
Germany (ex West)
Ghana
India
Indonesia
Israel
Italy
Jordan
Kenya
Malaysia
Malta
Netherlands
New Zealand
Nigeria
Norway
Pakistan
Portugal
Singapore
Spain

Sri Lanka
Sudan
Sweden
Switzerland
Thailand
Turkey
Yugoslavia
Zambia
Zimbabwe

PAL M
Brazil

PAL N
Argentina
Paraguay
Uruguay

PAL D/PAL K
China
Korea (North)
Romania

SECAM B/G
Cyprus
Egypt
Germany (ex East)
Greece
Iran
Iraq
Lebanon
Saudi Arabia

Syria
Tunisia

N SECAM
France
Luxembourg
Monaco

SECAM D/K
Africa (most)
Bulgaria
Cameroon
Hungary
Poland
Romania (not all)
USSR
Vietnam

NSTC
Bahamas
Barbados

Bermuda
Canada
Chile
Columbia
Cuba
Dominican Republic
Haiti
Honduras
Jamaica
Japan
Korea (South)
Mexico
Nicaragua
Panama
Peru
Philippines
Taiwan
Trinidad & Tobago
USA
Venezuela

These may seem a hopeless jumble, but all is not lost. Firstly, the difference between the PAL systems and between PAL and SECAM is relatively little. A TV repair shop should be able to make the adjustment for under £20. NSTC is a different case and cannot be made to work in other countries.

Secondly, some foreign suppliers stock a variety of systems, for example in the US you can buy PAL and SECAM TVs (see the *Directory* for details).

Be sure to check carefully BEFORE you order any video equipment. If you are going to have a piece of equipment converted, get a firm quote before sending off for the goods and make quite sure that the shop understands exactly what model you are getting and how you want it converted. The latest hi-tech TV is useless if it won't receive pictures in your country.

Video Tapes

Tapes differ in two ways: the format (i.e. VHS, Super VHS, 8mm) and the system used to record on them (PAL, SECAM, NSTC). When they are blank they are compatible with any system but once they have been recorded on they will only work with the system which did the recording. So while blank tapes are fine, pre-recorded ones may not be – again check with the above list.

The only way round the problem of incompatible pre-recorded tapes is to buy either a complete foreign system or a multi-player. This is a video machine that plays a number of different formats, including PAL, SECAM and NSTC. These have been very expensive but are now coming down in price – selling for around £350 in the UK.

If you do have one of these then pre-recorded films from, say, the US may well be a bargain – and you can certainly get new releases before they come out here. Getting tapes professionally transferred from one system to another is also possible but expensive (between £15 and £20 per hour).

7   *Your Rights*

Mail order transactions are protected in two ways: by general consumer legislation and by any additional guarantees offered by the supplier or manufacturer.

CONSUMER LEGISLATION

When buying something from abroad you are protected under the consumer law of the country where the contract was made. For example, if you order an item from the USA and have it sent to the UK you are protected under American, not British, legislation.

The law varies from country to country, although there are obvious similarities. Here we cover the main points of the countries most involved in international mail order.

European Community

The position in Europe is muddled. In theory there is supposed to be harmonised consumer legislation so all member states share the same basic rights which can be implemented in any given country. Thus a complaint against, say, an Italian supplier could be heard in a British court.

However, in reality this is not the case. At present, if a problem arises and goes to court, it has to be contested in the country of the defendant, i.e. where the goods were purchased, and according to that country's own legislation. This can be both costly and confusing and is rarely worth the effort.

To make things worse, the EC Directive, COM (92) 11, the legislation dealing directly with mail order, has not yet been either signed or ratified.

A voluntary code of practice has been drawn up by the European Mail Order Traders' Association. While this is laudable, it only covers companies who are members of Mail Order Traders' Associations in their own countries (at present a minority). It is also unfortunate that EMOTA are lobbying AGAINST the ratification of the EC legislation that would compel all mail order companies to comply with similar practices.

It is nevertheless worth knowing the EMOTA code of practice and asking whether specific companies adhere to it.

EMOTA GUIDELINES
- Consumers must know:
  the exact nature of the offer and its terms
  the features of goods and services
  the terms of delivery, exchange, return, reimbursement, after sales service, guarantees and any restrictions of rights

- If goods are unable to be dispatched then money must be returned as soon as possible and with a time limit of thirty days. If goods are returned then a refund must be made within seven working days.

- Consumers should be allowed fourteen days in which to return unwanted goods.

- Consumers have a right to privacy (in other words their name must not be sold on to another company without permission).

The code also allows individual consumers to take up problems with the Mail Order Traders' Association in their own country. These in turn will liaise with the sister organization in the supplier's country and investigate the claim.

Members of EMOTA are drawn from all over Europe and not restricted to EC countries. For addresses of EMOTA members, see *Appendix VI, Useful Addresses.*

Members of EMOTA

Austria
Belgium
Denmark
Finland
France
Germany
Great Britain
Italy
Netherlands
Norway
Portugal
Spain
Sweden
Switzerland

The UK

UK consumer law is in many instances tougher than that in other EC countries and covers goods bought here, regardless of where they are sent.

Most of the legislation is covered in the Sale of Goods Act, 1979. All goods sold have to satisfy three requirements: they must be 'of merchantable quality', 'fit for the purpose they are intended' and be 'as described'. These purposefully wide definitions are intended to prevent companies evading their responsibilities.

- Merchantable quality: products must be in good order. They shouldn't be damaged, scratched or broken.

- Fit for the purpose they are intended: this simply means the goods must do what they are supposed to do. The CD player must play CDs, the iron must heat up, the fax must fax.

- As described: goods must be as described in promotional literature. This is true not just of basic features (for example a 'TV with teletext' must indeed have this facility) but also of properties. For example, if a tent or jacket are described as waterproof then they must indeed be so, and not simply shower proof.

This clause refers both to written AND verbal descriptions. If, therefore, you are conducting a transaction entirely over the phone it is as well to record the conversation if possible. If not, insist on a written description.

These requirements are law – suppliers cannot avoid them simply by posting notices or including small print at the back of a catalogue disclaiming responsibility.

If goods are faulty in any way the consumer can legally insist on a replacement or a refund. You are not obliged to take a credit note, but if you do accept one you cannot change your mind later and ask for a refund.

A supplier can also offer to repair the product. This can be perfectly acceptable but make sure there is a written understanding that you retain the right to reject the goods if you feel the repair is not satisfactory. Without this you can end up with a botched repair and no further rights.

In some cases companies will offer compensation instead of a refund or replacement. For example, a pair of shoes might have a slight blemish on them and the company offers a small amount of money in compensation. This could be fine but you do not have to accept it – it is a legal right to insist on a replacement or full refund.

It is the responsibility of the supplier to make sure the goods arrive safely and in good condition. If they are faulty, do not try to repair them yourself but immediately contact the trader and ask for a replacement. It is also the supplier's responsibility to pay the return postage.

However, the consumer does not have the legal right to return an item simply because he or she does not like it. While many suppliers operate a 'no-questions-asked' policy, this is not enshrined in law.

In addition to national legislation, there are a number of trade associations which regulate the industry on a voluntary basis.

• Mail Order Traders' Association – an umbrella organization which has, with its European partner, EMOTA, drawn up the code of practice described above. They also have a domestic code of practice, a copy of which is available to consumers. Its main drawback is its lack of members.

- The Advertising Standards Authority – oversees all advertisements in the UK, which must be 'honest, decent and true'.

- The Mail Order Protection Scheme – or MOPS, an organization set up by the Fleet Street papers to vet companies advertising in the main national papers. If a registered company fails to deliver goods or defrauds you in some way you can request a refund directly from MOPS. They can also help with companies who have gone bust.

- Periodical Publishers Association – similar to MOPS but for magazines.

Full addresses of these organizations can be found under *Useful Addresses*, below.

The USA

Consumer law in the US is quite tough and offers protection in a number of ways. Federal laws cover the whole country and lay down basic codes of practice while each State also has its own legislation.

The relevant national legislation is the Federal Trade Commission's Mail Order Rule and the Code of Federal Regulations on Commercial Practices: Mail Order Merchandise. Briefly, these require companies to:

- dispatch goods within the time that is stated on the order form. If no such time is stated then this must be within 30 days of receiving the order.

- notify customers if dispatch is delayed, offering them the option to cancel the order (and receive a refund) or wait for a specified period of time (no longer than 30 days).

- give refunds within seven working days if by cheque; credit card orders must not be charged until the goods have been shipped. If a credit card refund is requested for some other reason then this must be made within seven days, under the Federal Truth in Lending Act.

The Civil False Representation Statute forbids misleading advertising, which includes descriptions in mail order catalogues, while the Mail Order Consumer Protection Amendments of 1983 speeds up prosecutions following from violations.

In addition to these federal laws, each State has its own legislation which is overseen by a State consumer office. While the laws differ in detail they share basic principles. The most important of these is that goods must be as described and perform in the manner intended. In other words if the supplier says it's a Sony CD player then it must indeed be one and it must play CDs properly.

For details of who to contact and how to complain see *When Things Go Wrong*, below. For addresses of US State consumer offices see *Appendix VI*.

Rest of the World

Consumer law in the rest of the world varies enormously. In keeping with the *laissez-faire* philosophy of Hong Kong, there is at present no consumer protection law. However, there is a Consumer Council which, despite having no legal teeth, does manage to get results. If you are ordering from places such as Thailand or South Korea you cannot expect much help from legislation.

In most cases you will have to rely on paying by credit card and taking out sufficient insurance. The companies listed in the Directory should be reliable and have proved to be so in the past but caution is the byword here.

PROTECTING YOURSELF

These are a few strategies which can make life easier if a dispute does arise.

• Keep the receipt. It may seem obvious but the simple receipt is a powerful ally. It proves what you bought, when, from whom and for how much. But not all receipts are created equal. Do not accept one that simply reads: 'Goods, £32'. Insist on details. You need to know the date, the name and address of the supplier and a brief description of the goods.

If the company won't send you such a receipt (which in itself should ring alarm bells) write the details in yourself at the time. And then keep the receipt for at least a year.

• If possible use a credit card. In the UK, the Consumer Credit Act states that for purchases over £100 made with a credit card the transaction is not between you and the supplier but between the credit card company and the supplier. This means that if there is a dispute you can claim the money back from the credit card company leaving them to take it up with the supplier.

♦ **WARNING!** This only refers to genuine credit cards and NOT to charge cards (e.g. American Express) or most gold cards.

Even for cheaper items it is still worth using a credit card for a number of reasons. Firstly, credit card companies tend not to do business with fly-by-nights – they will already have made certain checks themselves. Secondly, information on the supplier is held by the credit card merchant services. And lastly, the credit card flimsy makes a good additional receipt. Note the word additional – you must still insist on an official receipt.

• Keep copies of all correspondence, including faxes.

• Keep a record of phone calls. If you can't record conversations (most answering machines have this facility) then do write down what was said. Keep a note of the name of the person you spoke to and at what time.

• If complaining by phone or fax, send a hard copy to confirm and place the matter on record.

• When ordering from the UK, write 'Time is of the essence' on the order form. This somewhat archaic phrase ensures that the delivery date you have agreed with the supplier (i.e. the one often written on the form itself) becomes legally binding. In its absence the delivery date has no legal standing.

• If returning a faulty item do so as quickly as possible. Delay may result in losing the right to a complete refund and only having

41

recourse to compensation, which may mean a replacement or repair only.

INTERNATIONAL GUARANTEES

♦ **WARNING!** Any guarantee is only valid if it is stamped by the supplier and, in many cases, returned by you to the manufacturer. Do this as soon as you receive the goods and keep a record in a safe place.

Manufacturers' Guarantees

Nearly all products come with a manufacturer's guarantee but these may only be valid within one country. Large multi-nationals do issue worldwide guarantees which in principle should cover you anywhere. However, there is no legal requirement for them to do so.

Many multi-nationals' products are not identical in all countries and in these cases they may not guarantee items not usually available in your country (for example a hi-tech cordless phone ordered from the US and sent to the UK).

The Consumers Association in the UK recently asked some large electronics companies for their policies within the EC and received the following responses:

Companies which honour EC-wide guarantees

Akai
Hitachi
JVC
Mitsubishi
Nikon
Panasonic
Pentax
Samsung
Sanyo
Sharp
Sony

Companies which may not

Canon
Minolta
Olympus

Having said this, in practice most multi-nationals are sympathetic and you should have no problem with local service agents. If the manufacturer is not well known then check the exact nature of the guarantee before you buy – ask for a copy to be posted or faxed.

Suppliers' Guarantees

The supplier may also issue some kind of guarantee. This is usually along the lines of your money back if you are not satisfied or if the product does not work. The exact nature of the cover varies from supplier to supplier but there are some general points to check.

- Is there a 'satisfaction or money back' guarantee? In other words can you send an item back simply because you do not like it? This is especially important in the case of clothes.

- In the event of a product being returned, for whatever reason, who pays the postage and insurance? And is it sent by mail or courier service?

- What is the policy on backorders? This is where the supplier does not have the ordered item in stock but agrees to send it later. The point to check here is who pays the extra postage? This can mount up because it may cost more to ship two separate items than to put them into one package.

- How is the standard code of practice affected by a shipment overseas? Most suppliers provide extensive customer services but check to see if these apply outside their own country. Ask for a copy to be sent.

MAIL ORDER PREFERENCE SCHEMES

Several countries operate mailing preference schemes, which give consumers the opportunity to have their names struck off mailing lists. Individuals who contact these services have their name entered on a central registry which is then distributed to participating companies. You may also have your name added if you wish to receive more mailings.

These systems do work but are not foolproof. Information takes about three months to filter through and can only offer protection from mailing lists originating from companies registered with the service. You will still receive mailings from businesses you have dealt with directly, as they do not have to register their lists unless they sell them on.

It is best to contact the domestic preference service in your own country even if you are receiving mail from abroad. This is because the list will be 'cleaned' in the country which uses the names and not in the country of origin. Names and addresses of mail preference schemes can be found in *Appendix VI, Useful Addresses.*

8 *When Things Go Wrong*

RETURNING GOODS

Most companies set out their return policy in their catalogue. If they do not, ask for written details.

More complex is the issue of any duty and VAT you may have paid. If the goods are being returned for a refund then you will not be able to reclaim either VAT or duty. So while you might get your money back from the supplier you will still be out of pocket.

In the case of replacement goods it depends on the reason for sending them back. If the goods are faulty then you will not have to pay VAT or duty on their replacement. To ensure that this is the case, the supplier has to write 'No value' on the package and indicate that the goods are indeed genuinely replacing goods that were faulty.

However, goods which are returned and then replaced simply because you do not like them (or they do not fit), ARE liable for VAT and duty. So in the case of clothes of the wrong size you will have to pay tax twice. At least this is the official position. In practice it is a grey area since it is possible to describe the items as 'faulty' on the grounds that they are not of the correct size. It is therefore important to persuade the supplier to document such goods as officially 'faulty', which will in turn ensure that you do not pay VAT and duty twice over.

COMPLAINING

The initial step is to contact the retailer in person, preferably by phone, and let them know the nature of the problem. If that doesn't yield the proper response, write an angry letter to include:

the problem
the date of purchase
a copy of the receipt
a copy of cancelled cheque or itemized credit card bill
what you would consider a fair and equitable settlement
a date by which you would like a response

It is best to write in the language of the supplier, but if this is not possible still write in your own language – at least it puts the matter on record. If there is no satisfactory response you will have to take things further: see below.

It may also be worth writing to the manufacturer. Strictly speaking your dispute is not with them but they may be able to mediate.

TOUGHER ACTION

Europe & the UK

- Contact The Mail Order Traders' Association of the country concerned (see *Useful Addresses*, below). They can help in resolving disputes but only deal with companies who are members of their organization.

- Contact The Direct Marketing Association of the country concerned (see *Useful Addresses*, below). Again, these associations can only deal with companies who are members.

- In the UK contact the Office of Fair Trading (see *Useful Addresses*, below).

USA

- Contact the Consumer Affairs Office in the State where the company is operating
These are government funded organizations which look after the interests of consumers. They operate rather like Citizen Advice Bureaux in the UK and are an invaluable source of information and help. Each State has a Consumer Affairs Office and although they operate under different (State) laws they are all concerned with protecting the consumer. A full list of addresses and phone numbers listed by State can be found in *Appendix VI*.

- Contact the Postal Inspection Service
The law enforcement arm of the Postal Service, they offer help if you experience difficulty with a company or suspect that you have been the victim of mail fraud. However, they do not chase up late deliveries. This is the responsibility of the supplier who should get in contact with the local Post Office. The Postal Inspection Service is to protect the consumer against the illegal use of the postal system.

- Contact The Direct Marketing Association
The Direct Marketing Association is the trade organization to which most mail order houses belong (unlike their sister organizations in the UK and Europe which have far fewer members). While they do not have any legal powers they are an influential body which self-regulates the industry. They will follow up complaints made against members.

- If you are suspicious about a company but do not have a specific complaint you can check to see if there have been any complaints about it by contacting the Better Business Bureau in the area. To find out addresses of local offices contact their headquarters in Arlington (see *Useful Addresses*, below).

Canada

Canada also has tough consumer legislation and you can follow up your complaint in a number of ways.

- Contact the Better Business Bureaux

There are offices all over Canada who will help with mediation and arbitration. For further details contact their main office.

- Contact the Canadian Direct Marketing Association
Like the equivalent in the US, this trade organization helps consumers with complaints against members.

- Contact the Consumer & Corporate Affairs Office
The CCA is a government agency with central offices in five geographical areas.

See *Useful Addresses* on page 368.

9   *The European Free Market*

From January 1st 1993 the European Community became a free market, as did the European Free Trade Association (see below for members). This has considerable impact if you are resident in a member country and order goods from within the Community.

In essence it means that as far as Import Tariffs are concerned Europe is now treated as one large country. Goods originating from outside pay the tariff only once, on entry into the EC. They can then be re-sold from country to country without attracting any further tax. Goods originating from within the EC are taxed only in the country of manufacture and not again as they cross borders.

MEMBERS OF THE EUROPEAN COMMUNITY

Belgium	Italy
Denmark	Luxembourg
France	Netherlands
Germany	Portugal
Greece	Spain
Ireland	United Kingdom

MEMBERS OF THE EUROPEAN FREE TRADE ASSOCIATION

Austria	Liechtenstein
Finland	Sweden
Iceland	Switzerland

IMPORT TARIFFS

Import Tariff has now been harmonised across the EC, i.e. the rate for various goods is the same in all member states. Tariffs are imposed once, as the goods enter the EC, after which they can move around freely. So if a Japanese TV is brought into Germany it will have the same tariff imposed on it as if it were brought into the UK. If it is then sold to an Italian consumer there is no more tariff to pay.

EXCISE DUTY

The same is not the case with Excise Duty. This tax, added only to tobacco, alcohol and oil, is NOT harmonised and varies from country to country. This accounts for cigarettes and wine being so much cheaper in France than in the UK.

Furthermore, Excise Duty is levied on all suitable goods as they enter the country, regardless of where they originated. Thus it is not possible to order cigarettes from France and not pay Excise Duty.

The situation is confusing because if you travelled to France in person and bought the cigarettes you COULD bring them back without attracting any duty. This apparent anomaly is a hangover from the idea of Duty Free for travellers. It originated in the nineteenth century when passengers on cold and windy ferries to France were allowed to consume duty free spirits on the boat to keep them warm. It has developed into the huge business which we know today.

Currently – and until June 1997 – travellers are allowed to bring back a large allowance of goods without attracting Excise Duty.

DUTY ALLOWANCES WITHIN THE EC

Spirits	10 litres
Wine	90 litres
Beer	110 litres
Cigarettes	800

We mention this because the position on mail order transactions is confused. While the above regulations reflect the official Customs and Excise view, not everyone agrees. In particular, the European Commission and the British MEP Ben Patterson, claim that there is no difference between mail order purchasing and buying something in person. They therefore argue that consumers should be given the same duty free allowances regardless of how the transaction was made. However, since Customs and Excise are the ones who open the parcels, it seems unlikely that the nicety of this point will win the day.

VAT

VAT is not currently harmonised across the EC, although this is one of the goals of the free market. For now, each country sets its own VAT rate, with some having double the rate of others.

There are two parts to VAT: the tiers, which determine which goods are 'rateable', and the rate itself. Both vary from country to country.

VAT TIERS

Standard Rate   i.e. the normal rate of VAT applied to the vast majority of goods

Increased Rate   applied to luxury goods

Reduced Rate   applied to goods which are felt to be more essential

Zero Rate   applied to goods which may have been traditionally tax free (e.g. children's clothes, books and newspapers in UK)

Only Ireland and the UK have widespread zero rating (again, this is set to change).

EUROPEAN VAT RATES

	Standard	Increased	Reduced	Zero
Belgium	19.5%	None	1, 6, 12%	Minimal
Denmark	25%	None	None	Minimal
France	18.6%	None	2.1, 5.5, 13%	None
Germany	15%	None	7%	None
Greece	18%	36%	4, 8%	None
Ireland	21%	None	10, 12.5%	Wide variety
Italy	19%	38%	4, 9, 12%	Minimal
Luxembourg	15%	None	3, 6%	None
Netherlands	18.5%	None	6%	None
Portugal	16%	30%	5%	Minimal
Spain	13%	28%	6%	Minimal
United Kingdom	17.5%	None	None	Wide variety

As these tables show, working out VAT can be complex. But the most important point is whose VAT rate do you pay? This can make a good deal of difference. For example, a person in the UK ordering goods from Italy might have to pay 38% Italian VAT or just 17.5% British VAT.

Whose VAT to Pay

The simple answer is the country of origin, i.e. where the goods were purchased. However, nothing is simple in the EC and if the company has a large turnover in your country then it must register for VAT there too. It then charges just 'local' VAT.

The level of turnover depends on the country, varying between 35,000 and 100,000 ECU (European Currency Units), i.e. £24,500 – £70,000 per year. The UK has chosen the upper limit.

In practice this means that all but the largest mail order companies will charge you VAT at the origin rate, i.e. the level set in their own country. VAT will be added to the invoice in the same way as it is within the UK and will not appear on a Customs' sticker, as it does with orders from outside the EC.

Cars

For some time cars in the UK have been more expensive than identical models in the rest of Europe. Obviously the difference depends on the current exchange rate but at the time of going to press it is still worth it for some makes.

By EC law manufacturers must supply dealers with right-hand drive versions anywhere in Europe. However, some make more of a meal of this than others. For an excellent, comprehensive guide to importing a car read the Consumers Association's book. *Action Pack: Importing a Car*. It costs £8.99 and is available direct from the CA (see *Useful Addresses*).

10 *Telephone Tips*

While the telephone is by far the easiest and fastest way to place an order with a foreign supplier, it can prove expensive. The following information will help to cut the cost of calls but refers mainly to readers in the UK.

COST OF BT CALLS

CALLS TO THE USA & CANADA

Band	Time	1 min	5 min	10 min
Cheap	M-F 8pm-8am			
	All weekend	47p	2.37	4.69
Standard	M-F 8am-8pm	50p	2.52	5.04

CALLS TO EUROPE

Band	Time	1 min	5 min	10 min
Cheap	M-F 8pm-8am			
	All weekend	30p	1.49	2.97
Standard	M-F 8am-8pm	35p	1.78	3.56

♦ **WARNING!** International time bands are different from those on the domestic system. Do not make the mistake of thinking that all calls after 6pm are cheap – they are not!

CHARGE ADVICE

(UK only)
If you have a tone phone (i.e. one which beeps when you press the buttons) you can programme it to call you back with the cost of the call when you hang up. This service costs just over 5p per call and can be very useful to keep track of costs.

To operate it simply pick up the phone and dial *411#. You will then hear a woman's voice saying: 'Charge advice will be given on further calls from this number'. Now hang up and make your call as normal. Once you have finished the phone will ring and the same woman's voice will tell you how much your call cost.

To cancel the service dial #411#. Your phone will now be back to normal for further calls.

This service may be available in other countries with digital exchanges; check with your phone company.

ELECTRONIC OPERATORS/VOICE MAIL

Many American and now some British companies use electronic operators or voice mail to divert calls. This means you are greeted with a recorded message asking you to press certain buttons to access various services. Typically a message might run: 'If you wish to place an order press 1, if you wish to discuss an existing order press 2, if you want to talk to Customer Services press 3' and so on.

Once you have pressed the appropriate button on your phone you get through to the next stage, which may be a human or sometimes another set of choices until you finally do get to talk to a real person.

This system only works with phones using the tone dialling system – i.e. where a beep sounds for each number pressed. The machine at the other end interprets these and diverts your call accordingly. All voice mail has an option for non-tone phones (in the US known as rotary, in the UK as pulse). This usually involves waiting until all the options have been played whereupon you are automatically put through to a human operator who will then manually transfer you.

Obviously it is quicker – and therefore cheaper – to press the buttons. If your phone does not make a noise when you dial, check to see if there is a switch on the handset which can change it from Pulse to Tone or MF (multi-frequency). Most modern phones now have this facility and most UK exchanges support tone dialling, though not quite all as yet. If in doubt, call BT on 150 or your local phone company.

MERCURY

(UK only)
If you make many international calls it can make sense to use Mercury rather than BT. This company operates a rival telephone system and can prove cheaper for long distance and international calls. There is a standing quarterly charge which you have to pay in addition to your regular BT bill. However, this is easily recouped on the savings you can make. To access the network you simply tap in a simple code on your tone phone. For further information call their toll free number: 0800 424 194. But also see *Discount Calls*, below.

TOLL FREE NUMBERS

Many businesses now have toll free numbers so that consumers may call them free of charge. In the US these are prefixed by 1-800 while in the UK they are either 0800 or 0500. However, toll free numbers only work in the country of origin. You cannot use a US 1-800 number outside the United States. International toll free numbers do exist – and some companies use them – but they have the same prefix as any other toll free number in the calling country. Thus an American business might have a toll free number in the UK to call the States, but it will be an 0800 number and not a 1-800 number.

Having said this, there are ways in which you can get access to toll free numbers from outside, in particular to American 1-800 calls. One method is to use an AT&T Calling Card.

AT&T is one of America's largest phone companies. They issue a Calling Card which allows users to call from any phone in the world and have the cost billed to a credit card. To use the system you call a local toll free number which does in fact put you through to an operator in the States. This operator can then connect you to the required 1-800 number.

However, you are NOT getting a free call. Indeed there is an extra handling charge for each call made with the card of around $2.50. But it is a way to access these otherwise impossible numbers. The Calling Card itself costs nothing and can be obtained from AT&T in Europe by calling their toll free numbers, listed below:

AT&T TOLL FREE NUMBERS

Austria	0014 881 011	Luxembourg	0 800 0111
Belgium	11 0010	Netherlands	06 022 9111
Denmark	8001 0010	New Zealand	000 911
France	19 0011	Norway	050 12011
Germany	0130 0010	Portugal	05017 1 288
Greece	00 800 1311	Saudi Arabia	1 800 100
Ireland	1 800 550 000	Spain	900 99 00 11
Israel	177 100 2727	Sweden	020 795 611
Italy	172 1011	Switzerland	155 00 11
Japan	0039 111	UK	0800 890011

Other companies, such as Sprint, offer similar cards. Their toll free number in the UK is 0800 890877. There are also 'callback' services which connect you directly to a line in the US – see *Discount Calls* below.

MONEY SAVING STRATEGIES

Apart from the above, and making your call at the cheap rate, there are other ways you can ensure you spend as little as possible on calls.

- Have all the information ready to hand – fill in the order form as if you were posting it. This not only means you will include ALL the information needed but also speeds up the process of the supplier taking your order. The chances are they will be filling in an identical form on the other end of the phone and to have the information given in the right order will save time.

- Have any questions written down. The most common ones are:
  Exact cost (in case there has been a price increase)
  Cost of shipping and insurance and what it covers
  Shipping date and likely delivery time
  Name of the person you are dealing with

- Be ready to say you are calling from abroad IMMEDIATELY. This is to avoid being put on hold – a very common and expensive practice.

- Try to call early in the morning local time – i.e. when the supplier is just opening for business. This is not always possible but does lessen your chances of being put on hold – most people do not call first thing so you should get straight through.

DISCOUNT CALLS

With the deregulation of the telecoms industry in the UK there are now a number of companies offering very competitive alternatives to both BT and Mercury. For example, one of these sells calls to the US at just 14p per minute day or night. This compares very favourably with just under 50p for BT or Mercury.

A guide called *The Deregulated Phone Book* gives comprehensive information on all the services currently available and is certainly worth buying if you intend to call abroad regularly. We used it extensively in researching this book. It is published by a company called Running Heads: see *Appendix VI, Useful Addresses.*

11   Tips on Specific Items

Duty refers to UK and EC only

CDS

Duty 4.9%

CDs are ludicrously over-priced in the UK. The average price of a new release CD in the States is $13 as opposed to £13 here. They are, therefore, an ideal item to order from the US.

However, there are also a number of points to watch for. First, some companies, such as Bose, charge an international handling fee for overseas customers. This can cancel out any savings. Secondly, most suppliers calculate air mail by the lb. It is therefore cheaper to order CDs in threes or fours, which is the number you get per lb (the exact number depends on the packaging a company uses).

To make importing CDs worthwhile follow these guide-lines:

- If you are not bothered by the long delay have them sent by surface mail.

- If using air mail, buy 3 or 4 at a time to make maximum use of your first lb of postage.

- If possible use companies who do not add on a handling charge, e.g. Tower Records and Roundup (the latter charge $15 for the first lb and then $3 for each additional item).

COMPUTERS

Duty 14%

Not all computers are worth importing. If you are after a cheap IBM clone you will be better off looking in one of the specialist magazines, such as *PC Direct*. However, it is worth it for more expensive models such as Apple and Toshiba, especially the lap-tops. For something this expensive it is best to use a courier service.

The position with Apple changes all the time. Officially the company does not allow its distributors to operate by international mail order. However, this policy seems to be enforced with varying strictness, mostly according to the exchange rate. At present there are several companies willing to ship you an Apple overseas, although this may change.

JEANS

Duty 10%

Jeans are another bargain. Again, it may be cheaper to order several pairs at once. Levi 501s can be ordered from Sheplers (see under CLOTHES in the Directory). If they come by surface there are no extra shipping charges, making them a particularly good buy. Mass Army & Navy Store also sells them (see under OUTDOOR).

SOFTWARE

Duty 0%

As intellectual property, software attracts no duty, although you do still have to pay VAT. There is also duty to pay on the physical devices that carry the software, i.e. the discs, and the manuals. It is important to make sure the invoice specifies these separately. For example, a $100 software package might be divided into $95 for the software and $5 for the discs and manuals. Duty is then only payable on the $5.

Not all software can be exported. Some companies protect their overseas distributors by prohibiting US suppliers from shipping abroad. However, this does not seem to stop certain mail order houses from doing so despite the ban.

12 *Quick User's Guide*

THE DIRECTORY

The Directory is organized alphabetically by type of product. A typical entry:

Smiths Clocks   Full name of company
234 Main Street   Address
CT 89708-2313   Post Code

Tel: 603 987 8971   Phone (includes city code but not country code). Not all companies have telephone numbers.
Fax: 603 765 9871   Fax
Catalogue: Free   Price of catalogue ($ denotes call for price)
Goods: Clocks   Brief description of type of goods
Countries sent to: World   Countries to which the company will ship
Methods of payment: Types of payment the company will accept.

STEP-BY-STEP ORDERING

1. Look up the products in which you are interested in the Directory.
2. Send off for catalogues from several suppliers, by phone, fax or letter.

3. Compare prices & products. Check shipping, insurance & guarantees. Estimate full cost, including Duty & VAT* if relevant.

4. Place your order by phone or fax at cheap rate.

*FORMULA FOR ESTIMATING TOTAL COST OF GOODS

Price of goods + Shipping & Insurance = Total A
Total A + Duty % =   Total B
Total B + VAT % =   GRAND TOTAL

For Shipping & Insurance costs see *Appendix I*
For Duty % see *Appendix III*
For VAT % see *VAT* above

Example

Goods	100.00
Shipping & Insurance	12.00
Total A	112.00
Total A	112.00
Duty @ 10%	11.20
Total B	123.20
Total B	123.20
VAT @ 17.5%	21.00
GRAND TOTAL	**144.20**

13 *Mail Order Facts*

While much of the mail order business is the same the world over, there are some differences. Here we go through the details pertinent to each country, such as address format, time zones and preferred methods of payment (but see each supplier for specific details).

AUSTRALIA & NEW ZEALAND

Australia and New Zealand have a small but well-organized mail order industry which operates very much like that in the US or Britain. Obviously delivery time can be a little longer to Western Europe but apart from that ordering is quite straightforward.

| International phone code | Australia | 61 |
| | New Zealand | 64 |

| Time | Australia | GMT +8/10 hours |
| | New Zealand | GMT +12 hours |

Cheques	Cheques in Australian $	Credit cards	Visa
	Cheques in NZ $		Access
			Mastercard
			Eurocard
			Diners
			American Express
Address	First name, last name	James Johnson
	Number of street, street	582 Kirby Drive
	City/town, state & code	Allambie NSW 2100
		Australia

First name, last name	Michael Little
Number of street, street	65 Hope Avenue
City/town & code	Wellington 1
	New Zealand

CANADA

Although Canada does have some large mail order businesses, it tends to specialize in smaller companies offering high-quality or unusual items. The pound seems to have held up better against the Canadian dollar than the equivalent in the US so there may be some bargains for UK consumers.

International phone code   1   Time GMT – 3½ – 9 hours

Cheques	Cheques in Canadian dollars	Credit Cards	Visa
	Cheques in US dollars		Access
			Mastercard
			Eurocard
			Diners
			Amex

Address	First name, last name	Mayo Inc.
	Number of street, street	582 Eglington Avenue
	Town/city, province in brackets	Toronto (ON)
	Post code (Letter, number, letter,	M4P 1B9
	space, number, letter, number)	

Canadian Province Abbreviations
AB Alberta
BC British Columbia
MB Manitoba
NB New Brunswick
NF Newfoundland
NW Northwest Territories
NS Nova Scotia
ON Ontario

PE   Prince Edward Island
PQ   Quebec
SK   Saskatchewan
YT   Yukon Territory

EUROPE

Although the mail order industry in Europe is larger and more widespread than in the UK, it has not yet fully appreciated the advantages of a world-wide market. The majority of companies are content to operate only in familiar territories. One reason may be language, although companies which have bothered to issue catalogues in English have benefited from a new wave of customers in the US and UK.

Another practical problem is the companies' reluctance to take credit cards. This alone puts off many potential buyers who rightly see cards as the easiest way to make foreign payments.

International phone code See below   Time   See below

Cheques Cheques in local currency Credit Cards Visa
         Eurocheques   Access
                                                  Mastercard
                                                  Eurocard
                                                  Diners
                                                  Amex

Address First name, last name   Franz Huber
         Street, number of street,   Beethovenstrasse 55
         Code (number) town or city 9200 Verviers
         Country   Belgium

TELEPHONE CODES & TIME ZONES

Country	Phone code	Time Difference GMT
Austria	43	+1
Belgium	32	+1
Denmark	45	+1
France	33	+1
Germany	49	+1
Greece	30	+2
Ireland	353 (Dublin 0001)	0
Italy	39	+1
Luxembourg	352	+1
Netherlands	31	+1
Portugal	351	0
Spain	34	+1

HONG KONG

Hong Kong is often thought of as a shopper's paradise and certainly in terms of sheer choice it is. However, the days of cheap cameras and watches have largely gone. The Hong Kong dollar is now tied to the US dollar and as a result prices are no longer spectacularly cheap.

However, there are several mail order companies in Hong Kong which between them sell virtually everything and they will ship anywhere. There are still bargains to be had with clothes, especially silks and traditional Chinese wear.

International phone code 852   Time GMT +8 hours

Cheques Cheques in Hong Kong $ Credit Cards Visa
                                                Access
                                                Mastercard
                                                Eurocard
                                                Diners
                                                American Express

Address	First name, last name	James Lee
	Number of street, street	582 Eglington Avenue
	Part	Kowloon
		Hong Kong

UK

Mail order in the UK has finally shed its image of cheap and nasty and is beginning to mature into the sort of industry the US has had for years. There are a huge number of companies operating, from the giant conglomerates down to the one-man-bands, often selling obscure but delightful products. Delivery times have improved tremendously and the Royal Mail can now genuinely claim to be the most efficient postal system in Europe. This, coupled with the widespread acceptance of credit cards, has meant that British mail order has come of age.

International phone code   44   Time   Oct 24 – March 28 GMT
                                             March 29 – Oct 25 GMT –1

Cheques	Sterling on UK banks	Credit Cards	Visa
	Eurocheques in Sterling		Access
			Mastercard
			Eurocard

Address	First name, last name	John Smith Ltd
	Number of street, street	12 Black Street
	Town or city	Brighton
	County	West Sussex
	Post code (Two letters	BN14 6AZ
	& number, space, number	
	& two letters)	

USA

Ever since Benjamin Franklin issued the first catalogue back in 1744 the US has led the way in mail order. With by far the most sophisticated and developed industry it is now increasingly turning its attention to foreign markets. Take L. L. Bean, the giant clothing supplier. They had always done a certain amount of business overseas, mostly by word of mouth, but two years ago they set up an international division specifically to woo foreign custom. Within two years they were conducting over $38 million worth of business, some 6% of their total sales.

♦ **WARNING!** Contact lenses are much cheaper in the US, even at the current exchange rate, and it is tempting to order a spare pair from across the Atlantic. However, there can be drawbacks. In the UK it is illegal to sell lenses through the mail. The Optical Act of 1989 forbids anyone but a qualified optician from selling or fitting lenses – this is to protect consumers who could do irreparable damage to their eyes.

It is not entirely clear whether this extends to overseas suppliers, although the Optical Council thinks that it does. Certainly people have successfully bought lenses from the US and have had no problems with Customs. However, in this case it may be best to err on the side of caution and spend a little more money – after all, you do only have one pair of eyes.

International phone code	1	Time	Eastern:	GMT–5
			Central:	GMT–6
			Mountain:	GMT–7
			Pacific:	GMT–8

Cheques	Dollars on US banks	Credit Cards	Visa
			Access
			Mastercard
			Eurocard

Address	First name, last name	John Smith Inc.
	Number of street, street	3500 Seventh Avenue
	Town or city	San Francisco
	State & Zip	CA 12345

Part 2
DIRECTORY

ART SUPPLIES

Curry's Art Store Ltd
755 The Queensway East, Mississauga, ON L4Y 4C5, Canada.
Tel: 416 798 7983 *Fax:* 416 272 0778

Catalogue:	$12
Goods:	Art supplies
Countries sent to:	World
Methods of payment:	Visa, Mastercard

Curry's issue a 377 page catalogue for artist, craft and graphic supplies. They say they are never undersold but as we went to press we had not received their catalogue so cannot comment on prices.

Fiesta Arts Corp
18 East View Lane, Glen Head, New York, NY 11545–2004, USA.
Tel: 516 671 6888

Catalogue:	$2
Goods:	Posters
Countries sent to:	World
Methods of payment:	Cheque, Bank Transfer

A glossy 9 pages, this brochure offers classic posters from the Belle Époque period. Each print measures 19½" x 27½" with work by artists such as Lautrec, Mucha and Redon. The founder of the House of Riccordi was a friend, publisher and patron to the artists of the period, including such luminaries as Bellini, Donizetti, Rossini and Puccini and this American company is now the direct importer of posters from his archive.

Esmond Hellerman Ltd

Hellerman House, Harris Way, Windmill Road, Sunbury on Thames, Middlesex TW 16 7EW, United Kingdom. *Tel:* 0932 781888
Fax: 0932 789573

Catalogue:	Free
Goods:	Drawing & drafting supplies
Countries sent to:	World
Methods of payment:	Cheque, Bank Transfer

This impressive 106 page catalogue contains over 4,000 products. Established in 1950, Hellerman specialize in modern drawing and drafting equipment for artists and engineers. The range covers everything from pens, through compasses and templates to drawing boards and tables. There is an excellent index to guide the reader and some generous discount offers to persuade them to place an order.

The International Pen Shop

PO Box 7820, Maspeth, NY 11378, USA. *Tel:* 718 628 0600
Fax: 718 628 0599

Catalogue:	$2
Goods:	Pens
Countries sent to:	World
Methods of payment:	Visa, Mastercard, Cheque, Bank Transfer

This 64 page colour catalogue has to be THE source for pens. Splendidly produced, it features an enormous range of pens from the world's finest manufacturers. These include Mont Blanc, Parker, Sheaffer, Waterman, Tombo, Dupont, Stipula, Lamy, Visconti, Cross, Platinum and Rotring amongst others. Prices vary enormously but do seem to be less than in the UK. They start at around $14 for a pencil and rise to a sobering $10,000 for a stunning white gold Mont Blanc fountain pen. They also sell refills for every model.

Rex Art
2263 SW 37th Avenue, Miami, FL 33145, USA. *Tel:* 305 445 1413
Fax: 305 445 1412

Catalogue:	$5.95
Goods:	Graphic art supplies
Countries sent to:	World
Methods of payment:	Mastercard, Amex, Diners Club, Bank Draft

Another large graphic arts catalogue selling just about everything available. You can buy from a simple pen or roll of sticky tape, through oil and watercolour paints, to easels, drawing boards and light boxes. Well produced and easy to follow.

Daniel Smith Inc.
4150 First Avenue South, PO Box 84268, Seattle, WA 98134–5568, USA. *Tel:* 206 223 9599 *Fax:* 206 224 0404

Catalogue:	$5
Goods:	Fine art materials
Countries sent to:	Asia, Europe, Africa, USA
Methods of payment:	Visa, Mastercard, Cheque

Daniel Smith's 164 page reference catalogue contains every item the aspiring or professional artist could desire bar the subject itself. It offers an enormous range of paints from boxed kits to individual tubes and crayons. An essential oil painting kit retails at $79.50. There are special offers on selected ranges e.g. W & N Watercolor Field Box $48.85 instead of $67. Apart from paints the catalogue boasts a vast array of brushes, painting knives, papers and canvas which include exotic hand-made lace papers and papyrus.

The catalogue has a strong selection of studio equipment with frames and framing tools, and goodies for the graphic artist's studio with portfolios from $28.88 (another special offer) to projectors at $719.80.

AVIATION

Aircraft Speciality Co.
201 West Truslow Avenue, Fullerton, CA 92632, USA.
Tel: 714 870 7551 *Fax:* 714 871 7289

Catalogue:	$20
Goods:	Aircraft parts & pilot supplies
Countries sent to:	World
Methods of payment:	Visa, Mastercard, Cheque, Bank Transfer

This company issues a 416 page catalogue featuring just about everything you could need for a plane plus a wide variety of accessories such as pilot's clothes, watches, gifts and so on. At least this is what they told us! The catalogue costs $20 and they would not send us either a complimentary copy or even photocopies of sample pages. We are therefore unable to give any further information.

Wag-Aero
PO Box 181, 1216 North Road, Lyons, WI 53148, USA.
Tel: 414 763 9586 *Fax:* 414 763 7595

Catalogue:	Free
Goods:	Aviation paraphernalia
Countries sent to:	World
Methods of payment:	Visa, Mastercard, Cheque, Bank Transfer

The Wag-Aero Group specializes in Aircraft Services. Its 1993 catalogue runs to an impressive 147 pages. Jam-packed with everything for the private pilot, the range covers muffler and exhaust systems, gas tanks, batteries and spark plugs, lighting, props and spinners, radios, tyres, brakes and wheels. It even includes kits to make your own aeroplane, a replica of the 1930s Sport Trainer, but it's not cheap at $2,495 and that's just for the wings.

Parts for most light aircraft are available from the latest in propeller engines at $14,550 to door latches at $42.95. Wag-Aero has been in business for 33 years, so if it's not in this catalogue, you probably don't need it.

BOOKS

Bibliagora

PO Box 77, Feltham, Middlesex TW14 8JF, United Kingdom.
Tel: 081 898 1234 *Fax:* 081 844 1777

Catalogue:	Free
Goods:	UK & US books
Countries sent to:	Asia, Europe, Africa, USA
Methods of payment:	Visa, Mastercard, Diners Club, Amex, Cheque, Bank Transfer, Bank Draft

Bibliagora specialize in tracing out of print books but also sell new British and American books. Ironically their own catalogue was out of print when we went to press, but apparently when it does appear again will be 16 pages in colour.

Book Call

59 Elm Street, New Canaan, CT 06840, USA. *Tel:* 203 966 5470
Fax: 203 966 4329

Catalogue:	Free
Goods:	American published books
Countries sent to:	World
Methods of payment:	Visa, Mastercard, Cheque, Bank Transfer

Book Call enables you to order any book in print in the US at any time of the day or night, seven days a week. Dispatch of your order is guaranteed within 48 hours. They also publish Bibliomania, an A5 gift catalogue. It runs to 40 black and white pages covering around 180 titles which range from glossy art books, such as *Maxfield Parrish: The Masterworks* ($75), through current fiction, like Donna Tartt's *The Secret History* ($23), to perennial reference works such as *The Times Atlas of the World* ($175).

Canadian Magazine Publishers Association

2 Stewart Street, Toronto, Ontario M5V 1H6, Canada.
Tel: 416 362 9662 *Fax:* 416 362 2547

Catalogue:	$5
Goods:	Magazines
Countries sent to:	World
Methods of payment:	Visa, Mastercard, Cheque

This isn't really a catalogue but a 92 page directory of Canadian magazines put together by their trade association. Strictly speaking it is for retailers but they do (sometimes!) send it out to individuals. Each publication is shown in a small photograph followed by an informative description and details of subscription rates and a contact address. The directory divides magazines into ten different areas of interest: The Arts; Business; Children's; Feminist; Literary; News & Opinion; People & Places; Scholarly; Special Interest and Sports & Outdoors. If it is published in Canada it is probably here.

Centre de Developpement d'Agrobiologie

224 rue Principale, Sainte-Elizabeth-de-Warwick, PQ J0A 1M0, Canada. *Tel:* 819 358 3850 *Fax:* 819 358 3859

Catalogue:	Free
Goods:	Agricultural & horticultural books
Countries sent to:	World
Methods of payment:	Visa, Mastercard, Bank Transfer

Over 1,200 titles are available from this specialist company, covering all aspects of agriculture and horticulture. They do issue a free catalogue but it was unavailable as we went to press.

Chater & Scott

8 South Street, Isleworth, Middlesex TW7 7BG, United Kingdom.
Tel: 081 568 9750 *Fax:* 081 569 8273

Catalogue:	Free
Goods:	Motoring books & video tapes
Countries sent to:	World
Methods of payment:	Visa, Mastercard, Amex, Cheque, Bank Transfer

Chater's produce a closely printed 28 page catalogue listing a huge range of books on motoring. It is divided into general interest, technical, motorsport, manufacturers, manuals and part lists and motorcycles. They also have an extensive range of videos (VHS PAL) on motorsport and motorcycle racing.

Classic Motorbooks

PO Box 1, GS/94, Osceola, WI 54020, USA. *Tel:* 715 294 3345
Fax: 715 294 4418

Catalogue:	$2
Goods:	Car books
Countries sent to:	World
Methods of payment:	Visa, Mastercard, Amex, Cheque, Bank Draft

With 120 pages in colour, this excellent catalogue has books on every aspect of classic cars. Organized by manufacturer, it covers virtually every car of interest, as well as tractors, buses, vans, watercraft, snowmobiles, motorbikes, steam engines and trucks. It is not just restricted to American models but includes all major European badges. Here you can find service manuals, original handbooks, histories, personal reminiscences, videos and a great deal more. Each book is described in a useful paragraph and prices seem reasonable. For once that characteristic American claim 'the world's largest selection of . . .' seems true.

Clouston & Hall Booksellers P/L

28 Kembla St, Fyshwick 2609, Australia. *Tel:* 06 280 4499
Fax: 06 239 1076

Catalogue:	Free
Goods:	Remainder books
Countries sent to:	Asia, Europe, USA, Australasia
Methods of payment:	Visa, Mastercard, Cheque, Bank Transfer

Clouston's regular catalogue is printed like a broadsheet newspaper, with 12 pages of close print describing academic remainders from all different disciplines. There are also some new books at substantial discounts.

Computer Booklist

50 James Road, Birmingham BA11 2BA, United Kingdom.
Tel: 021 706 6000 *Fax:* 021 706 3301

Catalogue:	Free
Goods:	Books on computers
Countries sent to:	World
Methods of payment:	Visa, Mastercard, Amex, Cheque

This excellent 48 page catalogue lives up to its name – a huge listing of over 3,500 computer titles. Divided into sections on Using PCs, Programming, Using Macs, Home & Games and Professional, new editions are issued every four months. If they don't have it, it probably doesn't exist. Expert advice, next day delivery and a shipping policy to cover the world round off a very professional service.

D & P Enterprises

Box 1117, Squamish, BC V0N 3G0, Canada. *Tel:* 604 898 3037
Fax: 604 898 3723

Catalogue:	Free
Goods:	Books on mail order
Countries sent to:	World
Methods of payment:	Visa, Cheque, Bank Transfer

Books on mail order are the mainstay of this company – the sort that tell you how to start and run a company selling goods through the post. Titles include: *The Spare Time Mail Order Tycoon* and *Self-Publishing Made Easy*. They also publish the newsletter *It's in the Mail*, which keeps track of who is selling what this way.

As a sideline, they stock The Baby Soother, a cassette tape which is designed to promote good sleep and stop crying, and Pipal Leaf Paintings from India, which are miniature paintings on leaves. (These also seem to be available from other small Canadian mail order companies.)

Dillons the Bookstore

82 Gower Street, London WC1E 6EQ, United Kingdom.
Tel: 071 636 1577 *Fax:* 071 580 7680

Catalogue:	Free
Goods:	Books
Countries sent to:	World
Methods of payment:	Visa, Mastercard, Amex, Cheque, Bank Transfer

Dillons claims to be Europe's largest bookstore and their mail order department must break some records too. Although they will send any book from stock (over 300,000), they also issue several catalogues with details of new publications. These are split into subject areas, such as medical, social science, fiction and so on. They have a thriving international business and will send books anywhere in the world.

The Field-Naturalist

1241 Broad Street, Victoria, BC V8W 2A4, Canada.
Tel: 604 388 4174

Catalogue:	$2
Goods:	Natural History books
Countries sent to:	World
Methods of payment:	Visa, Mastercard, Diners Club, Cheque, Bank Transfer

The 52 page, simple catalogue concentrates on a wide range of books and recordings of natural history. However, the company also sells binoculars, telescopes and microscopes, details of which are available on request.

The Folger Shakespeare Library
201 East Capitol Street S.E., Washington, DC 20003, USA.
Tel: 202 675 0308

Catalogue:	Free
Goods:	Shakespeare-related books
Countries sent to:	World
Methods of payment:	Visa, Mastercard, Amex

The famous Folger Shakespeare Library issues a catalogue featuring books, music and gifts all related, naturally, to Shakespeare. As we went to press this was being up-dated so we were unable to see it.

Karl Franger Books
13295 Amblewood Drive, Surrey, BC V4A 6M4, Canada.
Tel: 604 538 5084

Catalogue:	Free
Goods:	New & secondhand books
Countries sent to:	World
Methods of payment:	Cheque, Bank Transfer

A mail order equivalent of the secondhand bookshop, this company specializes in Canadian and Latin American fiction and non-fiction. We were sent some sample pages from the catalogue with details of each book and its condition. However, it is not clear what the complete catalogue would look like or how large it is.

Books seem to start as low as Canadian $8.50 on top of which there is a charge of $2 for the first volume and $1 for additional ones, plus postage.

Gamblers Book Club
630 S. 11th Street, Las Vegas, NV 89101, USA. *Tel:* 702 382 7555
Fax: 702 382 7594

Catalogue:	Free
Goods:	Gambling books
Countries sent to:	World
Methods of payment:	Visa, Mastercard, Cheque

Based in Las Vegas (where else) this fascinating store issues a catalogue in the shape of a 32 page tabloid newspaper. There are thousands of titles covering all types of gambling, from casinos through racing to one-armed bandits and even the latest video machines. They also stock some intriguing books on con tricks, psychology, travel and fiction – all with a gambling theme of course.

The Good Book Guide
Unit 1, City Central II, Seward Street, London EC1V 3PB, United Kingdom. *Tel:* 071 490 9903

Catalogue:	Free
Goods:	Books & videos
Countries sent to:	World
Methods of payment:	Visa, Mastercard

The Good Book Guide offers two services. First it is an international book ordering company, which will ship books, cassettes and videos anywhere. They will even wrap them specially if they are gifts. Secondly, they publish *The Good Book Magazine* six times a year. This is an unbiased review of the latest books, all of which can of course be ordered. Subscriptions to this are £17 in the UK, £20 for Europe and £25 worldwide. This is NOT a bookclub and you are not obliged to order anything at all. One of the great benefits to overseas readers is that it keeps them up-to-date with the latest books and sells them at British prices. There are already 30,000 subscribers to this excellent scheme.

Harmony Foundation of Canada
202A 145 Spruce Street, Ottawa, ON K1R 6P1, Canada. *Tel:* 613 230 5399 *Fax:* 613 238 6470

Catalogue:	Free
Goods:	Books & videos
Countries sent to:	World
Methods of payment:	Cheque

Harmony is a charity which develops environmental education programmes. To this end it publishes and distributes a number of books and videos on the subject. For example, for Canadian $25 there is *Workplace Guide: Practical Action for the Environment*, which is a

176 page book to help environmental organizations. They do not have a catalogue but a simple leaflet in French and English describing their publications.

Heffer's Children's Bookshop
30 Trinity Street, Cambridge CB2 1TB, United Kingdom.
Tel: 0223 356200 *Fax:* 0223 410464

Catalogue:	Free
Goods:	Children's books
Countries sent to:	World
Methods of payment:	Visa, Mastercard, Cheque, Bank Transfer

'Choices' is a range of catalogues on children's books published by Heffer's: Children's Bookshop. It's a great idea, particularly for parents who don't have access to the larger bookstores. Catalogues in the series cover reference books, poetry, videos and foreign language titles. Although the catalogues are small (ranging from 4–6 pages) Heffer's can provide a more comprehensive list of titles on request.

The reference catalogue includes such staples as *The Oxford Children's Dictionary* (£4.99), *The Blue Peter Green Book* (£4.99 or £2.99 pb) and *Collins Illustrated Encyclopaedia of Famous People* (£15.00). The poetry catalogue includes *The Oxford Nursery Rhyme Book* (£12.95).

Home Services
Box 477 – GS, Chetwynd, BC V0C 1J0, Canada. *Tel:* 604 780 2364

Catalogue:	US$2
Goods:	Unusual books
Countries sent to:	World
Methods of payment:	Cheque, Bank Transfer, COD

'Unique Books' is a catalogue of books with a strong emphasis on self-help and 'inspirational' titles, many of which are not available in bookstores. Titles such as *How to Achieve Total Success* (Canadian $12.95) and *Your Thoughts Can Change Your Life* (Canadian $7) give a good indication of the type of product carried. They also have an extensive range of money-making books, mostly on mail order schemes.

A thin 24 pages, the catalogue makes inventive use of a range of spot colours. It contains a useful section on mail order titles such as the *Importer's Guide to Singapore Products* ($15) and the *USA Wholesale Sources Directory* ($10).

Map Marketing Ltd

92/104 Carnwath Road, London SW6 3HW, United Kingdom.
Tel: 071 736 0297 *Fax:* 071 371 0473

Catalogue:	Free
Goods:	Maps
Countries sent to:	World
Methods of payment:	Visa, Mastercard, Amex, Diners Club, Cheque, Bank Transfer

A nicely produced 72 page colour catalogue, this shows the wide variety of maps the company sells. For the UK there are the normal Ordnance Survey, road maps and city maps, along with more specialist versions such as post codes maps and even satellite maps. There is a similar stock of international maps covering most parts of the globe in great detail.

MENCAP Books

123 Golden Lane, London EC1Y 0RT, United Kingdom.
Tel: 071 696 5569 *Fax:* 071 608 3254

Catalogue:	£1
Goods:	Books on learning disability
Countries sent to:	Asia, Europe, Australasia
Methods of payment:	Visa, Mastercard, Cheque, Bank Transfer

MENCAP is a British charity for the mentally ill and in this 112 page catalogue sells books on all aspects of learning disability. In addition they hire out videos and have an excellent reference section with useful addresses.

The Military History Bookshop

2 The Broadway, Friern Barnet Road, London N11 3DU, United Kingdom. *Tel:* 081 368 8568 *Fax:* 081 368 8568

Catalogue:	Free
Goods:	History books
Countries sent to:	World
Methods of payment:	Visa, Mastercard, Cheque, Bank Draft, International Money Order

This specialist bookshop already has customers all round the world and it is not difficult to see why – it is an excellent source for all manner of military history books, both new and secondhand. The main catalogue, issued four times a year, is a densely printed listing over some 70 pages or so. In addition, there are two other catalogues published annually – one on Germany in World War II, the other on American military history.

The Nautical Mind Bookstore

Radisson Plaza Hotel, 249 Queen's Quay West, Toronto, ON M5J 2N5, Canada. *Tel:* 416 203 1163 *Fax:* 416 203 0729

Catalogue:	Free
Goods:	Nautical books & charts
Countries sent to:	World
Methods of payment:	Visa, Mastercard, Bank Transfer

A beautifully produced 128 page catalogue entitled 'The Nautical Mind Reference Book of Nautical Titles', describing hundreds of books of interest to professional and amateur sailors. Subjects covered include charts, cruising guides, boat design, history, knots, navigation and so on. There is also a selection of videos and fiction titles.

Oxbow Books Ltd
Park End Place, Oxford, Oxon OX1 1HN, United Kingdom.
Tel: 0865 241249 *Fax:* 0865 794449

Catalogue:	Free
Goods:	History books
Countries sent to:	World
Methods of payment:	Visa, Mastercard, Diners Club, Cheque, Bank Transfer

Oxbow specialize in books on archaeology, ancient and medieval history, art and literature. They produce an excellent 50 page catalogue which is issued on a regular basis. Each title is accompanied by a useful synopsis and many are unavailable in the US and elsewhere outside the UK. They also have a USA sales office which produces a version priced in $.

Oxbow Books
David Brown Book Company, PO Box 5605, Bloomington, IN 47407, USA. *Tel:* 812 331 0266 *Fax:* 812 331 0277

Postscript
22a Langroyd Road, London SW17 7PL, United Kingdom.
Tel: 081 767 7421 *Fax:* 081 682 0280

Catalogue:	Free
Goods:	Discounted books
Countries sent to:	World
Methods of payment:	Visa, Mastercard, International Money Order

Postscript deal in bargain books, that is, publishers' overstocks. This enables them to sell at extremely low prices, well under half the normal charge and sometimes much less. They publish excellent monthly catalogues of around 32 pages, divided into subject areas with each book receiving a helpful and informative description. Areas include Reference, Social History, History, 20th Century, Science, Art, Biography, War, Cookery and Travel. They also issue a separate academic catalogue.

Marga Schoeller Bucherstube gmbH

Knesebeckstr 33 (Ecke Mommsenstr), D 10623 Berlin, Germany.
Tel: 030 881 1122 *Fax:* 030 881 8479

Catalogue:	Free
Goods:	Books
Countries sent to:	World
Methods of payment:	Cheque, International Money Order

This German-language 44 page catalogue lists books on film from around the world, most in German but some in English.

Edward Stanford

12–14 Long Acre, London WC2E 9LP, United Kingdom.
Tel: 071 836 1321 *Fax:* 071 836 0189

Catalogue:	n/a
Goods:	Maps, travel guides & literature
Countries sent to:	World
Methods of payment:	Visa, Mastercard, Cheque

Stanford's are a well-known, long-established bookshop who specialize in travel. They stock an enormous range of maps from all round the world and even outside it – you can buy a map of the moon – plus travel books, guides, globes and so on. Although they do not currently publish a catalogue they do send goods anywhere. Simply contact the helpful staff directly.

Tartan Book Sales

500 Arch Street, Williamsport, PA 17705, USA. *Tel:* 717 326 2461
Fax: 717 326 6769

Catalogue:	Free
Goods:	Discounted books
Countries sent to:	World
Methods of payment:	Visa, Mastercard

This 83 page black and white catalogue is set out as a directory with a linear entry layout to help make its contents easy to read. With some 3,400 recent hardcover titles, it is pretty comprehensive. They have a large selection covering Crime, Self Help Manuals, Politics, Westerns,

Large Print and Finance.

Prices seem very competitive, with Peter Carey's recent novel *The Tax Inspector* selling at $5.98, as against the retail price of $21. Kathryn D. Cramer's *Staying On Top: When Your World Turns Upside Down* is just $4.98 as opposed to $17.95 in the shops. A great place to buy books.

Traveller's Bookstore
22 W. 52nd Street, New York, NY 10019, USA. *Tel:* 212 664 0995 *Fax:* 212 397 3984

Catalogue:	$2
Goods:	Travel books & accessories
Countries sent to:	World
Methods of payment:	Visa, Mastercard, Amex

This slim, 20 page catalogue is full of fascinating travel books covering the whole world. While the selection is not very extensive it is discerning and each book is given a complete and helpful description. Divided into sections on different countries, the catalogue also has a small range of travel goods such as irons, clocks and an ingenious voltage converter ($27.50).

Yes! Bookshop
1035 31st Street N.W., Washington, DC 20007, USA.
Tel: 202 338 7874 *Fax:* 202 338 8150

Catalogue:	$
Goods:	Books on inner development, Zen etc.
Countries sent to:	World
Methods of payment:	Visa, Mastercard, Amex, Cheque, Bank Draft

The Yes! catalogue was not ready as we went to press but features a good range of books on a wide range of 'alternative' subjects. These include inner development, holistic lifestyle (sic), health, meditation, yoga, psychology, philosophy, Buddhism and Zen.

BOOTS & SHOES

Caput Magnum Designs

Station Street, Holbeach, Spalding, Lincolnshire PE12 7LF, United Kingdom. *Tel:* 0406 24124 *Fax:* 0406 26129

Catalogue:	Free
Goods:	Shoes & sandals
Countries sent to:	Europe, USA
Methods of payment:	Visa, Mastercard

This nicely produced 19 page colour brochure carries a good range of interesting footware. They have a comprehensive range of Ecco shoes as well as German Servas court shoes, Remonte ladies' casuals, Mephisto outdoor shoes and Birkenstock sandals. For dancers, they have a variety of pumps and jazz shoes.

A typical ladies' sandal costs £47.95, ballet pumps are £29.95 and men's lace ups £59.95.

Double Eagle Custom Crafted Boots

5320 Cameron Road, Austin, TX 78723, USA. *Tel:* 512 454 6154

Catalogue:	$2.50
Goods:	Custom made boots
Countries sent to:	World
Methods of payment:	Visa, Mastercard, Amex

Double Eagle produce custom made cowboy boots in a variety of styles and leathers. The 4 page catalogue has colour photographs of the boots themselves and the types of materials available. These include alligator, elephant, ostrich, shark, lizard, camel, French calf, eel, kangaroo, python, anaconda, water buffalo and even anteater and hippopotamus (some of these species may be forbidden for import into certain countries). You can choose both the styling and stitching and the very detailed order form, running to some 6 pages with about 30 separate questions, ensures that each boot is genuinely custom fit.

Prices vary according to the leather, but start at around $500 for African antelope, $550 for French calf, and rise to some $1,900 for alligator.

Lee Kee Boot & Shoe Maker Ltd

19–21B Hankow Road, Kowloon, Hong Kong.
Tel: 376 1180 & 364 4903

Catalogue:	Free
Goods:	Handmade boots & shoes
Countries sent to:	World
Methods of payment:	Cheque, International Money Order

Lee Kee will tailor boots and shoes to any design. These include jodhpur boots, half-wellingtons, cowboy boots and riding boots. They will also copy any design from a drawing or photograph. These can be made in a variety of leathers, from standard calfskin through buckskin to the more exotic kangaroo, shark and even ostrich skin (though some of these may be banned from import into certain countries).

The brochure consists of a simple, typewritten sheet and prices are in US$. Shoes start at around $120 and rise to over $500 if made of alligator skin. Boots are a little more, starting at just under $150 rising to almost $800.

John Lobb Bootmaker

9 St James's Street, London SW1A 1EF, United Kingdom.
Tel: 071 930 3664/5

Catalogue:	n/a
Goods:	Handmade boots & shoes
Countries sent to:	World
Methods of payment:	Visa, Mastercard, Amex, Cheque, Bank Transfer

John Lobb's boots and shoes are handmade to measure. They do not issue a catalogue but will send photographs of previous work to interested customers. They add 'Our prices are beyond the reach of most people'!

Mark's Athletic Soles

4028 S.W. 57th Avenue, Miami, FL 33155, USA. *Tel:* 305 665 8601
Fax: 305 663 5885

Catalogue:	Free
Goods:	Running & leisure shoes
Countries sent to:	World
Methods of payment:	Visa, Mastercard, Amex, Cheque, Bank Transfer

This company offers the unusual service of re-soling shoes. These include running shoes, such as Nike and Reebok, as well as leisure shoes. They also sell New Balance, Rockport and even Timberland. However, they do not publish a catalogue and did not provide us with a price list so it is probably best to call direct to discuss your requirements.

Sally Small Shoes Ltd

71 York Street, London W1H 2BJ, United Kingdom.
Tel: 071 723 5321 *Fax:* 071 723 5321

Catalogue:	Free
Goods:	Adult women's shoes in very small sizes
Countries sent to:	Europe, USA, Australasia
Methods of payment:	Visa, Mastercard, Amex, Diners Club, Cheque, Bank Transfer

Sally Small have a London retail outlet specializing in women's shoes in small sizes but they also run a good mail order operation. Their 1 page, fold-out colour brochure features 27 different styles of shoes, all in total-leather and available in sizes 1–2½, 32–34 and 13–2½. Shoes include high-heels, pumps, sandals, low boots, dress shoes and slip ons all in attractive designs. Many also come in extra-wide fittings. Prices start around £28 rising to £75 with £1.75 for p+p, waived if you pay in cash (though be sure to send money by registered post).

Shelly's Shoes
1–3 Edgware Road, London NW2 6JZ, United Kingdom.
Tel: 081 450 0066 *Fax:* 081 208 4340

Catalogue:	£2
Goods:	Fashion shoes
Countries sent to:	World
Methods of payment:	Visa, Mastercard, Amex, Diners Club, Cheque, Bank Transfer

Shelly's have a large shoe store in Oxford Street, London, but also have a thriving international mail order side. A number of colour catalogues come in an impressive folder, all glossy, attractive and simple to follow. The £2 charge is refundable against orders and international customers can join the Shelly Club which gives further discounts. The text is in English with translations into French, German and Spanish.

There is an excellent range of Doc Martens, in a variety of styles for both men and women, as well as other high quality makes. Prices start at around £30 and go up to £60 or so for high boots.

Shipton & Heneage Ltd
117 Queenstown Road, London SW8 3RH, United Kingdom.
Tel: 071 738 8484 *Fax:* 071 924 2470

Catalogue:	Free
Goods:	Shoes & shoe accessories
Countries sent to:	World
Methods of payment:	Visa, Mastercard, Diners Club, Cheque, Bank Transfer

Shipton & Heneage produce beautiful, traditionally made shoes for men. Their attractive small catalogue features shoes in many different styles, although the emphasis is on the formal. They have a large international customer base which has been built up through word of mouth over the years – testament to the quality of their products.

Prices may seem on the high side but are in fact much lower than similar products in the shops. Shoes start at around £63 rising to just under £100. Non-EC readers may subtract VAT from these, at present 17.5%. Postage is £4.65 per pair in the UK, within the EC around £15, £17 to the US and Canada, £19 to Australia and £21 for elsewhere.

White's Boots & Work Clothes
N 6116 Freya Street, Spokane, WA 99207, USA. *Tel:* 509 487 7277

Catalogue:	Free
Goods:	Boots
Countries sent to:	World
Methods of payment:	Visa, Mastercard, Cheque, International Money Order

White's have been making their marvellous, hardwearing work boots for over 100 years. Their excellent 24 page colour catalogue features a range of men's boots mostly for outdoor use. However, they do make a 'dress' version for general wear in a variety of leathers. These include calfskin, water buffalo, ostrich, python and even beaver tail (though some of these may come under import restrictions in certain countries). All are custom made to your own measurements.

Laceup cowboy boots start at $245, dress boots at just over $500 and work boots at around $300.

CARS & MOTORBIKES

American Car Imports
57 Coburg Road, Wood Green, London N22 6UB, United Kingdom.
Tel: 081 954 9605 *Fax:* 081 889 7500

Catalogue:	n/a
Goods:	Cars
Countries sent to:	World
Methods of payment:	Visa, Mastercard, Amex, Diners Club, Cheque, Bank Transfer, Bank Draft

This company is not strictly speaking a mail order house but it does offer an interesting service. They will find and import specific cars from the US. Customers simply supply details of make, model and year (they can supply new and secondhand vehicles) and the company does the rest. It's particularly useful for people searching for classic cars, unusual models only available in the US, or motorhomes. Of course most cars will be left-hand drive.

British Cycle Supply Company Ltd
PO Box 119, Wolfville, NS B0P 1X0, Canada. *Tel:* 902 542 7478
Fax: 902 542 7479

Catalogue:	$5
Goods:	Parts for British motorcycles
Countries sent to:	World
Methods of payment:	Visa, Amex, Mastercard, Diners Club, Cheque, Bank Draft

It may seem strange to order parts for British bikes from Canada, but in fact this is one of the best sources for hard-to-find spares anywhere. Their 120 page catalogue lists some 15,000 parts for Triumph, Norton and BSA motorcycles. The company can also provide factory 'parts books' for specific bikes – just send them the details of your bike, the make, model and year along with the frame and engine number, and they will mail back this invaluable guide. The owner is an enthusiast and what he doesn't know about British bikes probably isn't worth knowing.

Early Birds
4256 Chesswood Drive, Downsview, ON M3J 2B9, Canada.
Tel: 416 630 8792 *Fax:* 416 630 8794

Catalogue:	$4
Goods:	Car parts for GMs
Countries sent to:	World
Methods of payment:	Visa, Mastercard, Cheque, Bank Draft

Early Birds specialize in restoration parts for G.M. 'muscle' vehicles between 1964 and 1981, i.e. Firebird, Camaro, GTO, Chevelle & El Camino, Cutlas & Buick and Chevy II & Nova. Their 150 page catalogue features just about every part you could wish for to keep these machines going, with clear line drawings of each item.

Light Brigade
1111 Stellar Drive, Unit 6, Newmarket, ON L3Y 7B8, Canada.
Tel: 905 853 1951

Catalogue:	Free
Goods:	Motorcycle/ATV/snowmobile parts & accessories
Countries sent to:	World
Methods of payment:	Visa, Mastercard, Bank Transfer, Bank Draft

Light Brigade sells many more items than featured in its 20 page catalogue. This seems to focus mainly on tyres, sprockets, chains and general accessories. In fact they stock a huge range of parts for ATVs, bikes and snowmobiles, from manufacturers such as Dunlop, Ferodo, Metzeler, Lockhart, Yuasa, Air Tech and Megacycle. Indeed they claim the 'widest selection anywhere', which seems quite a boast but may be true. Interested readers should simply give their very helpful staff a call.

George Moir Antique Auto Parts Ltd
11308 142 Street, Edmonton, AB T5M 1T9, Canada.
Tel: 403 454 2113 *Fax:* 403 455 1537

Catalogue:	$10 + p
Goods:	Reproduction Ford antique auto parts
Countries sent to:	World
Methods of payment:	Visa, Mastercard, Amex

George Moir Antique Auto Parts catalogue contains thousands of spares and accessories for the Ford range through the Model T of 1913 to the 1950s.

The catalogue runs to 264 glossy black and white pages and makes good use of top quality line drawings. It also contains a useful collection of shop manuals, service bulletins and restorer's guides which start at a few dollars.

Rocky Mountain Motorworks
901 Rampart Range Road, Woodland Park, CO 80863, USA.
Tel: 719 687 1003 *Fax:* 719 687 3064

Catalogue:	Free
Goods:	Parts & accessories for Volkswagens
Countries sent to:	World
Methods of payment:	Visa, Mastercard, Cheque, Bank Transfer, Bank Draft

This nicely produced 84 page catalogue specializes in parts for Volkswagen Beetles, both sedans and convertibles. It also does some parts for Karmann Ghias and other convertible VWs such as Rabbits (known as Golfs here in the UK). A separate Ghia catalogue was being produced as we went to press.

SLS IM- UND Export-Handelsgesellschaft mbh

Ahrensburgerstrasse 103 A, 22045 Hamburg (Wandsbek), Hamburg, Germany. *Tel:* 040 657 1004 *Fax:* 040 657 1042

Catalogue:	Free
Goods:	Parts for classic Mercedes
Countries sent to:	World
Methods of payment:	Visa, Mastercard, Cheque, Bank Transfer

SLS specialise in restoration parts for classic Mercedes such as the 230SL, 250SL and 280SL. They produce two excellent A4 catalogues with clear illustrations of each part. Although the text is in German, the layout makes it very easy to follow and for foreign customers there is an introductory letter in English explaining how to order, the cost of shipping and so on. They are used to shipping worldwide and provide an invaluable service for Mercedes enthusiasts.

Walridge Motors Ltd

6–5 Routledge Street, Hyde Park, ON N0M 1Z0, Canada. *Tel:* 519 641 2770 *Fax:* 519 473 3960

Catalogue:	$5 + p
Goods:	British motorcycle parts
Countries sent to:	Asia, Europe, USA, Australasia
Methods of payment:	Visa, Mastercard, Bank Transfer

Walridge Motors is a Canadian company dealing exclusively in spare parts for British motorcycles such as the Triumph, Norton and BSA. Its British Parts Catalogue (90 pages) has literally hundreds of reconditioned or newly made parts from the smallest 'o' ring to seats and carburettors. It also has a good range of workshop manuals, posters and wall charts.

CHILDREN & BABIES

Baby Love Products
5015–46 St, Unit R, Camrose, AB T4V 3G3, Canada.
Tel: 403 672 1763 *Fax:* 403 672 6942

Catalogue:	Free
Goods:	Baby goods
Countries sent to:	World
Methods of payment:	Visa, Mastercard, Amex, Cheque, Bank Draft

This 356 page colour catalogue stocks a vast range of products for babies, from 'diapering needs' (i.e. nappies), through safety items, toys and carriers to exercisers, bedding, breast-feeding equipment and books. It is one of the most extensive catalogues of its type and well worth a look.

Bébésecure Inc.
PO Box 1, Beaconsfield, PQ H9W 5T6, Canada. *Tel:* 514 485 2323

Catalogue:	$5
Goods:	Children's safety products
Countries sent to:	World
Methods of payment:	Visa, Cheque, Bank Draft

We did not receive the catalogue of this company in time for insertion so do not really know what they mean by 'children's safety products' but imagine it must be harnesses, door locks, stove protectors and so on. Perhaps an inquisitive reader could enlighten us!

Born To Love
15 Silas Hill Drive Dept GS, North York, ON M2J 2X8, Canada.
Tel: 416 499 8309 *Fax:* 416 499 5606

Catalogue:	Free
Goods:	Mother & baby products
Countries sent to:	World
Methods of payment:	Visa, Cheque, Mastercard, Bank Transfer

This 56 page black and white catalogue is printed on recycled newsprint-like paper which sets the tone for the products it describes. All are environmentally friendly and, as the blurb somewhat mysteriously claims, are 'real products for real people' (where is the catalogue of unreal products for unreal people?!)

But what this turns out to mean is an excellent range of goods for babies and mothers. There are plenty of reusable diaper (nappy) supplies, all sorts of breast-feeding equipment and books, maternity wear and various creams and lotions. They also sell baby clothes, carriers and ingenious devices to babyproof the home.

Bummis
10 Pine Ave W. #219, Montreal, PQ H2W 1P9, Canada.
Tel: 514 528 9438

Catalogue:	Free
Goods:	Diaper covers
Countries sent to:	World
Methods of payment:	Mastercard, Cheque

This small company just sells diaper (nappy) covers for use with cotton diapers. There are two models featured in their one page brochure plus a pair of 'plastic' pants, in fact made of much more comfortable nylon. The diaper covers come in red, yellow, blue or white and can be made of either nylon or cotton. Prices are around Canadian $8.

Dear-Born Baby Furnishing Inc.
72 Doncaster Avenue, Thornhill, ON L3T 1L5, Canada.
Tel: 416 881 3334 *Fax:* 416 881 2288

Catalogue:	Free
Goods:	Baby & youth furniture
Countries sent to:	World
Methods of payment:	Visa, Mastercard, Bank Transfer

Dear-Born's 40 page colour catalogue sells what it calls 'baby furniture', by which it means all sorts of accessories such as chairs, pushchairs, carriers, swings and safety harnesses. The range starts with products for the newborn and goes up to beds for sizeable toddlers.

Although some items are too large to ship, there are many interesting smaller products which may well be worth importing.

Doux Moments
381 Rang des Chutes, Ham-Nord, PQ G0P 1A0, Canada.
Tel: 819 344 2978 *Fax:* 819 344 2825

Catalogue:	$3
Goods:	Natural healthcare for mothers & babies
Countries sent to:	World
Methods of payment:	Cheque, Bank Transfer

Kathleen Nugent, the founder of this French Canadian company, is a mother of four and a professor in special educational needs and childbirth. Her catalogue, which is in French, sells a wide variety of environmentally sound, 'natural' products for mothers and babies. These include bras, baby carriers, nappies, shoes and so on. They also sell a selection of herbal remedies, crystals and tarot cards. The 34 page catalogue is of course printed on recycled paper.

Katie Gardiner Ltd

PO Box 29, Guildford, Surrey GU4 8EF, United Kingdom.
Tel: 0483 303453 *Fax:* 0483 68608

Catalogue:	Free
Goods:	Items for children
Countries sent to:	Europe, Africa, USA
Methods of payment:	Visa, Mastercard, Cheque, Bank Transfer

It is difficult to describe the range of products in this 24 page colour
catalogue, or as they insist on calling it 'katalog' (they also refuse to
use capital letters which can be a bit of a strain). In short it is 'things
for children', from foldaway potties and nightlights, through to toys,
books, shoes and clothes.

Many of the goods are unique to this catalogue and anyone with
small children will find something of interest. 'diggers' (sic) are
lightweight, breathable overalls which allow children to get dirty
without making them boil (£4.99). A range of tough shoes made out
of baseball leather are particularly attractive and come with three inner
soles to custom fit children's feet (£30).

Hearth Song Inc.

170 Professional Center Drive, Rohnett Park, CA 94928–2149,
USA. *Tel:* 707 585 9688 *Fax:* 707 585 9964

Catalogue:	Free
Goods:	Toys, books, games
Countries sent to:	World
Methods of payment:	Visa, Mastercard, Amex, Cheque, Bank Transfer

'A Catalog for Families', Hearth Song's publication is 64 pages in
colour featuring mostly toys and 'playthings'. All are well produced
and to a certain extent educational. The age range is from baby to 10
or so and includes games, puzzles, painting kits, books, stilts, jewellery
making equipment and so on. A well produced informative catalogue.

Ideas Mail Order Inc.
250 Bourget, Montreal, PQ H4C 2M3, Canada. *Tel:* 514 931 2240
Fax: 514 931 0059

Catalogue:	Free
Goods:	See below
Countries sent to:	World
Methods of payment:	Bank Transfer, Cheque, International Money Order

No catalogue but three fact sheets on three different products. The Baby Soother is a cassette tape which is designed to promote good sleep and to stop crying. If it really works then the Canadian $9 seems a snip. The second sheet details Pipal Leaf Paintings from India, which are miniature paintings on leaves. They sell for $1 each. The last item is a dietary supplement of herb foods, known as NBC packs. The information is a little sketchy but like all such foods they are said to balance the body in some mysterious way.

Mothercare Home Shopping
PO Box 145, Cherry Tree Road, Watford, Herts WD2 5SH, United Kingdom. *Tel:* 0923 210210 *Fax:* 0923 240944

Catalogue:	Free
Goods:	Clothes & accessories for babies and children
Countries sent to:	World
Methods of payment:	Visa, Mastercard, Amex

Mothercare is a very well-known high street chain in the UK, selling good quality clothes and accessories for mothers and babies up to toddlers. They now issue an excellent 124 page colour catalogue featuring a wide range of their products. It is organized chronologically, i.e. starting with maternity wear for the pregnant woman, going through early days with the new baby, through to venturing out (pushchairs and carriers) to 'Growing Up' – clothes and toys for the toddler. In short, just about everything you need to bring up a baby except for infinite patience and the ability to go without sleep.

Moyer's
25 Milvan Drive, Weston, ON M9L 1Z1, Canada. *Tel:* 416 749 2222
Fax: 416 749 8640

Catalogue:	$7
Goods:	Educational goods
Countries sent to:	Asia, Europe, Africa, USA
Methods of payment:	Visa, Mastercard, Amex, Cheque

Moyer's have been supplying Canada's educational needs since 1884, both through a number of shops and mail order. These days they produce a massive 460 page, colour catalogue with thousands of products aimed at the education market. These include books, toys, games, puzzles, furniture, bicycles, sports equipment, videos, stationery and much, much more. Thoroughly professional this is a marvellous catalogue intended primarily for schools and teachers but useful for anyone with small children.

Offspring Outfitters
PO Box 21051, Southcrest Postal Services, London, ON N6J 4W2, Canada.

Catalogue:	Free
Goods:	Children's clothes
Countries sent to:	Europe, USA, Australasia
Methods of payment:	Visa, Cheque, Bank Transfer

A 12 page colour catalogue with photographs of children's clothes from infant to toddlers. The emphasis is on simple, practical and comfortable designs made from cotton.

A pair of jeans costs just Canadian $7.99, a shirt $7.49. A long-sleeved button down boy's shirt is $30.99 while an embroidered dress is $29.32.

The Pack Parka
c/o Andermans, RR #4, Killaloe, ON K0J 2A0, Canada.
Tel: 613 757 3044

Catalogue:	Free
Goods:	See below
Countries sent to:	World
Methods of payment:	Cheque, Bank Draft

A small company, Pack Parka only sell the one product: the Pack Parka. This is an insulated cloth bag which attaches to a baby back carrier to keep the child warm outdoors without having to bundle up. Originally designed by a couple who didn't want to have to zip their child into cumbersome outdoor clothes every time they went out, it has proved very popular. Ingenious and effective, it costs Canadian $70 plus $5 to ship overseas.

Sienna Alternatives
49 Raymond Street, Ottawa, ON K1R 7A2, Canada.
Tel: 613 230 0894

Catalogue:	$2
Goods:	Alternative supplies for children & babies
Countries sent to:	World
Methods of payment:	Cheque, Bank Transfer

This 30 page black and white catalogue specializes in household goods which are environmentally friendly. It carries a large range of items, from chemical-free insect repellent through cotton diaper covers to homeopathic medicine, breast-feeding supplies and books.

Twins & More Supplies
3769 204A Street, Langley, BC V3A 6A7, Canada.
Tel: 604 530 6233 *Fax:* 604 530 6802

Catalogue:	Free
Goods:	Books & novelties for multiple births
Countries sent to:	Europe, USA, Australasia
Methods of payment:	Visa, Cheque, Bank Draft

This 32 page black and white catalogue is for parents with twins or 'multiples'. Most of it features helpful books on the subject, both for the parents and the twins themselves. But there are also some useful accessories such as a breast-feeding pillow specifically designed to make feeding twins easier. They also carry a range of 'novelties' such as T-shirts, mugs and stickers proclaiming the fact that you've got twins, which seems an odd thing to do but may appeal to some.

Wonders
183 Avenue Road, Toronto, ON M5R 2J2, Canada. *Tel:* 416 923 4942
Fax: 416 923 5677

Catalogue:	Free
Goods:	Children's casual wear
Countries sent to:	Asia, Europe, USA
Methods of payment:	Visa, Mastercard, Amex, Bank Transfer

Wonders sell designer children's clothes from babies up to 10 or so. All are bright, modern, attractive and mostly made from cotton. The 12 page colour catalogue also features some matching items for adults, for parents who enjoy this dubious practice.

An attractive red paisley shirt for a toddler is Canadian $22, a romper suit $25, a girl's dress $8 and turtlenecks $18.

CLOTHES

Alexandra Workwear plc

Alexandra House, Britannia Road, Patchway, Bristol, Avon BS12 5TP, United Kingdom. *Tel:* 0272 690808 *Fax:* 0272 799442

Catalogue:	Free
Goods:	Workwear & leisurewear
Countries sent to:	World
Methods of payment:	Visa, Mastercard, Amex, Cheque, Bank Transfer, Bank Draft

As Europe's largest supplier of workwear and 'careerwear', Alexandra mostly cater for businesses. Their 148 page colour catalogue is stuffed with uniforms for virtually every profession, from nurse to waiter, from dentist to workman. High fashion it is not but the quality is good and the designs practical. They also custom embroider a number of items such as sweatshirts, baseball hats and rugger shirts – useful for clubs and associations.

Anoraks are around £51, fleece jackets £18.75. A custom baseball hat is £6.99 with sweatshirts at £15.50.

Americana Clothing Corp.

511 Victor Street, Saddle Brook, NJ 07662, USA. *Tel:* 201 843 6471 *Fax:* 201 843 5723

Catalogue:	Free
Goods:	American 'classic' clothes
Countries sent to:	World
Methods of payment:	Visa, Mastercard, Amex

Americana sell 'America's best sportswear direct to you', which includes Levis, Lee, Champion and Harley-Davidson (yes, they make clothes too). Their simple brochure gives brief details of a limited stock.

A pair of Levi 501s is $43, while 550s (relaxed fit) are $38. Lee jeans start at $28, a jacket at $55.

Hanna Anderson

1010 N.W. Flanders, Portland, OR 97209, USA. *Tel:* 503 242 0920
Fax: 503 222 0544

Catalogue:	Free
Goods:	Women's & children's clothes up to 12 years
Countries sent to:	World
Methods of payment:	Visa, Mastercard, Amex, Cheque, Bank Transfer

An excellent glossy, 75 page catalogue with clothing for children and women. The designs are colourful, durable and sufficiently original to last through fashion fads. A particularly nice feature is the 'Hannadowns' idea. To help save money they offer a 20% credit return for clothes sent back, once children have outgrown them. These clothes – which must still be in good condition – are then donated to a child in need.

A pair of suitably named Wiggle Pants for newborns are $17, children's sweatshirts a reasonable $22. Brightly coloured leggings and tights are $13 while an adult print dress is around $30.

Arctic Trading Company

Box 910, Churchill, MB R0B 0E0, Canada. *Tel:* 204 675 8804
Fax: 204 675 2164

Catalogue:	Free
Goods:	Clothes & gifts
Countries sent to:	World
Methods of payment:	Visa, Mastercard, Amex, Cheque, Bank Transfer

This 24 page colour catalogue may not appeal to all – it contains a number of fur items. These include boots trimmed with Arctic fox fur (Canadian $195), fur parkas and jackets and a number of hats and slippers ($75). They also sell books on the frozen North and rather bizarre 'paintings' made out of caribou hair.

Ascot Chang Co. Ltd
5/F. Focal Industrial Centre – Block B, 21 Man Lok Street, Hunghom, Kowloon, Hong Kong. *Tel:* 344 384 *Fax:* 765 7349

Catalogue:	US$10
Goods:	Shirts, blouses, pyjamas
Countries sent to:	World
Methods of payment:	Visa, Mastercard, Amex, Cheque, Bank Draft

Ascot Chang is one of the classier shirt makers in Hong Kong. They have a long tradition of custom-made garments going back some 45 years and in 1982 started to make off-the-peg shirts as well. Their glossy 22 page brochure is beautifully produced with plenty of photographs. There was no price list enclosed.

L.L. Bean Inc.
Freeport, ME 04033 0001, USA. *Tel:* 207 865 3111 *Fax:* 207 878 2104

Catalogue:	Free
Goods:	Clothes and much else
Countries sent to:	World
Methods of payment:	Visa, Mastercard, Amex, Cheque, Bank Transfer

L.L. Bean is virtually synonymous with American mail order. By far the most famous catalogue company in the US it now has a very large international customer base too. Their enviable reputation is based on well-designed, high quality clothes and the amazing money-back guarantees: if products fail to satisfy in any way you can return them at ANY TIME for a full refund. They always honour this pledge but rarely have to – the quality of Bean products is legendary.

Catalogues are issued four times a year to coincide with the seasons and are on average 216 pages, in colour. Apart from a wonderful range of clothes for men and women – mostly in preppy styles – they also stock luggage, sports goods, camping equipment and clothes for children. In addition there are four specialist catalogues which can be requested separately: Fly Fishing; Hunting; Home and Camp and Winter Sports. If you intend to order just one catalogue from the USA, make it Bean's.

Far too many prices to mention, but generally good value for money. Fleece jackets are $58, Gortex windproof jackets $130, a chamois cloth shirt $28, jeans $43, field boots (similar to Timberland) $95.

Biobottoms

617-C 2nd Street, PO Box 6009, Petaluma CA 94953, USA.
Tel: 707 778 7152 *Fax:* 707 778 0619

Catalogue:	Free
Goods:	Children's clothes
Countries sent to:	World
Methods of payment:	Visa, Mastercard, Amex, Cheque, International Money Order

Biobottoms was started by two mothers who discovered an excellent diaper (nappy) cover. Made out of soft wool, it fastened with velcro for a perfect, leak-proof fit and could be used over and over. From simply selling this one item to friends they built up what has become a well-known business the world over. They now stock a range of practical clothes for babies and children up to around 10 years old. All are colourful, well designed and practical. Well worth a look.

The Blue Heron Company Ltd

Box 9, Tobermory, ON N0H 2R0, Canada. *Tel:* 519 596 2888
Fax: 519 596 2304

Catalogue:	Free
Goods:	Signal flag clothes
Countries sent to:	World
Methods of payment:	Visa, Mastercard, Cheque, Bank Transfer

This unusual company manufactures 'signal flag clothing', which consists of sweatshirts with words spelled out in nautical flags on the front. Obviously mainly for the boat enthusiast, you can have any words provided that they are not too long! The flags come in two sizes, one and two inch, and can also be printed on sweatpants, T-shirts and golfshirts. The company also sells large flags, mugs and stickers.

Sweatshirts are Canadian $40, T-shirts $23.

Boden

2 Pembroke Buildings, Cumberland Park, Scrubs Lane, London NW10 6RE, United Kingdom. *Tel:* 081 964 2662 *Fax:* 081 964 2598

Catalogue:	Free
Goods:	Clothes
Countries sent to:	World
Methods of payment:	Visa, Mastercard

Boden's publish a personable, 30 page catalogue with an engaging foreword by the founder and owner, Johnnie Boden. One of the principles behind the company is to produce modern classics using traditional materials and manufacturing methods. They seem to have pulled this off pretty well, with a selection of original and attractive clothing for men and women. One nice feature is that the models used are not professional clotheshorses but friends of the company. If you like comfortable but stylish clothing this is an excellent catalogue.

A 'bachelor shirt', so called because it does not need ironing, costs £38, a beautiful red waistcoat £45, a straight checked shirt £75 and an Aran jersey £45.

Boston Proper

6500 Park of Commerce Boulevard, N.W., Boca Raton, FL 33487, USA. *Tel:* 407 241 1700 *Fax:* 407 241 1055

Catalogue:	Free
Goods:	Contemporary fashions for women
Countries sent to:	World
Methods of payment:	Visa, Mastercard, Amex, Cheque, Bank Transfer

Boston Proper aim to sell clothes for 'women who have audacious, individual style'. They should add 'young' to that description, since all the clothes are clearly for women under 40 and the models look around 20. The clothes themselves are up-market and stylish, ranging from swimsuits through trouser suits to skirts, dresses and blouses. The look is casual but trendy, in an outdoors, American way. Recommended.

Boutique Minuit
Galerie du Centre 60, Bruxelles, 1000-BR, Belgium.
Tel: 02 223 09 14 *Fax:* 2 223 10 09

Catalogue:	300BF
Goods:	Sexy lingerie
Countries sent to:	World
Methods of payment:	Visa, Cheque, Bank Transfer

Despite the name, this 56 page colour catalogue is Belgian, not French. It features a collection of fantasy underwear predominantly for women. Outfits are skin-tight, see-through and in the main red, black or white.

The lingerie range includes sheer baby-doll night-dresses, see-through pyjamas and lace bodies. There is a large selection of camisoles, cupless bras and crotchless panties, stockings, suspenders and basques. Novelty outfits include waitress, maid and sub/dom pvc and leather sets. For the men there are a variety of G-strings and briefs in a range of styles and colours.

Prices range from 2000BF for a lycra cocktail dress to 550BF for a male G-string. Definitely one for the broad-minded.

John Brocklehurst
Bakewell, Derbys DE45 1EE, United Kingdom. *Tel:* 0629 812089
Fax: 0629 814777

Catalogue:	Free
Goods:	English country clothing
Countries sent to:	World
Methods of payment:	Visa, Mastercard, Amex, Cheque

Brocklehurst sell traditional English country clothing of the highest quality and their well-produced catalogue reflects this. Forty pages in colour, it features shirts, trousers, jackets and shoes modelled in suitably rustic locations. All the clothes are for men and would suit the 'hunting, shooting, fishing' fraternity.

Prices are not cheap but quality of this sort is always expensive and each item should last for many years. A pair of traditional full brogues cost £99.95, a moleskin waistcoat £45 and a classic Newbury shirt £9.95.

Brooks Brothers
350 Campus Plaza, Edison, NJ 08818, USA. *Tel:* 908 225 4870
Fax: 908 225 1520

Catalogue:	Free
Goods:	Classic American clothes
Countries sent to:	World
Methods of payment:	Visa, Mastercard, Amex, Diners Club, Cheque, International Money Order.

Brooks Brothers is one of the oldest and most respected clothing companies in the US. They have a large international business and ship all goods by Federal Express. The clothes are 'modern classical'. For men there are suits, shirts, ties, shoes, casual and beach wear. The range is similar for women and the clothes are attractive and well made.

A linen sports coat is $250, a poplin suit about the same. Shirts are around $45, a Regatta windcheater $135. A print dress costs $145 while a pair of women's shorts is $45.

Burberrys By Post
18–22 Haymarket, London SW1Y 4DQ, United Kingdom.
Tel: 071 930 7803 *Fax:* 071 839 2418

Catalogue:	Free
Goods:	Clothes, accessories & coats
Countries sent to:	World
Methods of payment:	Visa, Mastercard, Amex, Cheque

Burberrys is one of the great names in British clothing and holds two Royal Warrants. Their mail order department publishes a splendid folder with loose, colour sheets giving full details of the products and a special international order form. These are by no means restricted to the famous raincoat. There is a good selection of other clothes, including blazers, knitwear and children's wear, as well as food (including hampers), watches, luggage, fragrances and general gifts.

Men's trenchcoats are around the £550 mark, a single-breasted blazer £265 and a polo shirt £43. Watches – Burberrys' own make – start at £175 and rise to just under £400.

The Cockpit

47–10 33rd Street, Long Island City, NY 1101, USA.
*Tel:*718 482 1860 *Fax:* 718 472 9692

Catalogue:	$5
Goods:	American clothes
Countries sent to:	World
Methods of payment:	Visa, Mastercard, Amex, Cheque

The Cockpit sells 'merchandise inspired by America's heritage'. This turns out to mean an excellent range of men's clothes with a particular emphasis on leather jackets. If you are after a genuine A-2 goatskin flight jacket, as issued to the USAF, this is the source. They also sell Airvex leather jackets modelled on older designs, MacArthur shirts (as in WWII), trousers, combat jackets and so on. Thrown in for good measure are model aeroplanes, watches, hats, T-shirts, sunglasses, boots, flying suits, raincoats, baseball jackets and a selection of contemporary clothes. A perfect place to find that American look.

A leather flight jacket sells for $275, a pilot's briefing bag $200, a MacArthur shirt $40, a baseball jacket $99 and a genuine WWII Norden Bomb Sight a hefty $3,000!

Collections

PO Box 882883, San Francisco, CA 94188–2883, USA.
Tel: 415 588 2220 *Fax:* 415 588 4374

Catalogue:	Free
Goods:	Classic clothes for men
Countries sent to:	World
Methods of payment:	Visa, Mastercard, Amex, Diners Club, International Money Order

Collections issue a glossy 27 page, colour catalogue of contemporary American fashions for men. These are up-market labels from designers such as Perry Ellis, Ralph Lauren, Alexander Julian, Nautica, Barry Bricken and Cole-Hann. The catalogue is well laid out and full of interesting clothes.

A Ralph Lauren print polo shirt is a reasonable $55, a pair of Perry Ellis corduroy trousers $87.50, a pair of handmade boots $185.

Cyrillus
5 Cite Trevise, Ville de Paris, 75009, Paris, France.
Tel: 1 45 23 07 53 *Fax:* 1 45 23 02 92

Catalogue:	Free
Goods:	Clothes for men, women and children
Countries sent to:	World
Methods of payment:	Visa, Cheque, Bank Transfer

This stylish French catalogue features equally stylish French clothes. The 92 pages in colour are divided into sections for women, men, children, teenagers, 'juniors' and mothers and babies. The photographs are large and clear and the French text easy to follow.

A man's blazer is FF1,380, a pair of women's trousers FF455, a sweater FF635 and a child's coat/jacket FF650.

Dale & Waters
Shop 25, Wesley Centre, Hay ST, Perth 6000, Australia.
Tel: 09 321 8642 *Fax:* 09 321 4245

Catalogue:	Free
Goods:	Ladies' wear in large sizes
Countries sent to:	Australasia
Methods of payment:	Visa, Mastercard, Amex, Diners Club, Cheque, Bank Draft

Dale & Waters are 'Australia's leading large fitting specialist', which means they supply clothes for women in larger sizes. Their 24 page colour catalogue is issued several times a year and features trousers, casual shirts, dresses and skirts in sizes up to 30. They also sell sleepwear, slips and underwear.

A seersucker shirt is Australian $65, a crêpe skirt suit $125, a jersey print dress $65.

Delia Marketing Ltd
24 Craven Park Road, London NW10 4AB, United Kingdom.
Tel: 081 965 8707 *Fax:* 081 965 4261

Catalogue:	Free
Goods:	Bras & lingerie, especially large sizes
Countries sent to:	World
Methods of payment:	Visa, Mastercard, Amex, Diners Club, Cheque, Bank Transfer

This 55 page colour catalogue is about the size of an average paperback and features women's underwear. It offers over 100 styles of bra up to H cup along with a range of lingerie and nightwear. Manufacturers include Fantasie, Triumph and Glamorise. Bras are grouped into categories such as Sports and Leisure, Special Occasion and Front Fastening.

A swimming costume in classic design with internal bra costs around £38, a camisole top £11 and half slips £12.99. The company also offers a fitting advice service and suggestions for bras to use after a mastectomy.

Dellaca Corp. Ltd
7 Lyndhurst Street, Westport, New Zealand. *Tel:* 3 789 7729
Fax: 3 789 7702

Catalogue:	Free
Goods:	Contemporary clothes
Countries sent to:	Australasia
Methods of payment:	Visa, Mastercard, Amex, Diners Club

A colourful, 144 page catalogue featuring clothes for men, women and children. Most of the styles are casual, with plenty of shirts, trousers and shorts. They also sell swimming costumes, dresses, skirts and some accessories such as watches and bags.

A polo shirt costs New Zealand $46, a cotton jacket $80, a cotton skirt $37 and a linen jacket $150.

Deerskin Trading Post
119 Foster Street, PO Box 6038, Peabody, MA 01961–6038, USA.
Tel: 508 532 6523

Catalogue:	Free
Goods:	Leather clothes
Countries sent to:	Europe, USA
Methods of payment:	Visa, Mastercard, Amex, Cheque, Bank Transfer

This company provides a 63 page colour catalogue offering a comprehensive range of leather clothing made mostly from deerskin, as one might expect. Some of the designs are a little brash but the majority are very attractive. It has a useful quick page guide at the front and the goods seem reasonably priced.

Men and women's leather jeans sell for $179, Pignappa bomber jackets for $275 and a selection of accessories such as gloves from $29.95.

Dublin Woollen Company
41 Lower Ormond Quay, Dublin 1, Ireland.
Tel: 01 677 0301 or 01 677 5014 *Fax:* 01 677 0835

Catalogue:	Free
Goods:	Traditional Irish knitwear
Countries sent to:	World
Methods of payment:	Visa, Amex, Mastercard, Diners Club, Cheque, Bank Transfer

The Dublin Woollen Company has been producing traditional sweaters since 1888. They now have a wide range of products including tweeds, kilts, Kinsale smocks, shawls and rugs as well as the ever popular Aran sweaters. The simple brochure has black and white photographs of the main lines.

A hand-knit Aran sweater costs around IR£75, depending on the size, while a loomed version is cheaper at IR£40. They also sell scarves for IR£20 and gloves for IR£8. Postage is a standard IR£6.35 to the UK and IR£11.90 to continental Europe.

EziBuy Limited

204–210 John F Kennedy Drive, Private Bag 11000, Palmerston North, New Zealand. *Tel:* 0800 800 350 (Toll free only) *Fax:* 06 3546 673

Catalogue:	Free
Goods:	Mostly women's clothes
Countries sent to:	Australasia
Methods of payment:	Visa, Mastercard, Amex, Cheque, Bank Draft

This New Zealand company publishes several large catalogues a year mostly featuring women's clothes although they do have a line for men and children. The 140 colour pages show a good selection, from dresswear to practical casual clothes. The styles tend to be simple – not the latest fashion perhaps but good quality. There are a couple of drawbacks: they only export within Australasia and do not supply a non-toll free phone number which makes it impossible for customers outside the country to telephone direct.

Foley & Foley Ltd

Unit 1, 1A Philip Walk, London SE15 3NH, United Kingdom. *Tel:* 071 639 4807 *Fax:* 071 277 5563

Catalogue:	Free
Goods:	Gentlemen's shirts
Countries sent to:	World
Methods of payment:	Visa, Mastercard, Amex, Cheque, Bank Draft

Run by a husband and wife team, Foley & Foley make high-class, high-quality shirts at reasonable prices. Their 12 page A5 colour catalogue features a number of 'classic' designs as well as a small range of women's shirts. All are made from two fold cotton available in many different patterns and colours and manufactured in Britain. There is just one price, £36.50. Carriage is free within the UK, £6 to Europe, £10 elsewhere.

French Creek Sheep & Wool

Elverston, PA 19520, USA. *Tel:* 215 286 5700 *Fax:* 215 286 0324

Catalogue:	$3
Goods:	Up-market sheepskin & wool clothing
Countries sent to:	World
Methods of payment:	Visa, Mastercard, Amex, Bank Transfer

French Creek produce an excellent range of casual clothes for men and women made out of wool and leather. All their goods reflect the traditional skills practised by generations of local craftsmen and neighbours. The 35 page catalogue is well illustrated with colour photographs of sweaters, jackets, skirts, dresses, slippers and rugs. They really have succeeded in combining old-fashioned craftsmanship with contemporary design.

Sweaters are around $150, slippers $40, dresses from $150, skirts a little less.

Fun Wear Brands

141 East Elkhorn Avenue, PO 2800, Estes Park, CO 80517, USA. *Tel:* 303 586 3361 *Fax:* 303 586 3302

Catalogue:	Free
Goods:	Western wear
Countries sent to:	World
Methods of payment:	Visa, Mastercard, Amex, Diners Club, Cheque, Bank Transfer

This 24 page black and white catalogue features tough, practical clothes from the American West. They have a particularly good range of Levis, with jeans, jackets and shirts, as well as OshKosh overalls, hats, boots, moccasins, Australian clothes (including the ubiquitous drover's coat) and some Nike shoes.

A pair of Levi 501s can be as low as $24, while a Levi jacket is $56. OshKosh overalls are $33, a denim shirt $49. All in all, good prices from an interesting catalogue.

Gleneagles Knitwear

Abbey Road, Auchterarder, Scotland PH3 1DP, United Kingdom.
Tel: 0764 662112

Catalogue:	Free
Goods:	Handmade knitwear
Countries sent to:	World
Methods of payment:	Visa, Mastercard, Amex, Diners Club, Cheque, Bank Transfer

A small, fold-out brochure with colour photographs of cashmere sweaters in a number of styles for men and women. Established in Scotland since 1850, the company also stocks clothes by Aquascutum, Burberry and Jaeger but these are not shown. Nor are any prices so it is probably best to call with individual requirements.

Great Expectations

78 Fulham Road, London SW3 6HH, United Kingdom.
Tel: 071 5843 2451

Catalogue:	Free
Goods:	Maternity wear
Countries sent to:	Europe
Methods of payment:	Visa, Mastercard, Amex, Diners Club, Cheque

An 8 page, colour catalogue features fashionable clothes for pregnant women. Prices are not cheap, with a single-breasted V-neck jacket retailing at £122.65 and crêpe wrap skirt £128.50, but quality and finish are high.

Handart Embroideries

Room 106, 1st Floor, Hing Wai Building, 36 Queen's Road Central, Hong Kong. *Tel:* 523 5744 *Fax:* 845 5174

Catalogue:	Free
Goods:	Embroidered clothes
Countries sent to:	World
Methods of payment:	Visa, Mastercard, Amex, Diners Club

Handart do not publish a glossy colour catalogue but instead send out

18 photocopied pages with photographs and descriptions. This is to cut costs and enable them to maintain their very reasonable prices. They sell a large range of hand-embroidered tablecloths, place mats, handkerchiefs, silk and cotton sheets, scarves, kimonos, smoking jackets, blouses, pyjamas, silk shirts, ties and so on. Only a fraction of their stock is shown and readers can contact them directly for further information. They also sell jade jewellery and offer a custom tailoring service for a small extra fee.

Cotton, hand-crocheted tablecloths start at US$10 and come in oval, square and oblong shapes. A lace parasol is $22, a baby's christening gown $35, a lady's silk nightshirt $30 and men's silk shirts $50 – custom made for $10 extra.

Joseph Harriman Ltd
Garenden Road, Shepshed, Loughborough, Leics. LE12 9NX, United Kingdom. *Tel:* 0509 502341 *Fax:* 0509 600139

Catalogue:	n/a
Goods:	Socks
Countries sent to:	World
Methods of payment:	Cheque, Bank Transfer, Bank Draft

Harriman sell good quality socks for men and women, including a range of hockey socks. However, they do not issue a catalogue so interested readers should contact them directly with their requirements.

Hayashi Kimono
International Arcade 2-1-1, Yuraku-Cho, Chiyoda-Ku, Tokyo 100, Japan. *Tel:* 03 3501 4012

Catalogue:	Free
Goods:	Kimonos, 'happi coats' & yukata
Countries sent to:	Europe, USA, Australasia
Methods of payment:	Bank Transfer

This small, 16 page catalogue is in English with colour photographs of traditional kimonos for both men and women. Hayashi Kimono is the largest single retailer of such items in Japan, stocking clothes made in silk and polyester.

There are no ordering instructions in the catalogue or indications of price, but the shop will respond to written requests for further information in English (this service is not available by phone).

Icewear
PO Box 310, 212 Gardabair, Iceland. *Tel:* 1 641 466 *Fax:* 1 450 28

Catalogue:	Free
Goods:	Sweaters
Countries sent to:	World
Methods of payment:	Visa, Mastercard, Amex, Cheque

Although this 16 page colour catalogue is in German, it comes with an English order form and price list. There are dozens of brightly coloured, patterned sweaters made from Icelandic wool along with mitts, scarves and hats.

Prices include shipping and are in either DM or US$. Men's pullovers start at just under $100 and rise to $150 or so. A full-length, lined jacket is $300 while gloves are $17 and scarves about $20.

Jimmys International
TS PO Box 95001, Kowloon, Hong Kong. *Tel:* 368 8030
Fax: 368 8030

Catalogue:	n/a
Goods:	Custom-made clothes
Countries sent to:	World
Methods of payment:	Bank Transfer, Bank Draft

Everybody has heard of the Hong Kong companies which will run up a copy of your favourite suit overnight but most assume you have to go there in person to take advantage of this service. Not any more! Jimmys International will make shirts, blouses and suits to order. They do not issue a catalogue but will send out swatches of cloth. In the first instance, contact them by letter, phone or fax outlining your requirements. They will then send the swatches and give you an idea of price.

Kid's Cosy Cottons

2367 Haddington Crescent, Ottawa, ON K1H 8J5, Canada.
Tel: 613 523 2679 *Fax:* 613 236 8258

Catalogue:	Free
Goods:	Cotton clothes for children
Countries sent to:	Australasia, USA
Methods of payment:	Visa, Mastercard, Cheque, Bank Transfer

This 32 page colour catalogue describes a range of cotton clothes for children. All are well made and modern-looking in bright colours. The company is run by Margaret Berry, a mother of two sons, and this practical background shows in the design of the clothes.

Sweatshirts are around Canadian $23, a turtleneck $23, cotton leggings $20 and a pair of trousers $35. They also sell a small range of hand-knitted sweaters for adults, retailing at $200.

Long Tall Sally Ltd

Unit B, Pioneers Industrial Park, Beddington Farm Road, Croydon, London CR0 4VB, United Kingdom. *Tel:* 081 689 9000
Fax: 081 665 0399

Catalogue:	Free
Goods:	Clothes for tall women
Countries sent to:	Europe
Methods of payment:	Visa, Mastercard, Diners Club, Cheque

These catalogues for clothes for tall women (over 5'8") are produced six times a year, with two major ones. Twenty-eight pages in colour show a selection of well-made, fashionable clothes such as jackets, skirts, dresses, sweaters, and trousers. Long Tall Sally also has shops throughout Britain.

Jackets sell for £60, denim skirts for £40, raincoats for £75 and cotton skirts for £40.

Le Tricoteur

Perelle Bay, St Saviours, Guernsey, Channel Islands. *Tel:* 0481 64040
Fax: 0481 64264

Catalogue:	Free
Goods:	Sweaters
Countries sent to:	World
Methods of payment:	Visa, Mastercard, Amex, Diners Club, Cheque, Bank Draft

The famous Guernsey sweater was traditionally knitted by seamen's wives. Well-known for their warmth and durability, the patterns were handed down from mother to daughter. Le Tricoteur still uses a number of these families to make their range of sweaters. Suitable for men, women and children, they come in several variations on the basic theme: standard, long, with a zip and so on. There is also a good selection of 12 colours, including traditional stripe, and they can be made in cotton or wool.

MacGillivray & Co

Baliuanich, Benbecula, Outer Hebrides, Scotland PA88 5LA, United Kingdom. *Tel:* 0870 2525

Catalogue:	$4
Goods:	Handmade sweaters, Harris tweeds, tartans, rugs
Countries sent to:	World
Methods of payment:	Visa, Mastercard, Amex, Cheque, Bank Transfer

MacGillivray's do not produce a full-blown catalogue but a four-page description of their products. There are no illustrations but they do include swatches of fabric. They sell Harris tweed and tartans by the yard and also a selection of clothes, such as hand-knitted sweaters, rugs, hats and gloves. They also act as distributors for the Hebridean Crofter Weavers, Knitters and Craftspeople.

Harris tweed is £10.50 per yard while clan tartans start at £20 rising to £26 per yard (stipulate your clan when ordering). Hand-knitted wool sweaters are £48, tartan travel rugs £28.50.

Macho's Di Pisoni Sergio
Via Sestese, 63/65, Firenze, Italy. *Tel:* 055 454 115 *Fax:* 055 450 025

Catalogue:	L17.000
Goods:	Sports clothes
Countries sent to:	Europe
Methods of payment:	Cheque, Bank Transfer, Bank Draft, COD

Macho's A4, 36 page colour catalogue sells a range of workout and sports clothes fashioned by a group of extraordinarily well-developed models, male and female. There are sweatpants, leotards, Lycra shorts and body suits, swimming costumes and bikinis. They also sell a selection of clothes for mountain biking. The text is in Italian but very simple to follow.

Madova Gloves
Via Guicciardini, 1r, 50125 Florence, Italy. *Tel:* 055 239 6526
Fax: 055 210 204

Catalogue:	Free
Goods:	Gloves
Countries sent to:	World
Methods of payment:	Cheque, International Money Order

This delightful if tiny 24 page colour catalogue comes direct from 'the only glove factory in Florence' and is written in English. There is an excellent range of leather gloves for both men and women, available in a variety of colours (a chart is printed on the inside cover).

Prices are in US$ and orders must be paid for in dollars. They start at around $15 and move up to $63 for a cashmere-lined version.

Mark, Fore & Strike
6500 Park of Commerce Boulevard, N.W., Boca Raton, FL 33487, USA. *Tel:* 407 241 1700 *Fax:* 407 241 1055

Catalogue:	Free
Goods:	Clothes for active women
Countries sent to:	World
Methods of payment:	Visa, Mastercard, Amex, Cheque, Bank Transfer

Mark, Fore & Strike also publish the excellent Boston Proper catalogue (see above). Here too the clothes are well made and designed but the emphasis is on a slightly more conservative look (though still casual) suitable for a wider age range. There are trousers, sweaters, skirts, dresses, sweatshirts and a small selection of shoes.

A slim twill skirt is $58, a jacket dress $148, a cotton cardigan $48.

James Meade Ltd
48 Charlton Road, Andover, Hants SP10 3JL, United Kingdom. *Tel:* 0264 333222 *Fax:* 0264 3632000

Catalogue:	Free
Goods:	Shirts
Countries sent to:	World
Methods of payment:	Visa, Mastercard, Cheque, Bank Transfer

James Meade make 'Jermyn Street quality at affordable prices', or so it says on the front of their 28 page colour catalogue. And judging from the contents they live up to their claim. While their shirts are not tailored they do come with seven different sleeve lengths and many collar sizes so the effect is virtually the same. There are a great many styles to choose from and you can also opt for the detailing of your choice. Apart from the standard office shirt, Meade also stock polo shirts, pyjamas, dressing-gowns, sweaters, underwear and a range of women's blouses. All goods are shipped anywhere and they have a thriving international business. So much so that they have opened an office in the Netherlands which publishes a catalogue in Dutch (see below).

Shirts are around £35, sweaters £50 and blouses from £30.
Dutch Office: *Tel:* 017 18 3 45 49 *Fax:* 017 18 349 49

Monaghans

15/17 Grafton Arcade, Dublin 2, Ireland. *Tel:* 677 0823
Fax: 679 4451

Catalogue:	Free
Goods:	Sweaters
Countries sent to:	Asia, Europe, USA, Australasia
Methods of payment:	Visa, Mastercard, Amex, Cheque

Monaghans is Ireland's leading sweater shop and also publishes a 14 page colour catalogue for mail order customers. While this does not feature all of their range the selection is wide. Manufacturers include Glenmac, Pringle and Monaghans themselves. There are cashmere sweaters for both men and women in a variety of styles and colours. They also sell hand-knitted Arans and lambswool pullovers.

Each item is well illustrated and comes in Irish, European and American sizes. However, there was no price list with our catalogue so we are unable to comment on value for money.

Modeversand Ritter International gmbH & Co.

Reitschulstrasse 7, 6923 Lauterach, Vorarlberg, Austria.
Tel: 0 55 74 38 6004 *Fax:* 0 55 74 38 6005

Catalogue:	Free
Goods:	Women's clothes
Countries sent to:	Europe
Methods of payment:	Bank Transfer

Ritter International sells women's fashions aimed at the younger age range (20–35). Their glossy German catalogue contains 90 pages of sophisticated business and leisure clothes of a much higher quality than expected from mail order clothing companies. Own label dresses start at Austrian S1793 while separates are usually around S750–850. Accessories include shoes, boots and watches and there are a few pairs of jeans for the chaps. Men's Levi jeans are S898 so get your calculators out and compare prices.

Murray Bros
17 Commercial Road, Hawick, Scotland, United Kingdom.
Tel: 0450 73420 *Fax:* 0450 77656

Catalogue:	Free
Goods:	Knitwear, men's & women's clothing
Countries sent to:	World
Methods of payment:	Visa, Mastercard, Amex, Diners Club, Cheque, Bank Transfer

Murray Brothers catalogue is a 12 page, glossy, full-colour brochure featuring its Scottish Woollen Mills collection, with an emphasis on the classic 'Balmoral' look. It comprises casual separates in natural and man-made yarns for both adults and children.

Examples include a lady's 2-ply lambswool high-button cardigan with set-in sleeves and brass buttons at £29.99, wax cotton jackets for both men and women at £24.99 and men's country cords at £21.

Neiman-Marcus
PO Box 2968, Dallas, TX 75221–2968, USA. *Tel:* 214 556 2221
Fax: 214 401 6306

Catalogue:	$15 per year, single issues free
Goods:	Women's clothes & accessories
Countries sent to:	World
Methods of payment:	Amex, Cheque

Neiman-Marcus issue a 54 page colour catalogue called 'Essentials'. This features up-market stylish women's clothes along with a few accessories such as shoes and handbags. The look is mostly young and the clothes contemporary. Silk shirts are $98, a double-breasted jacket $188, turtleneck $158, a weekend bag $78. Great looking clothes in an attractive, well produced catalogue.

Robert Norfolk

67 Gatwick Road, Crawley, West Sussex RH10 2RD, United Kingdom.
Tel: 0293 553381 *Fax:* 0293 533832

Catalogue:	Free
Goods:	Designer sweatshirts & co-ordinates
Countries sent to:	Europe
Methods of payment:	Visa, Mastercard, Cheque, Bank Transfer

If you do not like printed sweatshirts then this is not for you. Their 32 page colour catalogue features rather cutesy designs, such as birds, mice and flowers, printed on several varieties of sweatshirt for men, women and children. They also sell matching trousers along with a selection of blouses, skirts and tops in rather more discreet style.

Sweatshirts start at around £30, with trousers at £20.

North Beach Leather Catalog Division

1335 Columbus Avenue, PO Box 94133, San Francisco, CA 94164, USA. *Tel:* 415 346 1113 *Fax:* 415 346 7320

Catalogue:	$4
Goods:	Designer leather clothing & accessories
Countries sent to:	World
Methods of payment:	Visa, Mastercard, Amex, Cheque, Bank Transfer

The North Beach catalogue is a large format, glossy designer product well suited to its up-market leather clothes. Fourteen colour pages feature exclusive designs for both men and women. Leather jackets with individual motifs cost around $695, leather jeans $350 and some stunning dresses in lambskin $450. If you have the money, these are tremendous clothes.

Una O'Neill Designs

30 Oakley Park, Blackrock, County Dublin, Ireland. *Tel:* 01 288 6272
Fax: 01 288 6272

Catalogue:	Free
Goods:	Hand-knitted sweaters
Countries sent to:	World
Methods of payment:	Visa, Amex, Cheque, Bank Transfer

Una O'Neill makes hand-knitted sweaters out of 100% Irish wool.
Her fold-out brochure has illustrations of many styles, including crew
necks, cross-over necks and with collars. She also sells crochet shawls
and ponchos, along with a selection of gloves, hats and scarves.
Although she has a large international clientele, there was no price list
with our brochure – possibly it fell out along the way!

Patagonia Mail Order

1609 W. Babcock Street, PO Box 8900, Bozeman, MT 59715, USA.
Tel: 406 587 3838 *Fax:* 406 587 7078

Catalogue:	Free
Goods:	Sportswear
Countries sent to:	World
Methods of payment:	Visa, Mastercard, Cheque

Patagonia is rightly world famous for its excellent range of outdoor
clothes. These are sold in high-class sports shops everywhere but they
also operate a large international mail order department. Indeed they
are so committed to this that they produce their catalogues in a variety
of different languages, including French, German, Italian and Japanese.

The 110 page catalogue is printed on recycled paper, part of the
company's commitment to the environment which it takes very
seriously. Beautifully presented, it features clothes for every outdoor
activity, from skiing to canoeing. All are designed and made by experts
who really understand the sports. They also issue a separate children's
catalogue. Thoroughly recommended.

A hiking parka sells for around $300, a fleece top $99, a canvas
shirt $56.

They also have an office in Paris – *Tel:* 1 41 10 18 18 *Fax:* 1 46 05
57 22.

Pentif Enterprises Ltd
PO Box 23029, Stratford, ON N5A 7VB, Canada. *Tel:* 519 273 2275
Fax: 519 272 1805

Catalogue:	Free
Goods:	Chemical-free bug jackets
Countries sent to:	World
Methods of payment:	Visa, Mastercard, Cheque, Bank Transfer

This is a brochure rather than a catalogue, describing the unique 'Nev-r-Bug' (sic) range of jackets this company manufactures. Designed to keep out all manner of bugs and insects, they are lightweight, breathable and while not totally waterproof do repel water. They even have a hood with netted face screen. Very useful if you live in a bug-infested area, as perhaps some Canadians do, or fish in such an environment.

Adult jackets are around Canadian $70, with trousers at $50. Male, female and children's sizes available.

The Peruvian Connection
Canaan Farm, Rural Route 1, Tonganoxie, KS 66086, USA.
Tel: 913 845 2450 *Fax:* 913 845 2460

Catalogue:	Free
Goods:	Woollen & cotton clothes
Countries sent to:	World
Methods of payment:	Visa, Mastercard, Amex, Cheque, Bank Transfer

All the clothes featured in this colour 32 page catalogue are handmade from cotton and wool in 'the ancient Andean textile tradition'. Almost exclusively for women – apart from the sweaters – they are well-made, beautifully designed high-class items. Some cloth swatches are also included.

A very attractive Cossack coat made from alpaca, lambswool and angora, sells for $735. 100% alpaca cardigans are $142 while V-necked versions for men are $165.

Pontiac Wool Works

Box 27, Shawville, PQ J0X 2Y0, Canada. *Tel:* 819 647 3749
Fax: 819 647 3068

Catalogue:	Free
Goods:	Woollens
Countries sent to:	World
Methods of payment:	Visa, Mastercard, Cheque, Bank Draft

This single colour sheet displays a small range of socks, mittens and slippers made from wool and felt. The company has a unique manufacturing system which ensures that the wool fibres are kept long and strong which in turn make the socks and gloves unusually warm, ideal for skiing and other outdoor activities. Ski socks are around Canadian $16.50, hats $25, mitts $20 and slippers $33.

Postina International B.V.

Vroenhof 24, B-3640 Kinrooi-Geistingen, Belgium.
Tel: 089 56 70 90 *Fax:* 089 56 84 57

Catalogue:	Free
Goods:	Clothes & gadgets
Countries sent to:	Europe, USA
Methods of payment:	Cheque, Bank Transfer

This French-language 48 page colour catalogue sells a strange combination of women's clothes and low-priced gadgets. The clothes are smart but not high fashion while the gadgets, for kitchen, household and garden, are all reasonably cheap. They include sets of knives, microwave dishes, loungers and that ubiquitous favourite of such catalogues – the electric nasal hair clipper (does anyone buy, let alone use, this thing?!).

Prince Fashions Ltd
Block B, 10th Floor, Unit 1005, 2–8 Watson Road, North Point, Hong Kong. *Tel:* 512 9809 *Fax:* 512 9488

Catalogue:	Free
Goods:	Discount clothing
Countries sent to:	World
Methods of payment:	Cheque, Bank Draft

Prince Fashions publish a 16 page colour catalogue of mainly women's clothing in wool, silk and cotton all at surprisingly low prices. An angora lambswool jumper, for example, is just £15.

Most of the designs have embroidered patterns and may not be to everybody's taste. Clothes include blouses, sweaters, jackets, skirts and trousers. There is also a small range of men's clothes, some traditional Chinese items and two pages of jewellery.

Chris Reekie & Sons
Old Coach House, Stock Lane, Grasmere, Cumbria LA22 9SL, United Kingdom. *Tel:* 05394 35221 *Fax:* 05394 35221

Catalogue:	n/a
Goods:	Woollen & mohair goods
Countries sent to:	World
Methods of payment:	Visa, Mastercard, Amex, Cheque, Bank Transfer

Reekie's sell unique woollen and mohair rugs, scarves, jackets and so on, all designed and made on the premises. They do not publish a catalogue but interested readers should contact them direct to discuss their requirements. They will then send swatches of fabric.

REI

International Dept, Sumner, WA 98352–0001, USA.
Tel: 206 891 2500 *Fax:* 206 891 2523

Catalogue:	Free
Goods:	Outdoor clothes & equipment
Countries sent to:	World
Methods of payment:	Visa, Mastercard, Cheque, Bank Transfer

REI has been outfitting campers and outdoor enthusiasts over 55 years and is one of the best suppliers in the US. The current catalogue runs to a very plush 108 pages of full colour. It features a superb range of outdoor clothing and equipment and contains detailed descriptions of every item. There is a large choice of own-label and other manufacturers' tents, sleeping bags, cooking equipment, water filters, binoculars, backpacks, watches, clothing and shoes.

REI is a co-operative which anyone can join and benefit from discounts on the goods. Lifetime membership is $10. If you are interested in hiking, skiing, walking or other outdoor activities, this catalogue is a must.

Seymours Shirts

136 Sunbridge Road, Bradford BD1 2QG, United Kingdom.
Tel: 0274 726520 *Fax:* 0274 735911

Catalogue:	Free
Goods:	Shirts
Countries sent to:	World
Methods of payment:	Visa, Mastercard, Amex, Cheque

Seymours don't so much have a catalogue as a whole package of goodies. A packed envelope contains two brochures with descriptions of shirts and blouses, a simple to follow order form, a wide selection of fabric swatches and even a free tape measure. All goods are fully made to measure and the materials used are of high quality.

For men there is a selection of styles, all fairly traditional with collars. These would be suitable for business or 'smart casual' wear. There is a smaller choice for women, with five styles again on the classical side. Pyjamas are also available.

Prices depend on the fabric used but start at around £35 for a cotton shirt, up to £69 for silk. Spare cuffs and collars come in at around £5.

Sheplers Inc.
6501 W. Kellogg, Wichita, KS 67209, USA. *Tel:* 316 946 3786
Fax: 316 946 3646

Catalogue:	Free
Goods:	Western style clothes
Countries sent to:	World
Methods of payment:	Visa, Mastercard, Amex, Cheque, Bank Transfer

If reclaiming the Wild West in classic rancho style clothing is for you, then this 67 page colour catalogue is the answer to your prayers. It is full of Western clothes, from cowboy boots, through jeans to shirts and even bolos (those strange things cowboys wear around their necks instead of ties). There is also a good selection of women's clothes as well as Levi 501s, which sell for under $30. All in all, an excellent catalogue.

Silvert's Clothing for Seniors
3280 Steeles Avenue West, Unit 18, Concord, ON L4K 2Y2, Canada. *Tel:* 416 738 4545 *Fax:* 416 738 6236

Catalogue:	Free
Goods:	Clothing for seniors and the physically challenged senior
Countries sent to:	World
Methods of payment:	Visa, Mastercard, Amex, Cheque, Bank Transfer

Silvert's is a company specializing in the clothing needs of 'seniors'. Its 34 page Fashion and Accessories catalogue comes with a 12 page supplement. Both are in colour throughout and are printed on high-grain gloss paper.

The emphasis is on comfort and practicality. Most of the clothes are made from cotton, polyester or flannelette. For women there are stylish day dresses, sportswear and casual combinations. Many items have Velcro fasteners at the back to ease dressing and undressing. Colours are bright and most fabrics are machine washable. For men there are trousers with Velcro flys, smart cardigans, dress and casual shirts. They also sell shoes and slippers and a good range of underwear and thermals.

Dresses are mainly in the Canadian \$40 – 70 range and men's shirts start from as little as \$19.98.

Sunveil Sunwear Inc.
355 Plains Road East, Unit 7A, Burlington, ON L7T 4H7, Canada.
Tel: 905 637 3029 *Fax:* 905 637 3391

Catalogue:	Free
Goods:	Sun protective clothing
Countries sent to:	World
Methods of payment:	Visa, Mastercard, Cheque, Bank Transfer, Bank Draft

Sunveil sells a fascinating range of clothing designed to offer protection from the sun. The founder, Marny Gall, wanted to continue with outdoor activities without having to smother herself in creams and lotions. The solution was a lightweight fabric which filters out up to 90% of the sun's harmful rays. It can be worn over bare skin, comes in white, yellow or navy and is virtually see-through. Garments include hats, shirts, sarongs, jackets and trousers for men, women and children. Prices start at around Canadian \$30 for a sarong and \$110 for a jacket.

Toil Hers Women's Workwear Ltd
Jondallah Farm SH 50 RD 5, Hastings, New Zealand.
Tel: 06 879 7971 *Fax:* 06 879 5864

Catalogue:	Free
Goods:	Women's clothes
Countries sent to:	World
Methods of payment:	Visa, Mastercard, Cheque, Bank Draft

This interesting New Zealand company sells 'Women's Working Clothes'. Specifically designed for women who work outside – mostly on farms – they include boots, overalls, hardwearing shirts, jeans, shorts, 'working' bras and so on. Their 12 page catalogue is printed like a colour tabloid newspaper and has articles as well as product descriptions and even readers' letters. It is issued several times a year and features clothes appropriate for summer and winter respectively.

European readers should therefore bear in mind that seasons in New Zealand are the opposite to those in Europe.

Town & Country Manor Ltd
Penrith, Cumbria CA11 9EQ, United Kingdom. *Tel:* 0768 899111
Fax: 0768 899222

Catalogue:	Free + p
Goods:	Classic countrywear
Countries sent to:	World
Methods of payment:	Visa, Mastercard, Cheque

As the company name suggests, this catalogue promotes fashion for the county set. There are 11 colour pages with photographs of unglamorous but practical clothes for men and women. Tartans seemed popular in the issue we saw.

Yorkshire corduroys are £39.99, a fleece-lined body warmer £19.99 and a padded coat £25.

Turu Mail Order
145 Princes Street, Hawera, Taranaki, New Zealand. *Tel:* 06 278 3034

Catalogue:	$4
Goods:	Outdoor clothing
Countries sent to:	Asia, Europe, USA, Australasia
Methods of payment:	Bank Draft

Turu is a New Zealand company which specializes in tough, practical outdoor clothing. Their 24 page colour catalogue has a good range of sweaters, shirts, trousers, socks, gloves, jackets, raincoats and jeans, many made in New Zealand. They also sell Dr. Marten's boots, trainers, an excellent range of work boots (many similar to Timberland) and gum boots from a number of different manufacturers.

Jeans start at around New Zealand $40, a check work shirt is $38, a waxed jacket $114 and a heavy, 100% wool sweater $70.

Charles Tyrwhitt Shirts

Saddlers Court, Camberley, Surrey GU17 7RX, United Kingdom.
Tel: 0252 860940 *Fax:* 0252 861677

Catalogue:	£1.50
Goods:	High quality shirts
Countries sent to:	World
Methods of payment:	Visa, Mastercard, Amex, Cheque, Bank Transfer

Charles Tyrwhitt operate entirely by mail and can therefore keep costs down on their large range of shirts. Most are suitable for the office and come in a variety of styles. They also sell polo shirts, ties, boxer shorts, braces, cufflinks and a few shirts for women.

Cotton shirts are £37.50, polo shirts £24.50, boxer shorts £11 and ties between £15 and £25.

R. Watson Hogg Ltd

52 High Street, Auchterarder, Perthshire, Scotland PH3 1BS, United Kingdom. *Tel:* 0764 62151 & 0764 662358 *Fax:* 0764 664007

Catalogue:	Free
Goods:	Knitwear
Countries sent to:	World
Methods of payment:	Visa, Mastercard, Amex, Diners Club, Cheque, Bank Transfer

A Scottish firm specializing in cashmere, tweeds and tailored clothing for both men and women, Watson Hogg produce a very attractive little catalogue of 28 colour pages. They sell clothes made by, amongst others, Ballantyne, Lampert, Viyella, Pierre Sangan, John Smedley, Barbour and Johnstons of Elgin. They also stock the Floris range of fragrances and Loofy waxed jackets and coats.

There are plenty of cashmere sweaters to choose from, as well as wool blazers, shirts, kilts and golfing wear. The company will also tailor-make any clothes to order. However, there was no price list with our catalogue – or indeed order form – so we are unable to give an idea of cost.

Woolen Wonders
Box 4511, RR #2, Corner Brook, NF A2H 6B9, Canada.
Tel: 709 688 2303

Catalogue:	$2
Goods:	Hand-knitted sweaters
Countries sent to:	USA
Methods of payment:	Bank Transfer

Woolen Wonders (sic) is based in Newfoundland and produces traditional hand-knitted Fisherman and Fair Isle sweaters. Their catalogue consists of a small postcard size folder containing 4 separate colour photographs of different sweaters, along with an order form and illustrations of a further two designs plus details of woollen mitts, leggings, socks and headbands. Sweaters start at Canadian $45 and rise to $115 for a 100% wool turtleneck.

Zig Zag Designer Knitwear Ltd
Riverford Mill, Stewarton, Kilmarnock, Ayrshire KA3 5DH, United Kingdom. *Tel:* 0560 485187 *Fax:* 0560 485195

Catalogue:	Free
Goods:	Knitwear
Countries sent to:	World
Methods of payment:	Visa, Mastercard, Cheque, Bank Transfer

Zig Zag design and make sweaters in Scotland. The 20 page catalogue shows off the bright, colourful styles to advantage. These are not the dour sweaters usually associated with Scotland, but full of dazzling reds, yellows and blues. They are available for men, women and children.

Most of the adult styles are priced at around £35 while the children's range is about half that.

COLLECTING

Canada Post Corporation

National Philatelic Centre, Antigonish, NS B2G 2R8, Canada.
Tel: 902 863 6550 *Fax:* 902 863 6796

Catalogue:	Free
Goods:	Stamps & related collectables
Countries sent to:	World
Methods of payment:	Visa, Mastercard, Cheque, Bank Transfer

The Canada Post Corporation publishes a 28 page A5 format colour catalogue detailing the latest Canadian stamps. The text, in English and French, gives plenty of useful information and stamps can be bought in a number of different packs, both loose and on first day covers. The catalogue is issued seasonally and comes with an informative pamphlet, also in French and English, entitled 'Windows of Discovery, The Joys of Stamp Collecting'.

Cinema City

PO Box 1012, Muskegon, MI 49443, USA. *Tel:* 616 722 7760
Fax: 616 722 4537

Catalogue:	$5
Goods:	Movie memorabilia
Countries sent to:	World
Methods of payment:	Visa, Mastercard, Bank Transfer

This company sells original movie posters, still photos and memorabilia mostly from 1975 onwards, although they can supply earlier material on request. The 62 page black and white catalogue lists films alphabetically with a brief description of each item available. They claim to provide a 'complete service for the cinema collector' and certainly they seem to be a very professional outfit. Up-dates to the catalogue are issued regularly featuring the very latest acquisitions. All goods are the genuine article – i.e. not reprints – and come from all over the world, not just the US.

A. Goto

1-23-9 Higashi, Shibuya-Ku, Tokyo, Japan. *Tel:* 3407 1759

Catalogue:	n/a
Goods:	Japanese & Chinese antiques
Countries sent to:	Europe, USA
Methods of payment:	Bank Transfer, Bank Draft

Goto sell small Chinese and Japanese antiques, many carved from horn and ivory. They do not issue a catalogue but will send a price list and colour photographs of current items. Prices are in US$ and seem reasonable. An elk-horn carved cosmetic box is around $100, a carved snuff bottle in amber $30.

The Movie Poster Place

PO Box 128, Lansdowne, PA 19050 0128, USA. *Tel:* 215 622 6062 *Fax:* 215 622 8050

Catalogue:	$1
Goods:	Movie posters & stills
Countries sent to:	World
Methods of payment:	Visa, Mastercard, Cheque

Produced like a newspaper with 43 pages of dense print, this catalogue is aimed firmly at the movie addict. With thousands of prints, posters, stills, magazines, press kits and programmes you can find something on virtually any film you care to mention. Large posters start at the $20 mark and rise according to rarity.

Jerry Ohlingher Movie Material

242 W. 14th Street, New York, NY 10011, USA. *Tel:* 212 989 0869
Fax: 212 989 1660

Catalogue:	Up to $10
Goods:	Movie posters and stills
Countries sent to:	World
Methods of payment:	Visa, Mastercard, Amex, Cheque, Bank Transfer

Ohlingher's produce a number of catalogues, from the free newspaper-like broadsheets, which are little more than price lists, up to the glossy, well-produced $10 edition. The free broadsheets specialize in certain areas, such as John Wayne, Marilyn Monroe, Elizabeth Taylor and so on.

All forms of movie memorabilia are available, such as posters, books, stills and programmes from all round the world. Posters start around $15 rising to $75 or so.

COMPUTER ACCESSORIES

Altec Lansing Multimedia
Route 6 & 209, Milford, PA 18337, USA. *Tel:* 717 296 2818
Fax: 717 296 1222

Catalogue:	Free
Goods:	Audio products for computers
Countries sent to:	World
Methods of payment:	Visa, Mastercard

Altec make speakers for computers used in audio-visual presentations.
Their well-designed products feature in a glossy brochure. No prices
available. They also have an office in the UK – *Tel:* 0763 247316
Fax: 0763 247317.

AlteCon Data Communications Inc.
7510 Bath Road, Mississauga, ON L4T 1L2, Canada.
Tel: 416 677 6500 *Fax:* 416 677 6505

Catalogue:	Free
Goods:	Data communication equipment
Countries sent to:	Europe, USA
Methods of payment:	Visa, Mastercard, Cheque, Bank Transfer

AlteCon's 80 page, A5 catalogue is packed with computer accessories
for data communication and networking. They also stock sophisticated
switches, cables, data splitters, surge protectors, interface converters,
Ethernet accessories and token ring equipment.

Computer Booklist
50 James Road, Birmingham BA11 2BA, United Kingdom.
Tel: 021 706 6000 *Fax:* 021 706 3301

Catalogue:	Free
Goods:	Books on computers
Countries sent to:	World
Methods of payment:	Visa, Mastercard, Amex, Cheque

This excellent 48 page catalogue lives up to its name – a huge listing
of over 3,500 computer titles. Divided into sections on Using PCs,

Programming, Using Macs, Home & Games and Professional, new editions are issued every four months. If they don't have it, it probably doesn't exist. Expert advice, next day delivery and a shipping policy to cover the world round off a very professional service.

Computer Express
31 Union Avenue, Sudbury, MA 01776, USA. *Tel:* 508 443 6125
Fax: 508 443 5645

Catalogue:	n/a
Goods:	Software & accessories
Countries sent to:	World
Methods of payment:	Visa, Mastercard, Bank Transfer

Computer Express do not issue a catalogue but welcome international enquiries, preferably by fax. They sell software and accessories for IBM, Apple, Amiga and Commodore. They do not sell the computers themselves but specialize in hard-to-find items and will answer all fax enquiries within 24 hours.

Computer Friends
14250 N.W. Science Park Drive, Portland, OR 97229, USA.
Tel: 503 626 2291 *Fax:* 503 643 5379

Catalogue:	Free
Goods:	Unusual computer accessories
Countries sent to:	World
Methods of payment:	Visa, Mastercard, Amex

Computer Friends publish a periodical newsletter as well as a catalogue. They specialize in unusual computer accessories to save money, and to make life easier and help cut down computer waste. For example, they stock a ribbon re-inker and a disc doubler, which will double the capacity of a 800k floppy.

Computer Plus

8182 Goldie Street, Walled Lake, MI 48390, USA.
Tel: 313 363 0100 *Fax:* 313 363 5150

Catalogue:	Free
Goods:	Computer supplies & accessories
Countries sent to:	World
Methods of payment:	Visa, Mastercard, Bank Draft

This company's catalogue was not ready as we went to press but we gather they sell computer supplies and accessories including software.

Dartek Computer Supply Corp.

949 Larch Avenue, Elmhurst, IL 60126, USA. *Tel:* 708 941 1000
Fax: 708 941 1106

Catalogue:	Free
Goods:	IBM/Mac supplies, software & accessories
Countries sent to:	Europe
Methods of payment:	Visa, Mastercard, Amex, Bank Transfer

Dartek publish two catalogues, one for IBM machines, the other for Macs. Both are around 72 pages, in colour, with a huge range of products. They sell not only software but also discs, drives, covers, stationery, monitors, modems – in fact everything except computers themselves. There is an emphasis on business use, so you can find a number of items here not available in the general-consumer catalogues.

Direct Micro

1782 Dividend Drive, Columbus, OH 43228, USA. *Tel:* 614 771 8771
Fax: 614 771 8772

Catalogue:	Free
Goods:	Modems & computer accessories
Countries sent to:	World
Methods of payment:	Visa, Mastercard, Bank Transfer

Direct Micro sell high speed modems and other accessories. Their catalogue was not available at the time of going to press, but interested readers can fax their request direct to the company for an up-to-date price list.

Global Microsystems

606 Venice Boulevard, Suite F, Venice, CA 90291, USA.
Tel: 310 822 2041 Toll free from UK: 0800 897 427
Fax: 310 822 0774

Catalogue:	n/a
Goods:	Software for Apples & IBM, some hardware
Countries sent to:	World
Methods of payment:	Visa, Mastercard, Bank Transfer

Global do not publish a catalogue but advertise extensively in the computer press, both in the US and UK. They sell a good range of software for both IBM and Apple machines and have a toll free number from the UK. An excellent source if you know what you are after.

Mac's Place

8461 154th N.E., Redmond, WA 98052, USA. *Tel:* 206 883 8312
Fax: 206 881 3090

Catalogue:	Free
Goods:	Mac hardware & software
Countries sent to:	World
Methods of payment:	Visa, Mastercard, Amex, Cheque, Bank Transfer

Mac's Place sells virtually everything for the Mac, from software through to accessories and even some printers. However, it does not sell Macs themselves. The 72 page colour catalogue is well laid out with plenty of information on all the products. Aside from the extensive software section, there are modems, memory, accelerators and general accessories.

WordPerfect 2.1 sells for $124, Lotus 1-2-3 Presentation Bundle for $138, the SupraFax Modem V.32bis for $258 and Norton Utilities 2.0 for $94. Some items of software may not be exportable because of copyright laws.

MacWarehouse

PO Box 3013, 1690 Oak Street, Lakewood, NJ 08701 3013, USA.
Tel: 908 370 3801 x 4000 & 908 370 4779 *Fax:* 908 905 9279

Catalogue:	Free
Goods:	Apple accessories & software
Countries sent to:	World
Methods of payment:	Visa, Mastercard, Cheque

MacWarehouse are a very large company specializing in software and accessories for Apple computers – but they do not sell the machines themselves. The 126 page colour catalogue is crammed full of products, all of which receive full and helpful descriptions. If it is made for the Apple, the chances are it is here.

Although the company in the US will export, they also have an operation based in the UK. They issue an almost identical catalogue but with British prices in £. Some of the items will therefore not be available in the UK and/or may be in American versions. It depends on the exchange rate and weight of the item as to whether it is best to order from the US or UK, so readers should probably consult both catalogues.

UK contact: *Tel:* 081 449 7113, or toll free: 0800 181 332, *Fax:* 081 447 1696.

Misco Canada Inc.

121 Ferrier Street, Markham, ON L3R 3K6, Canada.
Tel: 416 477 4055 *Fax:* 416 477 9239

Catalogue:	Free
Goods:	Computer supplies & accessories
Countries sent to:	World
Methods of payment:	Visa, Mastercard, Amex, Cheque

A 106 page colour catalogue full of every conceivable accessory for computers. Here you can find ribbons, toners, discs, monitors, scanners, keyboards, software, modems, cables and so on – everything, in fact, apart from computers themselves. Since this is a Canadian operation, UK readers may find the exchange rate makes it a better bet than similar catalogues from the US.

Multiple Zones International Inc.
17411 N.E. Union Hill Road, Suite 140, Redmond, WA 98052, USA.
Tel: 206 883 1975 *Fax:* 206 881 3421

Catalogue:	Free
Goods:	Software & peripherals
Countries sent to:	World
Methods of payment:	Visa, Mastercard, Amex, Cheque

Multiple Zones sell a large range of software for both IBM and Apple computers along with some peripherals. Unfortunately their catalogue was not ready as we went to press.

COMPUTERS

Action Computer Supplies

5th Floor, Alperton House, Bridgewater Road, Wembley, Middlesex
HA10 1BR, United Kingdom. *Tel:* 081 900 2566 *Fax:* 081 903 3333

Catalogue:	Free
Goods:	Hardware, software & accessories
Countries sent to:	World
Methods of payment:	Visa, Mastercard, Amex, Diners Club, Cheque

This 544 page catalogue is printed like a fat paperback and stocks virtually everything you could need for a computer. As far as hardware goes, they sell Toshiba laptops, Compaq, AST, IBM, Sanyo, Texas Instruments, Hewlett Packard, Tandon and other brand leaders. They do not, however, stock Apples.

They also sell software, furniture, discs, printers, ribbons, fax machines, photocopiers, laser toners and just about every other accessory. All are said to be at 'low low prices' and this seems to be true. A Toshiba T1000LE is just over £1,000, discounted to £830 if you buy other products at the same time. An IBM 70-081 is £2,550, an HP DeskJet 500 as low as £300.

Computers Direckt

4300 Linden Drive, Midland, MI 48640, USA. *Tel:* 517 835 3771
Fax: 517 835 7481

Catalogue:	Free
Goods:	Hardware & accessories
Countries sent to:	World
Methods of payment:	Visa, Mastercard, Bank Transfer

Although we had not seen this company's catalogue at the time of going to press, we gather they sell a full line of IBM and Apple hardware along with accessories and software.

Delo Computer gmbH

Mainstrasse 7, D-45663 Recklinghausen, Germany. *Tel:* 02361 60990
Fax: 02361 6099 12

Catalogue:	Free
Goods:	Computers & accessories
Countries sent to:	Europe
Methods of payment:	Cheque, Bank Transfer

Reseller News is a glossy 32 page brochure selling a broad range of
computer hardware and accessories. Written in German this is for the
seriously electronically minded. Software such as NewWare 386 is
available in both English and German versions. They also sell the
latest CD-ROM systems from Philips, NEC and Mitsumi. Graphic
systems include the Miro Tiger and Rainbow ranges and the SPEA
HiLite and FIRE systems. There is a good range of network adapters
and monitors including Philips 4CM 6099 Brilliance 1710 for German
M2199 and the Goldstar 1710 plus for DM1299.

Educalc Corporation

27953 Cabot Road, Laguna Niguel, CA 92677, USA.
Tel: 714 582 2637 *Fax:* 714 582 1445

Catalogue:	Free
Goods:	Technical calculators
Countries sent to:	World
Methods of payment:	Visa, Mastercard, Amex, Cheque, Bank Transfer

Educalc mainly sell technical calculators, that is machines capable of
a lot more than simply adding and multiplying. Their 72 page catalogue
details machines by Franklin, Psion, Sharp, Hewlett Packard and
others. They also sell a good range of books and some HP computer
printers.

Focus Enhancements
800 West Cummings Park, Suite 4500, Woburn, MA 01801–9648, USA. *Tel:* 617 938 8088 *Fax:* 617 938 0818

Catalogue:	Free
Goods:	Mac computer software & accessories
Countries sent to:	World
Methods of payment:	Visa, Mastercard, Amex, Cheque, Bank Transfer

Although Focus is an American company it produces a catalogue for the UK market priced in pounds sterling. It also has a toll-free number from the UK direct to the States. The 36 page colour catalogue details 'Mac enhancements', such as Ethernet, cables, software, books, memory chips and hard drives. Many of these are made by Focus themselves and sold direct to the public, thus cutting out the middleman.

They also have a fax-back service. This is where you call their fax number in the USA, enter digits which specify a particular product and then hang up. You are faxed back with information sheets on the item.

120Mb hard drives are £269, optical drives are £819 for 128Mb. Virex, a virus protection programme, sells for £43 while Mac books such as 'Dr Macintosh' are a reasonable £12.

Front Porch Computers
4742 Highway 52 Alt, Chatsworth, GA 30705, USA.
Tel: 0800 899 650 (toll free from UK) *Fax:* 706 695 1990

Catalogue:	n/a
Goods:	Brand name & custom computer systems
Countries sent to:	World
Methods of payment:	Visa, Mastercard, Amex, Diners Club, Cheque, Bank Transfer

Front Porch do not publish a catalogue but have toll free numbers from 23 countries so that customers can discuss their needs at no charge to themselves. They stock both brand name and custom computer systems from very simple set-ups to highly complex ones.

Toll free numbers include: Germany 013 081 9471, Italy 167 875 252, Portugal 050 181 3700, Netherlands 060 228 274

Hal Computers

18 Belsize Park, London NW3 4DU, United Kingdom.
Tel: 071 435 0108 *Fax:* 071 435 0108

Catalogue:	n/a
Goods:	Computers & software
Countries sent to:	World
Methods of payment:	Cheque

Hal Computers do not publish a catalogue but will source any computer
or accessory at a price which they claim to be the lowest in the country.
Simply call them with your requirements and they will give you a
quote. All products come with full guarantees and can be sent anywhere
in the world. They specialize in Apple computers but also supply other
makes including IBM. A good service but do not expect to have a long
chat – they are there just to provide the goods, not the advice!

Komentokeskus Oy

PO Box 391, FI 90101 Oulu, Finland. *Tel:* 981 371000
Fax: 981 371011

Catalogue:	Free
Goods:	Computers & accessories
Countries sent to:	Europe, Africa
Methods of payment:	Visa, Mastercard, Diners Club, Cheque, Bank Transfer

Although in Finnish, this newspaper-style catalogue is easy to follow.
It lists an extensive stock of computers, software and accessories.
Machines include Amiga, Atari, Commodore, PCs and others but not
Apple. They also sell Sega and other game modules.

Misco Computer Supplies Ltd
Faraday Close, Park Farm Industrial Estate, Wellingborough, Northants NN8 6XH, United Kingdom. *Tel:* 0933 400000
Fax: 0933 401520

Catalogue:	Free
Goods:	Computers & accessories
Countries sent to:	World
Methods of payment:	Visa, Cheque, Amex

Misco is a large company which sells computer consumables, supplies, accessories, hardware, software and even furniture. Their comprehensive catalogue is sent out free of charge every month to UK customers and quarterly worldwide.

P W Computer Supplies
Dawlish Drive, Pinner, Middlesex HA5 5LN, United Kingdom. *Tel:* 081 868 9548 *Fax:* 081 868 2167

Catalogue:	Free
Goods:	Hardware & software
Countries sent to:	World
Methods of payment:	Visa, Mastercard, Cheque, Bank Transfer

Computers, laptops, printers, fax machines, software and accessories are all represented in this 80 page catalogue. There is even some office furniture. Manufacturers include Ambra (i.e. IBM), Amstrad, Olivetti, Panasonic, Sanyo and Toshiba, but not – at present – Apple.

An Ambra Treka 386 SL notebook is £1099, a Toshiba T1850C £1795 and a HP LaserJet 4L printer £519.

CRAFTS

Baines Orr (London) Ltd

1–5 Garlands Road, Redhill, Surrey RH1 6NX, United Kingdom.
Tel: 0737 767363 *Fax:* 0737 768627

Catalogue:	£1
Goods:	Components for jewellery & other crafts
Countries sent to:	Europe
Methods of payment:	Visa, Mastercard, Cheque, Bank Transfer

Baines sell semi-precious stones and other components for DIY jewellery along with parts for other crafts. Their catalogue was unavailable as we went to press but should be out in early 1994.

Beckfoot Mill

Clock Mill, Denholme, Bradford, W. Yorks BD13 4DN, United Kingdom. *Tel:* 0274 830063 *Fax:* 0274 834430

Catalogue:	£1
Goods:	Soft toy kits
Countries sent to:	World
Methods of payment:	Visa, Cheque, Bank Transfer

Beckfoot Mill sell a good selection of parts to make soft toys and dolls. As well as complete kits, their small colour brochure stocks individual parts such as fabric, filling, eyes, noses, joints and so on. They also sell some needlepoint and macramé materials, quilts and even sleeping bags.

Bunka with Flair

49 Broadbridge Drive, West Hill, ON M1C 3K5, Canada.
Tel: 416 282 9257 *Fax:* 416 282 0580

Catalogue:	Free
Goods:	Embroidery kits & supplies
Countries sent to:	World
Methods of payment:	Visa, Mastercard, Bank Transfer

This company is both an importer and manufacturer of Bunka Shishu Art, which apparently is Japanese Punch Embroidery. The 64 page catalogue consists mainly of full page, colour plates of embroidery examples which can be made with the kits supplied. They also sell all necessary accessories.

Canadian Handcrafted
PO Box 940, Minden, ON K0M 2K0, Canada. *Tel:* 705 286 3305

Catalogue:	$5
Goods:	Equipment for timber frame buildings
Countries sent to:	World
Methods of payment:	Visa, Cheque, Bank Transfer

This highly informative 56 page catalogue is for the frontier man or pioneer who wants to build his own home, preferably out of wood. Printed on recycled paper and with a nice selection of black and white photographs, it features all the tools you'll need to build your dream house. They also stock a wide range of books and give plenty of advice on how to start, including a useful list of addresses of advice groups and so on.

Code's Mill Factory Outlet
Dept. R, Box 130, Perth, ON K7H 3E3, Canada. *Tel:* 613 267 2464 *Fax:* 613 264 0261

Catalogue:	$
Goods:	Felt, vinyl, burlap
Countries sent to:	World
Methods of payment:	Visa, Mastercard, Cheque, Bank Draft

Code's produce a large folder containing swatches of their dozens of felts and burlaps. They come in a wide range of colours and are sold by the metre and yard. They also sell bundles of scraps which may be useful for modelmakers (Canadian $4 per lb for felt ends, $2 per lb for felt strips).

Craft King Mail Order

Craft King Inc., PO Box 90637, Lakeland, FL 33804, USA.
Tel: 813 686 9600 *Fax:* 813 688 5072

Catalogue:	$5
Goods:	Arts & crafts supplies
Countries sent to:	World
Methods of payment:	Visa, Mastercard, Cheque, Bank Transfer

At 180 black and white pages this bumper catalogue contains every item the keen craftsperson could require. The range covers artists' materials from paintbrushes to easels, a huge variety of paints and colouring tools, earring kits, dollshouse accessories and adult miniatures, bead kits, craft books, basketry supplies, bridal knick-knacks, boxes to decorate and many many more fun things to do at home.

Apart from requiring a full day just to leaf through, this catalogue will supply hours of good ideas for the ardent hobbyist.

Creatively Yours, Handpainting on Silk

5550 Hastings Street, Burnaby, BC V5B 1R3, Canada.
Tel: 604 298 6744 *Fax:* 604 298 6744

Catalogue:	Free
Goods:	Silk scarves & dyes
Countries sent to:	World
Methods of payment:	Visa, Bank Draft, Cheque

This 9 page catalogue is printed on A4 sheets stapled together. There are no illustrations but clear descriptions of each item. The company specializes in supplies for the DIY silk dyer and sells silk by the yard as well as pre-formed articles such as ties and scarves. They also supply the necessary dyes and equipment which can then be used in conjunction with a microwave to produce the finished piece. Kits, books and videos are also available.

Grey Owl Indian Craft Sales Corp.
132 – 05 Merrick Boulevard, PO Box 468, Jamaica 34, USA.
Tel: 718 341 4000 *Fax:* 718 527 6000

Catalogue:	Free
Goods:	Indian craft supplies
Countries sent to:	World
Methods of payment:	Visa, Mastercard, Amex, Cheque, Bank Transfer

'The largest exporter of Native American items in the world' may seem like yet another American company claiming first prize, but in this case it's probably justified. The 209 page colour catalogue features just about everything connected to Native American Indians. There are full costumes, complete with wigs and feathers, along with craft supplies, kits, beads, books, music videos, animal skins, leather crafts, posters, jewellery and so on. There is even a range of tomahawks 'for the mountain man and buckskinner'.

Knitters of Australia
625 Hampton Street, Brighton, Victoria 3186, Australia.
Tel: 03 593 1433 *Fax:* 03 593 2161

Catalogue:	$5
Goods:	Knitting patterns
Countries sent to:	World
Methods of payment:	Cheque, International Money Order

Knitters of Australia is a club with members all round the world. The Australian $10 annual fee provides the large format, 24 page colour catalogue and discount prices on its patterns. These are for a wide range of clothes, for men, women, children and babies, in many styles. Prices are very reasonable, at under Australian $5, and you can also order wool from them.

Laila's Arts and Crafts
7860 Tranmere Drive, Mississauga, ON L5S 1L9, Canada.
Tel: 416 672 6577 *Fax:* 416 672 6595

Catalogue:	$20 + p
Goods:	Kits, frames & accessories for 3-D pictures
Countries sent to:	World
Methods of payment:	Visa, Mastercard, Amex, Cheque

Laila's 'Paper Tole Kit Catalog' runs to 12 loose pages stapled together. They feature colour illustrations of kits for paper toles from 6" x 8" up to 12" x 16". Subjects vary a great deal, from pictures of animals, through rather cutesy children, to trains, ships, flowers and cartoon characters.

Nowetah's American Indian Store and Museum
Route No. 27, Box 40, New Portland, ME 04954, USA.
Tel: 207 628 4981

Catalogue:	Free
Goods:	American Indian arts & crafts
Countries sent to:	World
Methods of payment:	Cheque, Bank Transfer

You need to send a stamped-addressed envelope to receive the otherwise free information on this interesting store. Owned and operated by Native American Indians of the Susquehanna-Cherokee tribes, it sells all sorts of crafts. These include sweaters, jewellery, knives, pelts, peace-pipes, rattles, dolls and so on.

The small, photocopied pamphlet also describes the 11 other specialist catalogues which they produce. These include ones on handwoven Indian rugs and wall hangings; Indian porcupine quill and bead jewellery; sterling silver and turquoise jewellery; Indian pottery; Indian toys and leather products. There is no charge for these but they are lent out on trust for two weeks at a time. This rather sweet touch seems to characterize the store.

Opulence Silks & Dyes Ltd

55 Lonsdale Avenue, North Vancouver, BC V7M 2E5, Canada.
Tel: 604 980 2120

Catalogue:	Free
Goods:	Silk & fabric dyes, silk & cotton, books & Japanese fabric art supplies
Countries sent to:	World
Methods of payment:	Visa, Mastercard, Bank Transfer

This simple 35 page catalogue is really more of a price list with brief descriptions of the products. The company sells natural fabrics, including a variety of silks, by the yard, as well as silk scarves. They also stock a wide selection of natural dyes along with the equipment needed to colour the fabrics. It is a specialized market well served by this knowledgeable and helpful company. There is an extensive list of books as well as patterns available.

Silk linen is Canadian $10.55 per yard, pure silk from $11.85 and Japanese kimono silk from $25 per yard.

Primavera

Studio 6 Workshop, Clos Menter, Excelsior Road, Cardiff, South Glamorgan CF4 3AT, United Kingdom. *Tel:* 0222 610584
Fax: 0222 521800

Catalogue:	£1
Goods:	Needlepoint kits
Countries sent to:	Europe, USA, Australasia
Methods of payment:	Visa, Mastercard, Cheque, Bank Transfer

Primavera sell a selection of needlepoint kits through their 24 page colour catalogue. Most of these are for cushions with original designs, which are also available just as canvasses. There are some tapestry kits along with accessories such as a magnifying lamp. Overseas orders are welcomed; a postal surcharge of £6 is added.

Pussy Willow Lace
407–9632 Cameron Street, Burnaby, BC V3J JN3, Canada.
Tel: 604 936 8632

Catalogue:	$3.50
Goods:	Lacemaking equipment
Countries sent to:	World
Methods of payment:	Visa, Cheque, Bank Transfer, Bank Draft

Pussy Willow specialize in hard-to-find equipment for making lace and fine needlework. Unfortunately, their catalogue was not available as we went to press, but we gather it runs to 60 black and white pages and will be available in 1994.

Rodin
36 Champs-Elysees, Paris VIII, France. *Tel:* 1 43 59 58 82
Fax: 1 45 61 13 07

Catalogue:	n/a
Goods:	Fabrics
Countries sent to:	Asia, Europe, Africa, USA
Methods of payment:	Cheque

Rodin do not produce a catalogue but will send out samples of their materials and fabrics which are suitable both for clothes and furniture.

I. Shor Canada Ltd
1111 Finch Avenue West #34, Downsview, ON M3J 2E5, Canada.
Tel: 416 665 8600 *Fax:* 416 665 0364

Catalogue:	$5
Goods:	Jewellery making equipment
Countries sent to:	World
Methods of payment:	Visa, Mastercard, Cheque, Bank Draft

Although we did not receive this catalogue before going to press, we understand it covers all sorts of supplies for people to make their own jewellery.

Tander Leather Co.
Box 13,000, 120 Brock Street, Barrie, ON L4M 4W4, Canada.
Tel: 705 728 2481 *Fax:* 705 721 1226

Catalogue:	$2
Goods:	Leathercraft supplies
Countries sent to:	Asia, Europe, Africa
Methods of payment:	Visa, Mastercard, Bank Draft

Tander have been in business for over 75 years, selling a huge range of leathercraft supplies, and now claim to be the largest such supplier in the world. Their current catalogue, running to 116 colour pages, is crammed full of interesting items for anyone who enjoys working in leather (or should I say with leather).

They have everything from simple starter kits for children, through supplies to make specific items, such as bags and wallets, to tools, hardware and of course the leather itself. There are kits to make briefcases, holsters, saddles, belts, boots, moccasins, even clothes. They also stock a range of jewellery supplies and a good selection of books. An excellent resource.

West Wind Hardwood Inc.
PO Box 2205, Sidney, BC V8L 3S8, Canada. *Tel:* 604 656 0848
Fax: 604 381 9663

Catalogue:	$
Goods:	Wood
Countries sent to:	USA, Australasia
Methods of payment:	Visa, Mastercard, Cheque, Bank Transfer

West Wind sells hardwoods, softwoods (marine grade), veneer plywoods and marine plywoods. While they do issue a catalogue it was out of print when we went to press.

Wild & Woolly Yarns
38 Victoria Road, Devonport, New Zealand. *Tel:* 445 3255

Catalogue:	Free
Goods:	Sweaters
Countries sent to:	World
Methods of payment:	Visa, Mastercard, Amex, International Money Order

Wild & Woolly's 12 page colour catalogue features dozens of 'knit-kits', complete kits to knit sweaters, including the wool. Each design is fully illustrated and available for men, women and children. The style is bright and colourful and the prices reasonable.

Men's sweaters start at around New Zealand $65 rising to just under $100. All goods are sent by 'sea and land', which keeps postage down to $15 per item and guarantees delivery within a month.

Wild Goose Chase
Box 1166, Grand Rapids, MI 49501, USA.
Tel: 616 363 8587/453 3200

Catalogue:	$2
Goods:	Quilting patterns
Countries sent to:	World
Methods of payment:	Cheque, Bank Transfer

Five loose pages describe a variety of quilting patterns for wall hangings, bags, sweatshirts and so on. All are illustrated with photographs.

The patterns sell for between $4–5.50 each plus postage of $4 for up to 3 and $6 for up to 6.

CYCLING

Bilenky Cycle Works Ltd

5319 North 2nd Street, Philadelphia, PA 19120, USA.
Tel: 215 329 4744 *Fax:* 215 329 4744

Catalogue:	Free
Goods:	Handcrafted bicycles
Countries sent to:	World
Methods of payment:	Bank Transfer, International Money Order

This small company handmakes bicycles and tandems. Using only the best Reynolds tubing, the machines can either be made to standard measurements or custom-built. Primarily they make frames but they also supply complete bikes. The catalogue is actually a series of brochures giving specifications, photographs, re-prints from reviews and a number of letters from satisfied customers. If you are serious about cycling, this is the place to come.

Frames start from $875 rising to $1,250 for a fully customized version. Tandem frames are between $1,900 and $2,350 and $3,250 – $3,650 for completed machines. Lead times are 6–8 weeks.

Performance Bicycle Shop

PO Box 2741, Chapel Hill, NC 27514, USA. *Tel:* 919 933 9113
Fax: 919 942 5431

Catalogue:	$2
Goods:	Bicycles, cycling clothes, equipment & accessories
Countries sent to:	World
Methods of payment:	Visa, Mastercard

This 72 page colour catalogue looks like a magazine and is very well laid out and produced. It has just about everything you could need for cycling, from high-performance bikes, through frames, handlebars, and pedals, to clothes, watches, pumps, tyres, saddles, speedometers and bags. They also have in-line skates, tents and sleeping bags.

Gortex jackets sell for around $200, panniers from $75, in-line skates $200, mountain bikes from $230 to $1,000.

ELECTRONICS

Billiards Old Telephones
21710 Regnart Road, Cupertino, CA 95014, USA. *Tel:* 408 252 2104

Catalogue:	$1
Goods:	Vintage telephones
Countries sent to:	World
Methods of payment:	Cheque, Bank Transfer, Bank Draft

This eccentric company sells old telephones and parts. The rather scrappy 16 page catalogue looks put together by hand and photocopied. However, it is clearly the work of an enthusiast who knows all there is about ancient phones. They also sell plans to modernize antique models and original old phone directories from across the USA, though why anyone would want one of these seems puzzling.

Art deco phones adapted for use on the modern network sell for around $200 while an older version, with separate mouthpiece, is $225. All orders are shipped within 24 hours.

Bi-Rite Photos & Electronics
15 East 30th Street, New York, NY 10016, USA. *Tel:* 212 685 2130
Fax: 212 679 2986

Catalogue:	n/a
Goods:	Electronics, cameras & phones
Countries sent to:	World
Methods of payment:	Visa, Mastercard, Bank Draft

Bi-Rite do not at present publish a catalogue but will send goods to overseas customers. They sell a good selection of cameras, video equipment (including games), telephones and electronics. Interested readers should contact them direct with their requirements.

Bonus-Postimyynti
Luhtat 6, FI-81701 Lieksa, Finland. *Tel:* 975 524644 *Fax:* 975 524644

Catalogue:	Free
Goods:	Electronics, parts & equipment
Countries sent to:	Europe
Methods of payment:	Diners Club, Amex

Bonus issue a small 24 page catalogue packed with electronic equipment, accessories and parts. They specialize in CB radio and carry a full range of radios, aerials and microphones. They also sell metering equipment and a wide selection of parts, including cables and adapters. Although in Finnish, each item is illustrated so it is relatively easy to understand.

Brunelle Instruments Inc.
73, 6th Range S., St Elie d'Orford, PQ J0B 2S0, Canada.
Tel: 819 563 9096 *Fax:* 819 569 1408

Catalogue:	Free
Goods:	Electrical & electronic measuring instruments
Countries sent to:	World
Methods of payment:	Visa, Cheque, Bank Transfer

Unfortunately we have not been able to see this catalogue before going to press. However, we gather it is 40 pages, in colour, and features a wide range of electronic measuring devices suitable for the professional and amateur.

Cambridge Soundworks

15 California Street, Newton, MA 02158 9954, USA.
Tel: 617 332 5936 *Fax:* 617 332 9229

Catalogue:	Free
Goods:	Hi-fi
Countries sent to:	World
Methods of payment:	Visa, Mastercard, Amex

This company doesn't simply happen to export abroad, they positively seek to. The excellent 62 page catalogue is full of the latest hi-fi equipment, from mid to high price. They specialize in surround-sound equipment for hooking up to TVs, as well as laserdisc players. Manufacturers include Sony, Pioneer, Philips and their own Cambridge SoundWorks brand. There is also a small range of portable stereos for cassettes and CDs.

A Sony state-of-the-art discman is $199, a CD/Laserdisc player by Pioneer $399 and a complete ProLogic surround system $1,775.

Copper Electronics Inc.

3315 Gilmore Industrial Boulevard, Louisville, KY 40213, USA.
Tel: 502 968 8500 *Fax:* 502 968 0449

Catalogue:	$15 for 12 issues, first free
Goods:	CB radios, electronics & computers
Countries sent to:	World
Methods of payment:	Visa, Mastercard, Cheque, Bank Transfer

Copper Electronics' 40 page black and white catalogue is printed on newsprint and comes out 12 times a year, complete with letters and 'articles'. The main emphasis is on CB kit and electronic equipment such as signal monitors and watt meters. However, they also stock a good range of radar detectors, scanners and some computer accessories along with an own brand PC.

A Uniden HR-2510 mobile transceiver is just $200, radar detectors are under $40 and scanners start at $90.

47th Street Photo
455 Smith Street, Brooklyn, NY 11231, USA. *Tel:* 718 722 4750
Fax: 718 722 3510

Catalogue:	$3
Goods:	Photographic & video equipment, TVs, computers & electronics
Countries sent to:	World
Methods of payment:	Visa, Mastercard, Amex, Cheque, Bank Draft

47th Street Photo call their 150 black and white catalogue 'The Source' and it certainly is one of the best places to buy a huge range of goods at excellent prices. They do not just sell cameras either, but also computers (including Toshiba laptops), video equipment, TVs, personal stereos, hi-fi, radar detectors, calculators, copiers and fax machines, home appliances (irons, vacuums, microwave ovens etc.), phones, watches and a lot more. And to make things even better, they stock video and TV systems in a variety of formats, so you can buy PAL equipment here.

Prices are far too numerous to mention but you can be sure that they are amongst the most competitive in the US. This is one of those catalogues you can't really do without.

MD Electronics
PO Box 241296, Omaha, NE 68124, USA. *Tel:* 402 554 0417
Fax: 402 392 0991

Catalogue:	$3
Goods:	Cable TV equipment
Countries sent to:	World
Methods of payment:	Visa, Mastercard, Cheque, International Money Order

MD Electronics sell a complete line of cable coverters and descramblers for the North American market, although these may work elsewhere as well. The 16 page colour catalogue also details video accessories – such as replacement and universal remote control units.

Sales Midden-Holland
Brocihweg 11, 2071 RM Schoonhoven, The Netherlands.
Tel: 01823 85498 *Fax:* 01823 84859

Catalogue:	Free
Goods:	Satellite system
Countries sent to:	Europe
Methods of payment:	Visa, Mastercard, Amex, Diners Club, Cheque, Bank Draft

While this company did answer our questionnaire and assures us that they ship their goods within Europe, they did not have a catalogue ready and did not give any information on their range other than 'satellite systems'. Curious readers might like to see if they get any further.

Techno Retail Ltd
Unit 9, Hampton Farm Industrial Estate, Feltham, Middlesex, United Kingdom. *Tel:* 081 898 9934 *Fax:* 081 894 4652

Catalogue:	Free
Goods:	Cameras, video & electronic goods
Countries sent to:	World
Methods of payment:	Visa, Mastercard, Amex, Diners Club, Cheque, Bank Transfer

Techno is a very successful high street chain in the UK but they also operate a mail order department. They carry a wide range of cameras and lenses along with accessories such as filters, film and cases. They also have an excellent selection of video equipment, from basic camcorders up to semi-professional machines, editing desks, monitors, VCRs and so on. Lastly, they stock personal hi-fis and palmtop computers such as the Psion Series 3 and Sharp ZQ machines. And of course they sell batteries, blank cassettes and videos.

A Canon EOS 1000FN 35mm SLR is £360, a Sony FX200 video camera £600 and a JVC HR-D980 VCR £500.

FISHING

Hook & Tackle Industries Ltd
PO Box 6, Dept C, Lethbridge, AB T1J 3Y3, Canada.
Tel: 403 328 5252 *Fax:* 403 328 7577

Catalogue:	$2
Goods:	Fly fishing equipment & books
Countries sent to:	Europe, USA, Australasia
Methods of payment:	Visa, Mastercard, Amex, Cheque, Bank Transfer

An informative, 48 page black and white catalogue selling a comprehensive range of hooks, tools and materials for making fishing flies. They also stock books and some interesting accessories, although not rods.

Jenson Fishing Tackle Co.
PO Box 9587, Austin, TX 78766, USA. *Tel:* 512 836 1788
Fax: 512 836 1269

Catalogue:	Free
Goods:	Fishing tackle & accessories
Countries sent to:	World
Methods of payment:	Visa, Mastercard, Amex, Bank Transfer

The catalogue was not ready as we went to press but sells all sorts of fishing tackle and accessories.

Kaufmann's Streamborn
PO Box 23032, Portland, ORE 97281–3032, USA.
Tel: 503 639 6400 *Fax:* 503 684 7025

Catalogue:	$6
Goods:	Fly fishing supplies
Countries sent to:	World
Methods of payment:	Visa, Mastercard, Amex, Bank Transfer

Another splendid fishing catalogue. Large format, 96 colour pages, it sells rods, flies, clothes, boots, videos, hooks and accessories. They have some particularly interesting 'float tubes', which are glorified inner tubes in which the angler can stand and wade out. They have a flourishing international clientele.

Le Baron Outdoor Products Ltd
8601 St Lawrence Boulevard, Montreal, PQ H2P 2M9, Canada.
Tel: 514 381 4231 *Fax:* 514 381 2822

Catalogue:	$8
Goods:	Outdoor equipment
Countries sent to:	World
Methods of payment:	Visa, Mastercard, Bank Draft

Le Baron produce two catalogues a year, Spring and Fall, which run to about 300 colour pages each. They stock a huge selection of goods for camping, fishing, hunting and general outdoor activities plus an excellent range of clothing. All are at discount prices and because this is a Canadian company, the exchange rate may be more favourable for UK readers than similar outlets in the US.

Michael & Young Fly Shop
10484 137th Street, Surrey (Vancouver Suburb), BC V3T 4H5, Canada. *Tel:* 604 588 2833 *Fax:* 604 582 9627

Catalogue:	Free
Goods:	Fly fishing products
Countries sent to:	Asia, Europe, USA
Methods of payment:	Visa, Mastercard, Amex, Cheque, International Money Order

This is more a listing of products than an illustrated catalogue. Its 46 pages give helpful but brief descriptions of all kinds of equipment for fly fishing. This includes flies themselves, rods and reels, clothing, boots, accessories and books. There is a minimum order of Canadian $35.

The Orvis Co.
Historic Route 7A, Manchester, VT 05254, USA. *Tel:* 802 362 3622
Fax: 802 362 3525

Catalogue:	Free
Goods:	Hunting & fishing equipment
Countries sent to:	World
Methods of payment:	Visa, Mastercard, Amex, Cheque, Bank Transfer

The catalogue was not ready as we went to press but sells all sorts of fishing tackle and accessories as well as hunting equipment.

Tom C. Saville
Unit 7, Salisbury Square, Nottingham NG7 2AB, United Kingdom.
Tel: 0602 784 248 *Fax:* 0602 42004

Catalogue:	£1.20
Goods:	Game fishing equipment
Countries sent to:	World
Methods of payment:	Visa, Mastercard, Cheque, Bank Transfer

This well-produced 136 page black and white catalogue is crammed with everything for the game angler, including rods, reels, hooks, fly tying equipment, clothes and books. All prices include VAT so this needs to be taken off for export orders.

Techsonic Industries
3 Humminbird Lane, Eufaula, AL 36027, USA. *Tel:* 205 687 6613
Fax: 205 687 4272

Catalogue:	Free
Goods:	Electronic fishing aids
Countries sent to:	World
Methods of payment:	Visa, Mastercard, Bank Transfer

Techsonic make instruments under the brand name 'Humminbird Wide'. These are fish-seeking devices to attach to boats. Using sound waves, they display an LCD image of the water either ahead, underneath or around the boat, complete with icons for fish. It may not seem very sporting but would certainly save a great deal of time. Prices on request.

FOOD & WINE

Abergavenny Fine Foods Ltd
4 Castle Meadows Park, Abergavenny, Gwent NP7 7RZ, United Kingdom. *Tel:* 0873 850001 *Fax:* 0873 850002

Catalogue:	Free
Goods:	Speciality Welsh cheeses
Countries sent to:	Asia, Europe, USA, Australasia
Methods of payment:	Visa, Mastercard, Cheque, Bank Transfer

This catalogue is really more of an illustrated price list consisting of several loose sheets with colour photographs of the produce. This includes an excellent range of Welsh cheeses as well as Cumberland sausages and Welsh Rarebit. They sell individual cheeses along with special postal gift selections. The text is in English and French. Remember: there may be restrictions importing cheese into some countries.

Adnams Wine Merchants
The Crown, High Street, Southwold, Suffolk IP18 6DP, United Kingdom. *Tel:* 0502 724222 *Fax:* 0507 724805

Catalogue:	£2.50
Goods:	Fine wines
Countries sent to:	World
Methods of payment:	Visa, Mastercard, Cheque, Bank Transfer

Adnams are a well-known merchant from Suffolk and have twice won *The Sunday Telegraph's* 'Wine Merchant of the Year' award – and should win something for their catalogue too (maybe we should instigate a prize of our own).

The beautifully designed 96 page catalogue has wines from all round the world and each region has a lengthy introduction. There is even an extraordinary money-back offer: if you don't like a wine – for any reason – you can request a full refund for up to a month later. Whether this applies to overseas customers is doubtful, but Adnams will dispatch their goods anywhere.

Carriage is free in the UK for two cases or more, £5 for smaller orders. They also offer a cellarage service for £5 per case per year.

Berkmann Wine Cellars Ltd

12 Brewery Road, London N7 9NH, United Kingdom.
Tel: 071 609 4711 *Fax:* 071 607 0018

Catalogue:	Free
Goods:	Wine
Countries sent to:	Europe
Methods of payment:	Visa, Mastercard, Cheque, Bank Transfer

Berkmann sell wines from France, Italy, Portugal, Spain, Australia, New Zealand, Chile and Argentina. Their catalogue was not ready as we went to press but should now be available.

Bridfish Ltd

Unit 1, The Old Laundry Industrial Estate, Sea Road North, Bridport, Dorset DT6 3BD, United Kingdom. *Tel:* 0308 56306

Catalogue:	Free
Goods:	Smoked foods
Countries sent to:	Europe
Methods of payment:	Visa, Mastercard, Cheque, Bank Transfer

This small Dorset smokery uses traditional methods involving no colouring or dyes. Much of the fish is locally caught. The attractive 12 page brochure gives details of salmon, trout, prawns and kippers as well as poultry and meat. All items are vacuum packed, chilled and packaged in polystyrene boxes with ice pads. Restrictions may apply to certain countries.

1lb of smoked, sliced Scottish salmon is £18.50, a 5lb pack of smoked kippers is £15.50 while a Bridfish Bumper Pack of trout, salmon, mackerel, chicken, duck and ham is £57.50.

Charbonnel et Walker

One, The Royal Arcade, 28 Old Bond Street, London W1X 4BT, United Kingdom. *Tel:* 071 491 0939 *Fax:* 071 495 6279

Catalogue:	Free
Goods:	Chocolate & sugar confectionery
Countries sent to:	World
Methods of payment:	Visa, Mastercard, Amex, Cheque, Bank Transfer

Charbonnel et Walker have been Britain's Master Chocolatiers since 1875 and currently hold a Royal Warrant from the Queen. Their beautiful catalogue, printed on 11 loose sheets, features a selection of plain chocolates, after dinner mints and sweets as well as luxury sugar confectionery and the best hot chocolate drink you're ever likely to come across.

A 1lb assortment of plain chocolates is £16.50, 8oz of Mocha Batons £10.50, 1lb of truffles £18 and 500g of drinking chocolate £7.25.

Collin Street Bakery

Box 79, Corsicana, TX 75110, USA. *Tel:* 903 872 8111
Fax: 903 872 6879

Catalogue:	Free
Goods:	Baked goods
Countries sent to:	World
Methods of payment:	Visa, Mastercard, Amex, Diners Club, Cheque, Bank Transfer

Texas's Collin Street Bakery produces the DeLuxe Fruitcake which is only available by mail order and has a very large international fan club. The DeLuxe is made from 27% pecans, with honey, cherries, pineapple and other fruits. Supplied in a decorative Christmas tin the DeLuxe comes in three sizes: small ($1^7/_8$ lb), medium ($2^7/_8$lb) and large ($4^7/_8$lb).

Prices start from $13.75 per cake, with postage from $4.95. Delivery takes 8–12 weeks so Christmas shoppers should think ahead.

Comtesse du Barry S.A.
Route de Touget, 32200 Gimont, France. *Tel:* 62 67 76 81
Fax: 62 67 85 92

Catalogue:	Free
Goods:	Delicatessen foods
Countries sent to:	World
Methods of payment:	Cheque, International Money Order

This terrific French company is a very high-class delicatessen selling over 200 wonderful products. These include foie gras, pâtés, preserves, wine, chocolates and even pre-cooked meals. The beautiful catalogue – in French and English – comes in a deep blue folder and has enticing colour photographs of the products. Hampers are available.

Corney & Barrow
12 Helmet Row, London EC1, United Kingdom. *Tel:* 071 251 4051
Fax: 071 608 1373

Catalogue:	Free
Goods:	Wines & spirits
Countries sent to:	Europe, USA, Australasia
Methods of payment:	Visa, Mastercard, Cheque

Corney & Barrow have been established as wine merchants since 1780 and boast three Royal Warrants. They stock predominantly French wine of which they have a wide range. Their discreet 115 page catalogue offers a highly intelligent guide to all aspects of wine production and consumption. Each area is described in detail and the wine summarized with wit and *savoir faire*.

Sampling cases containing 3 bottles of house red, 3 of claret, white and sparkling wine are £58. House wine can be bought for as little as £3.64 while Dom Perignon Champagne with an 1985 vintage is £56.52 per bottle or £288.60 half a case.

Fauchon

26 Place de la Madeleine, Paris VIII, France. *Tel:* 1 47 42 60 11
Fax: 1 47 42 28 71

Catalogue:	Free
Goods:	Grocery
Countries sent to:	World
Methods of payment:	Visa, Mastercard, Amex, Diners Club, Cheque, Bank Transfer

Fauchon is THE French food store and this magnificent 144 page colour catalogue does them proud. Although in French it is very easy to follow even for non-speakers and is beautifully illustrated throughout with excellent photographs. The produce ranges from beer, wine and spirits (including champagne) to cheese, conserves, fruit, caviar and chocolates – in short all you would expect from a high-class delicatessen. There are also a number of hampers in different sizes and you can even have complete meals sent, served on special trays which arrive in a gift box!

Prices are what you might expect – on the high side. Six bottles of wine cost from around 500F up to several thousand. A small hamper is 130F, larger ones between 400F and 750F, truly splendid ones 22,000F (that's over £2,000!).

Fortnum & Mason

181 Piccadilly, London W1A 1ER, United Kingdom.
Tel: 071 465 8666 *Fax:* 071 437 3278

Catalogue:	£
Goods:	High-class foods & wine
Countries sent to:	World
Methods of payment:	Visa, Mastercard, Amex, Diners Club, International Money Order

One of the most famous food shops in the world, Fortnum & Mason have supplied the Royal Family for years. They produce both a standard catalogue and a special one for Christmas. Both are beautifully produced, with excellent photographs. As one might expect, all the goods are of very high quality with prices to match. Several of the hampers have been specially designed for export in mind, i.e. they do not contravene import regulations on certain types of meat and fruit.

A simple gift box with two bottles of wine, cheese, salmon, biscuits, venison and several other goodies, comes to £100. A single York Ham, weighing 14lb, is an astonishing £78 while the export hampers range from £50 to £100. Most come in traditional wicker baskets.

Gazin's

2910 Toulouse Street, New Orleans, LA 70119, USA.
Tel: 504 482 0302 *Fax:* 504 827 5391

Catalogue:	$2
Goods:	Louisiana gourmet food
Countries sent to:	World
Methods of payment:	Visa, Mastercard, Amex

This 32 page colour catalogue carries both Cajun Creole cuisine and a range of kitchen appliances. Unlike other companies listed here, Gazin's sell more ingredients than finished items. These include fish, bread, biscuits, oil, rice and soup mixes as well as various condiments and a range of coffee.

A box of Cajun Seafood Pie Mix sells for $6.95, 8oz of Pecan Praline Dessert Coffee for $8.50 and Cajun spices for $3.50 per jar.

Ferdinando Giordano SPA

Via Cane Guido 58, 12050 Valle Talloria di Diano d'Alba, Cuneo, Italy. *Tel:* 0173 231 731 *Fax:* 0173 231 794

Catalogue:	Free
Goods:	Italian wine & food
Countries sent to:	Europe
Methods of payment:	Visa, Mastercard

This excellent 64 page colour catalogue is in Italian but nevertheless is easy to follow for non-speakers. There's a good range of 'house' wines and grappa along with Italian food specialities such as mushrooms, cheese, sauces, pâtés, truffles, honey, cakes and chocolates.

Wines start at around L4,000, grappa at L5,000. Giordano olive oil is L60,000 for six bottles and a large jar of 'misto funghi' (mushrooms) is L10,850.

The Hamper People of Norfolk

Strumpshaw, Norwich, Norfolk NR13 4AG, United Kingdom.
Tel: 0603 716815 *Fax:* 0603 715440

Catalogue:	Free
Goods:	Food & wine hampers
Countries sent to:	World
Methods of payment:	Visa, Mastercard, Amex, Diners Club, Cheque, Bank Transfer

The Hamper People produce three catalogues, two for the domestic market, the other for overseas customers, called 'Gifts International from H. L. Barnett'. All are in colour and beautifully illustrated with photographs of the magnificent food hampers. Packed in traditional wicker baskets, they contain a variety of food and wine, such as cheese, biscuits, salmon, chocolate, preserves and so on. In addition, the international catalogue has gardening gifts, stationery, china, wines, clothes and some toys. Some food items cannot be sent overseas. There is a separate catalogue for high-class Christmas decorations.

Hampers start around £15, rising to £350.

Lay & Wheeler Ltd

6 Culver Street West, Colchester, Essex, United Kingdom.
Tel: 0206 764446 *Fax:* 0206 560002

Catalogue:	Free
Goods:	Wine
Countries sent to:	World
Methods of payment:	Visa, Mastercard, Amex, Cheque, Bank Transfer

This splendidly produced 124 page colour catalogue is far more than simply a list of products and prices. Extensive and informed notes describe each region and wine in great detail. There are over 1,000 wines in total, from 120 countries. A must for the serious wine drinker.

Prices are too various to detail but postal charges are £4.75 for one bottle £6.50 for up to three. Orders of a case or more are sent by special carrier, the charge being £5.05. Two cases or more and carriage is free. Export charges are available on request.

MacVicar View Maple Products

c/o Mark & Sarah MacVicar, Box 1252, Brownsburg, PQ JOV 1A0,
Canada. *Tel:* 514 533 5103

Catalogue:	Free
Goods:	Maple syrup products
Countries sent to:	World
Methods of payment:	Cheque, Bank Transfer

This small company produces a very simple, 1 page price list-cum-
brochure detailing its maple syrup products. All are made 'the old-
fashioned way' from pure ingredients. Maple butter is Canadian $3.50
for 150g, while 500ml of syrup is $8 and a 4 litre jug $40.

Manor Bakery

PO Box 193610, Little Rock, AR 72219, USA. *Tel:* 501 562 4783
Fax: 501 568 4215

Catalogue:	Free
Goods:	Baked goods
Countries sent to:	World
Methods of payment:	Visa, Mastercard, Amex, Cheque, Bank Transfer

'Rich, red cherries, hearty chunks of pineapple, tasty pecans and golden
raisins . . . all in a delicious butter-rich cake.' Thus runs the description
of the world-famous Manor Texas Fruit Cake. Located in the now
presidentially famous Little Rock, Arkansas, the Bakery has produced
a glossy 12 page brochure featuring a host of goodies all of which
would make ideal Christmas or birthday gifts.

The range covers 'Southern Tradition' cakes such as Macadamia
Surprise or Southern Pecan to an assorted three-pack of Chocolate,
White Chocolate and Original Fruit Cake. Some of the cakes are
available in special gift tins but the good news for those with a sweet
tooth is that they can all be bought either individually or in cases of
twelve. Prices range from $10.95 for a 12oz box of Texas Fruit Cake
Miniatures to $160.20 for a case of 12 gift-boxed Chocolate Cherry
Rapture.

Matthews 1812 House Inc.

Box 15, 250 Kent Road, Cornwall Bridge, CT 06754, USA.
Tel: 203 672 6449

Catalogue:	Free
Goods:	Food gifts
Countries sent to:	World
Methods of payment:	Visa, Mastercard, Amex, Cheque, Bank Transfer

This 32 page catalogue has colour photographs of delicious-looking cakes, cookies, tortes and preserves. All can be shipped anywhere, though you need to speak to them personally for postal charges.

The Lemon Rum Sunshine Cake is $21 for the large size, while a Chocolate Raspberry Liqueur Cake is $23 if in a presentation tin, $20 without (though it is not sent loose).

Moravian Sugar Crisp Co. Inc.

431 Friedberg Church Road, Clemmons, NC 27012, USA.
Tel: 910 764 1402 *Fax:* 910 764 8637

Catalogue:	Free
Goods:	Cookies
Countries sent to:	World
Methods of payment:	Visa, Mastercard, Cheque, Bank Transfer

In the way of American companies, the product is said to be 'just the most delicious cookie in the world', presumably a claim based on faith rather than exhaustive research. The 8 page catalogue shows all 6 flavours: ginger, sugar, chocolate, lemon, butterscotch or black walnut. Each cookie is hand-rolled according to the recipe of the founder, a Mrs Travis.

A 1lb tin of assorted shaped chocolate crisps is $14, while a 2lb tin is $24. There are also special gift packs from $14 up to $72.

North Country Corp.
52 New Street, PO Box 193, Cambridge, MA 02238, USA.
Tel: 617 547 0657 *Fax:* 617 354 4951

Catalogue:	$
Goods:	'Natural' foods
Countries sent to:	World
Methods of payment:	Visa, Mastercard, Amex, Cheque, Bank Transfer

This interesting 48 page colour catalogue has the rather bizarre title 'Rent Mother Nature'. This refers to the idea of being able to 'rent' a particular fruit tree, bee hive or even lobster trap and have some of the produce sent to you, along with a special 'lease document'.

However, aside from this the catalogue is full of high quality foods such as maple syrup, honey, coffee, food hampers and cookies as well as a number of interesting gifts. Three jars of honey are $14.95, a hamper of Vermont cheese $34.95 and a giant New England Hamper $124.95.

Pepperidge Farm Mail Order Co.
PO Box 931, Clinton, CT 06413, USA. *Tel:* 203 664 6000
Fax: 203 664 4401

Catalogue:	Free
Goods:	Speciality foods
Countries sent to:	World
Methods of payment:	Visa, Mastercard, Amex, Diners Club, Cheque

Pepperidge Farm sells a range of delightful biscuits, chocolates and cakes along with soups and even smoked salmon. The 40 page colour catalogue is well laid out and easy to follow. Goods are sent in traditional tins and the order form includes deadline dates for Christmas, Halloween and so on. They also send out hampers and 'Monthly Assortments' – mini-hampers dispatched every month with a different selection of items. These make excellent, year-round gifts.

A 15oz tin of biscuits comes in at $19.50; 11oz of chocolate truffles is $20 while a Christmas plum pudding will cost $17.95. The monthly assortments are $79 for four months, $109 for six months and $205 for a year.

Prince Edward Island Preserve Co.

1 Cow Cabbage Lane, Charlottetown, PE C1E 1B0, Canada.
Tel: 902 368 2697 *Fax:* 902 368 7347

Catalogue:	Free
Goods:	Preserves, coffee, hampers
Countries sent to:	World
Methods of payment:	Visa, Mastercard, Amex, Diners Club

This small 10 page colour brochure has enticing photographs of a range of preserves, coffee, tea and hampers. While they definitely export to the USA it is not clear from their literature (or the questionnaire they sent us) whether they cover the rest of the world so it might be best to check in person.

Reinhardt & Laird

102-H Commonwealth Court, Post Pox 5549, Cary, NC 27512 – 5549, USA. *Tel:* n/a *Fax:* 919 481 9369

Catalogue:	Free
Goods:	Gourmet food
Countries sent to:	World
Methods of payment:	Visa, Mastercard, Amex

This small 16 page colour catalogue contains gourmet foods from around the US. These include cakes, biscuits, coffee, preserves, nuts and sweets. All goods are sent surface mail, which is a drawback since this can take 12 weeks to Europe.

Cakes are around $35, a package of biscuits $27 and 1lb of coffee $21.

Roger's Chocolates Ltd
913 Government Street, Victoria, BC V8W 1X5, Canada.
Tel: 604 384 7021 *Fax:* 604 384 5750

Catalogue:	Free
Goods:	Chocolates
Countries sent to:	Europe, USA, Australasia
Methods of payment:	Visa, Mastercard, Amex

A mouthwatering 8 pages of high-class chocolates. Roger's have been producing these handmade wonders since 1885 and now offer them worldwide. There are various boxes of Victoria Creams, from 1lb (10 chocolates) to 5lb (50 chocolates). They also sell gift boxes and tins containing a selection of items.

Yapp Brothers plc
The Old Brewery, Mere, Wiltshire, United Kingdom. *Tel:* 0747 860423
Fax: 0747 860929

Catalogue:	Free
Goods:	Wines
Countries sent to:	Europe
Methods of payment:	Visa, Mastercard, Diners Club, Cheque, Bank Transfer

Yapp's 50 page catalogue mostly features French wines. Each region is described in detail, with the aid of maps, and the blurb on the wines is refreshingly honest and straightforward. Carriage on more than two cases is free, otherwise £3. They also offer olive, walnut and hazelnut oil.

FURNITURE

3 Falke Mobler

Howitzvei 2, 2000 Frederiksberg, Denmark. *Tel:* 31 873 030
Fax: 31 873 181

Catalogue:	Free
Goods:	Furniture & lamps
Countries sent to:	World
Methods of payment:	Visa, Mastercard, Amex, Cheque, Bank Transfer

The company issues a number of catalogues featuring different types of furniture. They supply international brand names 'at affordable prices'. However, we cannot confirm this as they did not send us any catalogues despite repeated requests. Perhaps persistent readers will get further!

Ashley Furniture Workshops

3A Dawson Place, London W2 4TD, United Kingdom.
Tel: 071 289 1731 *Fax:* 081 318 1439

Catalogue:	Free
Goods:	Traditional leather furniture
Countries sent to:	World
Methods of payment:	Cheque, Bank Draft

Ashley's make custom-made classic English furniture in 18th and 19th century styles. They do not hold any stock as each piece is made individually after consultation with the customer. Using traditional materials and skills, they produce wonderful chairs, sofas and stools, mostly covered in fine leather. There were no prices in the lavish 32 page catalogue but I imagine this quality of workmanship does not come cheap.

Cohasset Colonials by Hagerty
38 Parker Avenue, Cohasset, MA 02025–2096, USA.
Tel: 617 383 0110 *Fax:* 617 383 9862

Catalogue:	$3
Goods:	Colonial wooden furniture
Countries sent to:	Asia, Europe, USA
Methods of payment:	Cheque, International Money Order

The subtitle to this 32 page colour catalogue is 'Affordable Museum Reproductions'. The company handmakes Colonial furniture using pieces from museums all over the USA as models. There are bookcases, four-posters, chairs, desks, tables and so on, all beautifully made and faithfully copied. There are also lamps, mirrors and cutlery. Obviously some of the items may be prohibitively expensive to ship but there is still much of interest here.

An eight piece set of flatware (cutlery) originally designed by Thomas Jefferson sells for $47, a pewter pitcher for $85, a four-poster bed for around $600 and a bowback Windsor chair $210.

Country Desks (Neils Ltd)
86 High Street, Berkhamsted, Hertfordshire HP4 2BW, United Kingdom. *Tel:* 0442 248270 *Fax:* 0442 872731

Catalogue:	Free
Goods:	Reproduction office furniture
Countries sent to:	World
Methods of payment:	Visa, Mastercard, Cheque, Bank Transfer

Country Desks are members of The Guild of Mastercraftsmen and produce high quality reproduction furniture. The look is traditional, with a wide variety of leather topped desks, bureaux and bookcases in mahogany, yew or oak (all from sustainable sources). They also produce dining-room chairs and tables as well as leather upholstered desk chairs.

Desks start at around £450, bookcases from £550 and chairs from £135.

Fundação Ricardo do Espirito Santo Silva
Largo das Portas do Sol 2, Lisbon 2, Portugal.

Catalogue:	Free
Goods:	Reproduction antiques
Countries sent to:	World

This foundation in Portugal runs a museum of the decorative arts along with 14 workshops dedicated to keeping alive the great tradition of classical Portuguese furniture making. They do not issue a conventional catalogue but send out a truly splendid folder containing information on their activities and 66 loose A4 colour plates each featuring one item. These range from chairs and cabinets to lamps, rugs and bureaux. All are exquisite reproductions of antiques, most of them held by the museum itself.

It is not clear how to order or how much pieces cost but interested readers should get in touch with the foundation directly – they do respond to enquiries in English.

Charlotte Horstmann & Gerald Godfrey Ltd
104 Ocean Terminal, Kowloon, Hong Kong. *Tel:* 735 7167
Fax: 730 9412

Catalogue:	n/a
Goods:	Handcrafted furniture
Countries sent to:	World
Methods of payment:	Visa, Mastercard, Amex, Diners Club, Cheque, Bank Draft

This company handmakes contemporary furniture in rosewood along with decorative accessories, Asian antiques, Chinese fine art and Primitive paintings. However, they did not send us a catalogue so we are unable to comment on quality.

Mallory's

PO Box 1150, Jacksonville, NC 28540, USA. *Tel:* 919 353 1828
Fax: 919 353 3348

Catalogue:	Free
Goods:	All kinds of household furniture
Countries sent to:	World
Methods of payment:	Visa, Mastercard, Cheque, Bank Transfer

Mallory's has a giant store in North Carolina, which they somewhat arbitrarily claim to be the 'furniture capital of the world'. There is no main catalogue but a simple brochure describing their service and listing the many manufacturers they represent. Most of these have their own literature which can then be requested. It is probably best to call and discuss your needs with a sales assistant who will then forward the appropriate details.

Martha M. House

1022 South Decatur Street, Dept GS94, Montgomery, AL 36104, USA. *Tel:* 205 264 3558 *Fax:* 205 262 2610

Catalogue:	$6
Goods:	Carved reproduction furniture
Countries sent to:	World
Methods of payment:	Visa, Mastercard, Cheque, Bank Draft, International Money Order

This company has been selling reproduction furniture for over 40 years. Their current catalogue runs to 40 pages in colour and features a large range of carved solid wood Victorian and French repro furniture, lamps, prints and accessories. Typical items are chairs, sofas, tables and stools in the sort of ornate styles which grace so many Westerns. Each piece is handcrafted to the customer's own specification, with a choice of over 300 fabrics. Prices seem very competitive but clearly shipping charges on the larger items can be high.

Shaker Workshops
PO Box 1028, Concord, MA 01742, USA. *Tel:* 617 646 8985
Fax: 617 648 8217

Catalogue:	Free
Goods:	Traditional Shaker furniture
Countries sent to:	World
Methods of payment:	Visa, Mastercard, Amex, Cheque, Bank Transfer, International Money Order

Shaker furniture is known the world over for its simple, elegant design. This company publishes a 56 page colour catalogue featuring chairs, tables, stools and beds as well as baskets, trays and other household items. You can order goods either complete or in kits to assemble at home (which is probably more practical for mail order).

A rocking chair kit is $97, a beautiful bookcase $385, a stool $45 and an unusual and elegant wooden candlestick $60.

GADGETS

Brookstone
Department M78, 1655 Bassford Drive, Mexico, MO 65265, USA.
Tel: 314 581 7777 *Fax:* 314 581 7361

Catalogue:	$3
Goods:	Household gadgets & products
Countries sent to:	World
Methods of payment:	Visa, Mastercard, Amex, Bank Transfer, Bank Draft

Brookstone subtitle their 64 page colour catalogue 'Hard-to-find Tools' but gadgets would be a better word. It is full of intriguing gizmos to make life easier. Some are familiar from the sort of catalogues which appear with credit card bills and Sunday papers, but others are more unusual.

A pocket deadbolt is a lock which can be attached to the inside of any door to prevent people getting in even if they have a key – useful in hotels. There are a number of electronic devices to keep pests – and pets – away from certain areas. One protects 3,000 sq feet from rodents, spiders, moths and other insects by emitting an ultrasonic sound. Another keeps cats and dogs out of rooms or off kitchen surfaces.

There are also plenty of gadgets for the garden, car, bicycle, kitchen and general household use. It would be hard not to find something of interest here.

Garant-O-Matic

Haansbergseweg 12, 5121 LJ Rijen, Netherlands. *Tel:* 1612 20200
Fax: 1612 20177

Catalogue:	$2
Goods:	Household gadgets
Countries sent to:	Europe
Methods of payment:	Cheque

This 32 page colour catalogue is at the lower end of the gadget market. Printed on newsprint-like paper, it features items like the copper bracelet, teeth whitening stick and nightvision glasses. However, amongst the tackier goods there are always a few gems and despite being in Dutch it is easy to follow for English readers. Strangely – though perhaps not considering this is from Holland – they also have a range of soft porn videos.

Hammacher Schlemmer

212 W. Superior Street, Chicago, IL 60610, USA. *Tel:* 312 664 8170
Fax: 312 664 8618

Catalogue:	$3
Goods:	Gadgets, gizmos & gifts
Countries sent to:	World
Methods of payment:	Visa, Mastercard, Cheque, Bank Transfer

Hammacher Schlemmer has been selling the latest gadgets and gizmos since 1848 and is something of an institution in the US. Its excellent 68 page catalogue is full of fascinating products, some familiar from similar publications here, others apparently unique. They range from a circular personal sauna ($1,600), through to TV goggles which give one the impression of watching a giant screen ($899), to virtual reality machines and replica 1920s phones ($219).

But not everything is expensive. A 100 year light bulb is $25 (though how they tested that is not clear) and a pair of shoes with headlights in the toes is $40 (who thinks of these things?!). A must for anyone hooked on gadgets.

Hedonics
195 Bridgeland Avenue, Toronto, ON M6A 1Y7, Canada.
Tel: 416 785 0262

Catalogue:	Free
Goods:	Gadgets
Countries sent to:	World
Methods of payment:	Visa, Mastercard, Amex, Cheque, Bank Transfer

Hedonics is yet another gadget catalogue but with the difference that many of the items seem genuinely exclusive. It is issued twice a year and runs to 16 pages in colour. Highlights of the last two catalogues include a portable answering machine which can be hooked up to hotel phones (Canadian $200), a caller ID phone ($190), leather condom case ($30) and a tape recorder adapter to automatically record mobile phone conversations ($50).

Le Catalogue de l'Homme Moderne
C.S.D.C. SA, 40 Lambroekstr Zavant, 1930 Zaventem, Belgium.
Tel: 02 725 08 65 *Fax:* 02 725 04 66

Catalogue:	Free
Goods:	Modern gadgets
Countries sent to:	Europe
Methods of payment:	Cheque

A typical gadget catalogue, this one has 68 colour pages with French text. But even for non-speakers, it is easy to follow – after all a nasal hair clipper is the same in all languages. Most of the items are familiar from other catalogues, but there are one or two originals.

Lighthouse Innovative Enterprises Ltd
'Innovations Improve Our Nations', 27 Ancaster Court, Dartmouth,
NS B2V 1J2, Canada. *Tel:* 902 435 1768 *Fax:* 902 435 1768

Catalogue:	Free
Goods:	Gadgets & inventions
Countries sent to:	World
Methods of payment:	Visa, Cheque, Bank Transfer, Bank Draft

This company sells a range of weird and wonderful gadgets, such as
the 'See Me' reflective arm band, and other medical, household and
children's products, some of which come as DIY kits. They also supply
evaluations of inventions for private and company innovators. Their
catalogue was not available as we went to press but should be by
1994.

Postina International B.V.
Vroenhof 24, B-3640 Kinrooi-Geistingen, Belgium.
Tel: 089 56 70 90 *Fax:* 089 56 84 57

Catalogue:	Free
Goods:	Gadgets & clothes
Countries sent to:	Europe, USA
Methods of payment:	Cheque, Bank Transfer

This French-language 48 page colour catalogue sells a strange
combination of women's clothes and low-priced gadgets. The clothes
are smart but not high fashion while the gadgets, for kitchen, household
and garden, are all reasonably cheap. They include sets of knives,
microwave dishes, loungers and that ubiquitous favourite of such
catalogues – the electric nasal hair clipper (does anyone buy, let alone
use, this thing?!).

The Sharper Image

650 Davis Street, San Francisco, CA 94111, USA. *Tel:* 415 445 6122
Fax: 415 788 1111

Catalogue:	Free
Goods:	High-class gadgets
Countries sent to:	Asia, Europe, USA, Australasia
Methods of payment:	Visa, Mastercard, Amex, Diners Club

Like Hammacher Schlemmer (see above), the Sharper Image is one of
the bibles of the gadget world. A very well produced 76 pages in
colour, its byline reads 'Welcome to the affordable fantasy'. Full of
wonderful gadgets for just about everything, it makes fascinating
reading. Here you can buy an electric toothbrush which cleans with
sonic waves, an automated, motorized tie-rack (how did you ever live
without one?), a laser sight which attaches to a putter, an ozone-based
air purifier, a fold-up sauna, a full-size replica of a 1940s jukebox
which plays CDs and yes, once again, the nasal hair cutter, but with a
difference – this one is in trendy matt black and waterproof so you can
remove those ugly hairs in the shower. A truly great catalogue.

The Sinister Shoppe

PO Box 261, Station 'C', Toronto, ON M6J 2P4, Canada.
Tel: 416 366 1790 *Fax:* 416 599 5461

Catalogue:	$2
Goods:	Goods for left-handed people
Countries sent to:	World
Methods of payment:	Visa, Mastercard, Bank Draft

This 16 page A5 catalogue carries all sorts of useful items for left-
handed people and even opens back to front to make it easier for them
to read. There is an excellent range of knives, scissors and other kitchen
equipment, including a potato peeler and ladle. An ingenious left-handed
ball point pen is bent into an 'S' shape, which is said to make writing
easier, there is a calculator designed to be held in the right hand and
even a pack of cards which takes account of the fact that left-handed
people fan cards differently from the right-handed, thereby blotting
out the pips in the corners.

GARDENING

Allwood Brothers
Mill Nurseries, Hassocks, Sussex BN6 9NB, United Kingdom.
Tel: 0273 844229

Catalogue:	2 x 1st class stamps
Goods:	Seeds
Countries sent to:	World
Methods of payment:	Visa, Mastercard, Cheque

An A5, 24 page catalogue, this sells just carnations and pinks. Each variety is given a brief description and can be sent as a plant or seed (seeds only for overseas customers).

Chiltern Seeds
Bortree Stile, Ulverston, Cumbria LA12 7PB, United Kingdom.
Tel: 0229 581137 *Fax:* 0229 584549

Catalogue:	50p in stamps
Goods:	Seeds
Countries sent to:	World
Methods of payment:	Visa, Mastercard, Cheque, Bank Transfer

One of the great names in seeds, Chilterns publish a rather strange looking catalogue. Very tall and narrow, it has over 270 tightly printed pages. It's a little like a phone book cut in thirds vertically.

The thousands of seeds are listed alphabetically with each receiving a full description. There is a particularly good selection from Australia and New Zealand.

Cruickshank's
1015 Mount Pleasant Road, Toronto, ON M4P 2M1, Canada.
Tel: 416 488 8292 *Fax:* 416 488 8802

Catalogue:	Free
Goods:	Flower bulbs and gardening accessories
Countries sent to:	World
Methods of payment:	Visa, Mastercard, Cheque, Bank Draft

Cruickshank's publish four catalogues a year, one for each season.

All are in colour and around 70 pages. The majority of those pages is filled with flowers, with splendid photographs and useful descriptions. There are also some gardening accessories, such as boots, watering cans and jackets. The latter, made by Barbour, are pricey (Canadian $430) and may be cheaper in the UK.

Deacons Nursery
Godshill, Isle of Wight, PO38 3HW, United Kingdom.
Tel: 0983 840750

Catalogue:	Free
Goods:	Fruit trees & bushes
Countries sent to:	World
Methods of payment:	Visa, Mastercard, Cheque, Bank Transfer

This is one of those catalogues which doesn't just list products but gives informative, helpful descriptions on each one. Specialising in fruit trees and bushes, it has 52 pages of well-written text. Fruits include a large variety of apples, plums, cherries, nuts, soft fruits, grapes and even kiwis and figs.

Gardens North
5984 Third Line Road, North, RR#3, North Gower, ON K0A 2T0, Canada. *Tel:* 613 489 065 *Fax:* 613 489 0065

Catalogue:	$5
Goods:	Seeds
Countries sent to:	World
Methods of payment:	Bank Draft

Gardens North's 79 page catalogue contains no pictures but very detailed text covering rare seeds from all over the world including border plants, alpines, ornamental grasses, native American species and wildflowers especially suited to the cold season gardener. Most seed packages are priced at under Canadian $2.50.

Gaze Seed Company Ltd

PO Box 640, 9 Buchanan Street, St John's A1C 5K8, Newfoundland.
Tel: 709 722 4590 *Fax:* 709 722 9945

Catalogue:	Free
Goods:	Seeds & plants
Countries sent to:	World
Methods of payment:	Visa, Mastercard

This large format, 64 page black and white catalogue from Newfoundland specializes in hardy plants for that country's climate. There are many useful articles as well as helpful descriptions. Along with seeds, Gaze also sell pesticides and garden accessories such as hoses, forks, hoes and so on.

L.S.A. Goodwin & Sons

Goodwin's Road, Bagdad, Sth 7030 Tasmania, Australia.
Tel: 002 686 233

Catalogue:	Free
Goods:	Seeds
Countries sent to:	World
Methods of payment:	Bank Draft

Goodwin's specialize in 'famous native strains of hardy outdoor cyclamen' from Australia. They issue a one page brochure with typed information and prices, which seem reasonable.

Halls of Heddon

West Heddon Nurseries, Heddon on the Wall, Newcastle upon Tyne NE15 0JS, United Kingdom. *Tel:* 0661 852445 *Fax:* 0661 852445

Catalogue:	£1
Goods:	Dahlia pot tubers
Countries sent to:	World
Methods of payment:	Bank Transfer

Halls concentrate on chrysanthemums and dahlias and send out a simple price list of the many varieties which they sell. The brief descriptions give details of the type of flower and when it should be planted. Individual plants are under £1 while they also stock 'special collections', from £6.25 up to £26.50 for 50 plants.

Henrietta's Nursery
1345 N. Brawley, Fresno, CA 93722–5899, USA. *Tel:* 209 275 2166
Fax: 209 275 6014

Catalogue:	$1
Goods:	Cactus & succulent seeds
Countries sent to:	Europe, USA
Methods of payment:	Visa, Mastercard, Cheque, Bank Draft

A 48 page black and white catalogue with very informative descriptions of a huge variety of cacti and succulents from all round the world. Helpful advice on what to grow when and where, as well as a range of books.

J. L. Hudson, Seedsman
PO Box 1058, Redwood City, CA 94064, USA. *Tel:* n/a

Catalogue:	$4
Goods:	Seeds
Countries sent to:	World
Methods of payment:	Cheque, Bank Transfer, International Money Order

This closely printed, 96 page catalogue has the title 'The 1994 Ethnobotanical Catalog of Seeds', which according to my dictionary means seeds used in connection with folklore and religion. According to Hudson themselves, ethnobotany is the 'study of the interactions of human cultures and plants' and the title of their catalogue is to re-affirm 'our long commitment to the distribution of seeds and knowledge'.

In practice this means a publication full of unusual seeds with full descriptions not only of cultivation but how many of them have been used by cultures in the past. A fascinating read even for the non-gardener, it is up-dated by periodic supplements. All seeds come in packets priced at $1.25 with a minimum order of $10 for overseas customers.

E. B. LeGrice Roses Ltd
Norwich Road, North Walsham, Norfolk NR28 0DR, United Kingdom.
Tel: 0692 402591 *Fax:* 0692 402591

Catalogue:	Free
Goods:	Roses
Countries sent to:	Europe, Africa, Asia, USA
Methods of payment:	Visa, Mastercard, Bank Transfer

LeGrice just supply roses and their 36 page colour catalogue has over 400 of them, many completely new varieties. They are divided into types, such as patio, shrub, climbing and so on. Each section has a lengthy introduction while the roses themselves also have useful descriptions.

Rawlinson Garden Seed
269 College Road, Truro NS B2N 2P6, Canada. *Tel:* 902 893 3051
Fax: 902 897 7303

Catalogue:	$2
Goods:	Seeds
Countries sent to:	World
Methods of payment:	Visa, Mastercard, Cheque, Bank Transfer

The policy behind producing this simple, though extensive (56 page) catalogue is to keep costs down. Seeds are chosen very carefully with a view to high germination rates. There is a wide selection of flowers, vegetables and herbs and the brief descriptions are helpful when making a choice. Postage is free within Canada. It is added for overseas customers, but they do not have to pay an internal tax (G.S.T.) which needs to be deducted from the catalogue prices.

Reid & Waterers

The Heath, 462 Staines Road, Middlesex TW4 5DS, United Kingdom.
Tel: 0345 626268 *Fax:* 081 572 5623

Catalogue:	Free
Goods:	Garden furniture
Countries sent to:	World
Methods of payment:	Visa, Mastercard, Cheque

Reid & Waterers came up with the idea of this catalogue after friends complained about how difficult it was to find good garden furniture. They have certainly solved the problem. Their 24 page colour catalogue is full of high-quality chairs, tables and benches as well as barbecue equipment, ornaments and accessories. The furniture is solid, well made and constructed from woods such as cherry and teak. They claim only to stock the best and the products seem to bear this out. They also sell a small range of tools, such as shears, secateurs and spades.

Teak benches start at around £160, a rocking deckchair is £70, a steamer chair with leg rest £345. Carriage is free in the UK and negotiable for other destinations.

Richters

357 Highway 47, Goodwood, Ontario L0C 1A0, Canada.
Tel: 905 640 6677 *Fax:* 905 640 6641

Catalogue:	$4
Goods:	Herbs & seeds
Countries sent to:	World
Methods of payment:	Visa, Mastercard, Cheque, Bank Draft

Richters' 84 page, colour A5 seed catalogue specializes in herbs for culinary and medicinal use. The text is highly informative and well illustrated throughout. They stock over 700 varieties of herb, many of which are difficult to find elsewhere. They also sell plants, dried herbs, some gardening accessories and a selection of books and videos. An excellent catalogue for the herb enthusiast or any kitchen gardener who wants to be a little more adventurous.

Stokes Seeds

PO Box 10, St Catharines, ON L2R 6R6, Canada. *Tel:* 416 688 4300
Fax: 416 684 8411

Catalogue:	Free
Goods:	Vegetable & flower seeds
Countries sent to:	World
Methods of payment:	Visa, Mastercard, Cheque, Bank Transfer

A 96 page catalogue crammed full of flower and vegetable seeds.
Each contains a full description and information on cultivation. There
are many varieties exclusively developed by Stokes, such as their
tomatoes, corns and carrots. The latter are around Canadian 68c for
10,000 pellets, while tomatoes are $1 per packet.

Suttons Seeds Ltd

Hele Road, Torquay, Devon TQ2 7QJ,United Kingdom.
Tel: 0803 612011 *Fax:* 0803 615747

Catalogue:	Free
Goods:	Seeds
Countries sent to:	Europe
Methods of payment:	Visa, Mastercard, Cheque

Suttons are probably Britain's most famous seed suppliers and their
128 page colour catalogue is no disappointment. Crammed with flowers
and vegetables, it is lavishly illustrated with brief but useful
descriptions. Exports are only available for European customers.

Thompson & Morgan Ltd
Poplar Lane, Ipswich, Suffolk IP8 3BU, United Kingdom.
Tel: 0473 688821 *Fax:* 0473 680199

Catalogue:	Free
Goods:	Flower & vegetable seeds
Countries sent to:	World
Methods of payment:	Visa, Mastercard, Cheque, Bank Transfer

Thompson & Morgan have been producing their Seed Catalogue for over 100 years. The 1994 catalogue is the first however, to carry a Quality Charter. Should seeds not germinate, be late in arrival or letters go unanswered T&M will issue gift vouchers in recompense.

The catalogue is A5 and runs to over 200 pages. It contains hundreds of colour photographs of flowers in full bloom and fully ripe vegetables and fruit. There are also good descriptions of the plants' habitats and how best to maximise their potential. Plant types are sub-divided into useful categories: annuals for hanging baskets and containers, borders and climbers; cut flowers; fragrant flowers; bonsai; plants for indoors and greenhouses; bulbs and vegetables.

Delphinium 'cardinale' seeds, which bloom in the first summer if sown in February, cost only £1.19 for 100. And if you fancy your hand at growing giant vegetables, seeds for Hercules BL7 Cabbage are also available – the largest weighed a record 127lb.

Tulipshow Frans Roozen
2114BB Vogelenzang, The Netherlands. *Tel:* 02502 47245
Fax: 02502 46320

Catalogue:	Free
Goods:	Flower bulbs
Countries sent to:	Asia, Europe, USA
Methods of payment:	Visa, Mastercard, Amex, Cheque

This 24 page colour catalogue is printed in both Dutch and English. It carries many varieties of tulip and other flowers, each of which is given a brief description. As far as we know, the only international mail order source for genuine Dutch tulips.

GIFTS

Atlantic Bridge Corporation Ltd

Ballybane, Dept GS, Galway, Ireland. *Tel:* 091 53657 *Fax:* 091 53443

Catalogue:	$2
Goods:	China & glass
Countries sent to:	World
Methods of payment:	Visa, Mastercard, Amex

This 32 page colour Irish catalogue has wide distribution in the US but also ships worldwide. There is a good selection of Waterford crystal along with Royal Doulton, Lladró and Wedgwood china. Porcelain figures feature widely, along with decorated plates and vases.

Prices are in US$. A Waterford crystal jug is $81, a Wedgwood small vase $32, and Royal Doulton figures from around $150.

Australian Geographic Pty Ltd

321 Mona Vale Road, Terry Hills, 2084 Australia. *Tel:* 02 450 2300 *Fax:* 02 986 3517

Catalogue:	Free
Goods:	Gifts & toys
Countries sent to:	World
Methods of payment:	Visa, Mastercard, Bank Transfer

The Australian Geographic is a charity which puts money into conservation and research. Profits from the 76 page colour catalogue go towards this work. It is full of fascinating gifts and toys oriented to the outdoors, nature and science. There are also such items as hammocks, telescopes, books, videos, tents and sleeping bags. The selection of Australian-made outdoor clothes is well worth a look.

A specially designed wool sleeping bag, which does not lose its thermal properties even when wet, sells for Australian $115, hi-tech insulated slippers are $34.95 and bushman's oilskin coats are $195.

Beautiful British Columbia

929 Ellery Street, Victoria, BC V9A 7B4, Canada. *Tel:* 604 384 5456
Fax: 604 384 2812

Catalogue:	Free
Goods:	Gifts made in British Columbia
Countries sent to:	World
Methods of payment:	Visa, Mastercard, Cheque, Bank Transfer

This 32 page colour catalogue specializes in gifts from British
Columbia on Canada's West coast. This remit allows them great variety
with products as diverse as CDs, chocolates, puzzles, mugs, jewellery,
posters and cuddly toys.

A beautiful jade bear sculpture will set you back Canadian $129
but most items are far less than this. A set of floating candles is $9, a
'Whale' sweatshirt $30 and a 4oz box of salmon $16.

Butler Distributing Company

730 Fairfield Avenue, PO Box 22, Kenilworth, NJ 07033, USA.
Tel: 908 241 3060 *Fax:* 908 298 9248

Catalogue:	$3, refundable
Goods:	Country & Western items
Countries sent to:	World
Methods of payment:	International Money Order

Butler specializes in Country & Western gifts, videos, CDs and
cassettes. They have a huge selection of 'How to' videos, concentrating
on Western dancing, rodeo riding, horse training and so on. All are on
VHS using the American NTSC system (i.e. not compatible with
European or British video players). They stock the latest Country &
Western music, using Billboard Magazine's Top Album & Singles
chart, up-dated weekly.

Videos are around $30, 45rpm singles $2.25, cassettes $9.98 and
CDs $15.98.

Canadian Geographic

39 McArthur Avenue, Vanier, ON K1L 8L7, Canada.
Tel: 613 745 4629 *Fax:* 613 744 0947

Catalogue:	Free
Goods:	Canadian-made gifts
Countries sent to:	World
Methods of payment:	Visa, Mastercard, Bank Transfer

A wide variety of goods are featured in this 40 page colour catalogue. Most are made in Canada and have some connection with the great outdoors. There's a small selection of clothes, such as sweatshirts, hand-knitted sweaters and socks. There's a good range of books on natural history along with a few toys and other gifts.

Cashs of Ireland

Mail Order Courier Centre, PO Box 158, Plainview, NY 11803, USA.
Fax: 21 964 552 (Ireland)

Catalogue:	Free
Goods:	Irish gifts
Countries sent to:	World
Methods of payment:	Visa, Mastercard, Amex, Cheque, Bank Draft, International Money Order

Although based in Ireland, Cashs does such a lot of mail order business in the US that it has a New York contact address. But strangely, if you want to order by fax you need to call direct to Ireland (see number above).

The 64 page colour catalogue features knitwear, cut glass, china and a good selection of general gifts from Ireland. Prices are in US$ and seem reasonable. A woman's Aran cardigan costs $89, a man's tweed hat $39. A Waterford crystal goblet is $42, a wine glass $39 and 'the Captain's Set' consisting of decanter plus six tumblers, $400.

Elephant House

67/12 Soi Phra Phinit (Off Soi Suan Phlu, Sathorn Tai Road), Bangkok 10120, Thailand. *Tel:* 286 5280 *Fax:* 213 2311

Catalogue:	Free
Goods:	Thai & Burmese gifts
Countries sent to:	World
Methods of payment:	Visa, Mastercard, Amex, International Money Order

This 24 page colour catalogue is in English with excellent photographs of the handmade gifts. Lacquerware features throughout, along with carvings in wood and celadon. All the items seem high-class and well made, although the prices, in US$ may be a little steep. A Burmese betelnut lacquered round box is $85, a small carved wooden horse $50 and a Bencharong pepper bowl with gold leaf detailing $130.

Emerald Mail Order

Ballingeary, Macroom, County Cork, Ireland.
Tel: 800 338 9790/26 47039 *Fax:* 26 47153

Catalogue:	Free
Goods:	Porcelain, glass & gifts
Countries sent to:	World
Methods of payment:	Visa, Mastercard, Amex

This is another Irish mail order house with its eye firmly on the American market, where it has a contact address and toll free phone number. The colour catalogue features all kinds of gifts but has a particularly good selection of china and glassware. Manufacturers include Waterford, Spode, Doulton, Wedgwood, Hummel and others. Some items may be on the twee side – such as the pottery cottages – but others are very attractive. There is also a selection of Christmas items and Peter Rabbit merchandise.

Prices are in US$. A Waterford goblet is $45, a decanter $207. Peter Rabbit Wedgwood plates are around $20 while a crew neck sweater is $45.

A. Gargiulo & Jannuzzi

80067, Sorrento, Naples, Italy. *Tel:* 081 781 041 *Fax:* 081 807 1263

Catalogue:	Free
Goods:	Inlaid wood products
Countries sent to:	World
Methods of payment:	Visa, Mastercard, Amex, Diners Club, Cheque, Bank Transfer

Gargiulo & Jannuzzi produce an English language series of colour brochures with the subtitle 'The oldest inlaid woodwork factory in Sorrento', which I take must be stuffed with them. They make a number of different items all intricately inlaid. Some are a little on the tacky side – especially the pictures for hanging on the wall. Others, such as boxes, chairs, table tops, trays and gaming tables are delightful. Prices on request.

Maritime Merchants

22 Crestview Drive, Charlottetown, PE C1E 1N4, Canada.
Tel: 902 566 1430 *Fax:* 902 566 1430

Catalogue:	Free
Goods:	Canadian crafts
Countries sent to:	USA
Methods of payment:	Mastercard, Cheque, Bank Draft

Maritime's catalogue was not ready as we went to press but will be published in 1994. Its 24 colour pages feature Canadian-made craft items out of pewter, wool and leather, including moccasins, toys, books, woollen blankets and gifts.

The Metropolitan Opera Gift Collection
70 Lincoln Center Plaza, New York, NY 10023–6593, USA.
Tel: 212 769 7010 *Fax:* 212 769 7007

Catalogue:	Free
Goods:	Opera books, gifts & recordings
Countries sent to:	World
Methods of payment:	Visa, Mastercard, Amex, Cheque, Bank Draft

This 24 page colour catalogue from New York's renowned Metropolitan Opera, interprets the brief of 'opera related gifts' pretty widely and includes many fascinating items. Along with the standard collection of books, CDs (around $16) and videos (American format), there are opera glasses, prints, cushions, pens, mugs and plates. There is a unique framed autograph of Puccini, selling for no less than $9,000 (assuming it hasn't already been snapped up) and a delightful sterling silver 'opera light' for $275. This comes on an elegant chain and is said to 'cast a subtle beam of amber light perfect for opera, theater or dining', though quite why one needs a beam of amber light while doing any of these things is not explained.

The National Trust (Enterprises) Ltd
The Stableblock, Heywood House, Westbury, Wilts BA13 4NA, United Kingdom. *Tel:* 0373 858787 *Fax:* 0373 827575

Catalogue:	Free
Goods:	Quality gifts
Countries sent to:	World
Methods of payment:	Visa, Mastercard, Amex, Diners Club, Cheque

The National Trust, set up over 100 years ago to preserve the UK's heritage, now issues a catalogue featuring a diverse range of household items and gifts. The 48 colour pages display such goods as pewter candlesticks, lead crystal glass, teddy bears, sweaters, picnic equipment, tapestry kits, stationery, books and hampers full of country preserves and sweets. All are high quality and reflect the Trust's interest in the best of British traditions.

The Nature Company
PO Box 188, Florence, KY 41042, USA. *Tel:* 606 342 7200
Fax: 606 342 5630

Catalogue:	Free
Goods:	'Natural' gifts
Countries sent to:	World
Methods of payment:	Visa, Mastercard, Amex

The Nature Company intends to issue a catalogue specifically for the UK market, but for now will send out either the US or Canadian editions. The 36 colour pages feature 'gifts for nature lovers'. These include both indoor and outdoor clothes, shoes (including Timberland), books, binoculars, birdbaths, kitchen equipment, gardening accessories, toys and general gifts.

Timberland shorts are $58 and jackets $140. A wooden lizard is $16 and a glass oil lamp $38.

New Internationalist
55 Rectory Road, Oxford, OX4 1BW, United Kingdom.
Tel: 0865 728181 Credit card orders: 091 491 0281
Fax: 0865 793152

Catalogue:	Free
Goods:	Books & gifts
Countries sent to:	World
Methods of payment:	Visa, Mastercard, Cheque, Bank Transfer

The *New Internationalist* is a magazine committed to campaigning for a fairer deal for the 'south', i.e. those living in the southern hemisphere. This brochure displays a number of gifts not generally available elsewhere and profits go towards furthering the work of the organization. There are T-shirts, hats, jewellery, books, games and toys. The minimum order for overseas orders is £6.

Stechers Ltd
27 Frederick Street, Port of Spain, Trinidad, WI *Tel:* 809 623 5912
Fax: 809 627 8444

Catalogue:	Free
Goods:	See below
Countries sent to:	World
Methods of payment:	Visa, Mastercard, Amex

This duty free shop in Trinidad does not publish a catalogue but sends
out a one page sheet with information on its services along with a list
of manufacturers represented. These include Cartier, Patek Philippe,
Waterford, Dunhill, Dartington, Hoya and so on. They sell watches,
clocks, china and porcelain, silverware, crystal, leather goods and
jewellery all at duty free prices said to be cheaper than virtually
anywhere else.

However, there was no price list included so we cannot verify this.
If interested, write or call with details of what you are after and they
will quote a price.

The Worn Doorstep
1411 Fort Street, Suite 1803, Montreal, PQ H3H 2N7, Canada.
Tel: 514 932 9319 *Fax:* 514 932 6385

Catalogue:	Free
Goods:	Canadian gifts
Countries sent to:	World
Methods of payment:	Visa, Cheque, Bank Transfer

The criteria for entry into this 32 page catalogue is simply that the
gifts must be made in Canada. As a result the products are very diverse,
from spoons to buckets, candles, mitts, placemats, books, paperweights
and so on.

Since they are in touch with many artisans they also run a service
to find or have made virtually any craft item you might request. For
example, custom-made Newfoundland sweaters, Cowichan sweaters,
toques and mitts, copper planters, bird's eye maple salad bowls and so
on. As they told us 'We like to do anything and we have an excellent
list of folk who can make most anything! Even big things, such as
canoes, skiffs, stained glass windows, etc.'

GLASSES

Hildago Sunglasses
Hildago Inc., 45 La Buena Vista, Wimberley, TX 78676, USA.
Tel: 512 847 5571 *Fax:* 512 847 2393

Catalogue:	Free
Goods:	Sunglasses & prescription glasses
Countries sent to:	World
Methods of payment:	Visa, Mastercard, Amex, Diners Club, Cheque, Bank Transfer

This 56 page black and white catalogue is well illustrated with clear, informative text. The range of sunglasses is enormous, including Ray-Bans, bollé, Revo, Laura Ashley, Ralph Lauren and Hildago's own excellent brand. There are several pages giving very useful information on how to choose the correct lenses and frame according to use. The result is you can virtually custom make your own sunglasses, including prescription lenses.

The company also sells spectacle frames and prescription lenses at reasonable prices. In addition there are watches, calculators, binoculars, blood pressure monitors and short wave radios. All in all, an excellent catalogue.

Revo sunglasses start around $120, bollé at $74, Hildago's own brand and Ray-Bans at $50.

National Contact Lens Centre
3527 Bonita Vista Drive, Santa Rosa, CA 95404, USA.
Tel: 707 545 6352 *Fax:* 707 545 6353

Catalogue:	Free
Goods:	Contact lenses
Countries sent to:	World
Methods of payment:	Visa, Mastercard, Cheque, Bank Transfer

Run by Dr Michael Talmadge, this company only deals in contact lenses which they send anywhere in the world. There is no catalogue but a simple price list with details of lenses by Bausch & Lomb, Sola Barnes-Hind, CIBA, Wesley Jessen and Johnson & Johnson (the Vistakon brand) amongst others.

There is some controversy over contact lenses by mail, with the UK authorities claiming it is illegal and certainly it is within this country. However, the position is not so clear if lenses are ordered from overseas and Customs are unlikely to seize them. The problem is that lenses must only be fitted by qualified practitioners and it is considered too risky for consumers to do this themselves.

However, many people order a second set from the USA, where prices are much cheaper. You simply need to send in your prescription number. Six disposable lenses start at $20, soft lenses at $42. One advantage to this company is that Dr Talmadge usually answers the phone himself so you can question him personally on details.

Sunglasses, Shavers & More
704 Main Street, Yarmouth Port, MA 02675, USA. *Tel:* 508 362 7005
Fax: 508 362 4220

Catalogue:	Free
Goods:	Sunglasses, shavers & more!
Countries sent to:	World
Methods of payment:	Visa, Mastercard

The 'more' of this 16 page black and white catalogue includes Braun
clocks, in-line skates, watches, pens and Swiss Army knives. But the
bulk is taken up by sunglasses from such manufacturers as Ray-Ban,
Levis and Serengetti.

A pair of Wayfarer Ray-Bans start at just under $50 while all Levis
are $30. In-line skates by Ultra-Glide are between $130 and $160.

GOLF

Austad's
4500 East 10th Street, PO Box 5428, Sioux Falls, SD 57196, USA.
Tel: 605 336 5393 *Fax:* 605 339 0362

Catalogue:	Free
Goods:	Golf equipment
Countries sent to:	World
Methods of payment:	Visa, Mastercard, Amex, Diners Club, Bank Transfer

Austad's have been in business for 30 years, selling a wide range of golf equipment, including clubs, bags, clothing and accessories. They have a thriving international section and even produce a special catalogue for overseas customers. Running to 48 pages in colour, it is issued several times a year. The selection of clubs in the catalogue is not that extensive but they keep far more in stock so it is worth calling for prices on specific items. Many of the gadgets and teaching aids never seem to make it to this country and there is always something for the golfer who has everything.

A Yamaha To Dawg carbon driver sells for $269, a set of Spalding Advance irons for $299. Golf bags start at $80 while balls are from $16 per dozen.

The Competitive Edge Golf Catalogue

526 W. 26th Street, 10th Floor, New York, NY 10001, USA.
Tel: 212 924 3800 *Fax:* 212 924 3838

Catalogue:	Free
Goods:	Golf clubs & accessories
Countries sent to:	World
Methods of payment:	Visa, Mastercard, Amex, Bank Transfer

Competitive Edge produce a 32 page colour catalogue full of interesting golf clubs and accessories. The clubs, which are not the usual makes, are hi-tech, state of the art models. For example, they stock the Samurai range of graphite clubs which are a cross between irons and woods, as well as SnakeSkin drivers. They have a good selection of putters, some ingenious accessories and training aids and a few golfing clothes.

A Samurai 'iron' is $99, while the 'woods' are $129. A SnakeSkin graphite driver is also $99.

Don's Discount Golf & Tennis

10880 Biscayne Boulevard, Miami, FL 33161, USA.
Tel: 305 895 0121 *Fax:* 305 895 0292

Catalogue:	n/a
Goods:	Golf & tennis equipment
Countries sent to:	World
Methods of payment:	Visa, Mastercard, Amex, Diners Club

Don's do not produce a catalogue but will send goods overseas. As their name suggests, they sell golf and tennis gear and interested readers should contact them direct with details of their requirements.

Golf Haus
700 N. Pennsylvania, Lansing, MI 48906, USA. *Tel:* 517 482 8842

Catalogue:	Free
Goods:	Golf clubs & accessories
Countries sent to:	World
Methods of payment:	Visa, Mastercard, Cheque, Bank Transfer

Said to be one of the cheapest sources of golf clubs in the US, this company does not issue a glossy catalogue but a simple price list updated every 6 weeks or so. If you order a full set of clubs and mention **The Global Shopper**, you even get a free set of headcovers!

Prices change continually: the last list we saw had a set of Mizuno Wings woods for $260, a Ping putter for $38, a set of Taylor Made irons (Burner Midsize) for $415. These seem very keen prices indeed.

Golfsmith
11000 North IH-35, Austin, TX 78753, USA. *Tel:* 512 837 4810
Fax: 512 837 1245

Catalogue:	Free
Goods:	Golf clubs & accessories
Countries sent to:	World
Methods of payment:	Visa, Mastercard, Cheque, Bank Transfer

Golfsmith produces two equally well-designed catalogues. The smaller of the two, 'The Golf Store', runs to 60 colour pages and stocks clubs, bags, balls, shoes, videos and a host of accessories many of which never make it to the UK. The second, much larger one (230 pages) is the 'Clubhead & Components Catalog'. This contains everything you need to build your own clubs: heads, shafts, grips and tools.

The clubs in both publications tend not to be the famous names but – reading between the lines – are accurate copies. For example, the Tour Mode II irons bear an uncanny resemblance to the latest Pings, but sell for a fraction of the price ($272 for 3-9 and PW). A Golfsmith lightweight bag is $77.50 and looks similar to much more expensive models.

They also have a European operation: Golfsmith Europe Inc., Upton Road, Upton, Huntingdon, Cambridgeshire.

The Golf Works
Box 3008, Newark, OH 43055, USA. *Tel:* 614 323 4193
Fax: 614 323 0311

Catalogue:	Free
Goods:	Components for golf clubs
Countries sent to:	World
Methods of payment:	Visa, Mastercard, Cheque, Bank Transfer

The Golf Works sell everything you need to make your own golf clubs. The fat, full colour catalogue has extensive descriptions of every product and includes advice and suggestions. They sell heads for both irons and woods, shafts, grips and an impressive array of equipment to put them together.

The makes are not well-known brands but are nevertheless very similar to them and of course can be fully custom made. They also sell clubs preassembled from your choice of components. A metal wood club head costs $22, shafts start at around $15 and grips from under $1.

Las Vegas Discount Golf & Tennis
Paradise Road 4405, Las Vegas, NV 89109, USA. *Tel:* 702 892 9999
Fax: 702 892 0230

Catalogue:	$5
Goods:	Tennis & golf equipment
Countries sent to:	World
Methods of payment:	Visa, Mastercard, Amex, Cheque, Bank Transfer, Other

No catalogue as we went to press, but apparently it features many different makes of tennis racquets, clothes and shoes as well as golf clubs, bags and accessories.

Edwin Watts
PO Box 1806, Ft Walton Beach, FL 32549, USA. *Tel:* 904 244 2066
Fax: 904 244 5217

Catalogue:	Free
Goods:	Golf clubs & equipment
Countries sent to:	World
Methods of payment:	Visa, Mastercard, Amex, Cheque, Bank Transfer

Edwin Watts nas over 30 shops in the USA and a well-established international mail order business. Their 32 page colour catalogue sells many of the famous names, such as Yonex, Callaway (makers of Big Bertha drivers), Taylor Made, Ben Hogan, Mizuno and so on. They also stock bags, putters, videos and balls.

A Yonex ADX Tour wood is $300, a set of irons $1,099. Big Bertha drivers start at $160 rising to $250 for the titanium shaft model. The catalogue, which is issued regularly, also carries sale items.

HEALTH

The Body Shop by Mail
45 Horsehill Road, Cedar Knolls, NJ 07927–2014, USA.
Tel: Toll free: 1 800 541 2535 *Fax:* 201 984 0035

Catalogue:	Free
Goods:	Skin & hair care preparations
Countries sent to:	World
Methods of payment:	Visa, Mastercard, Amex, Cheque

The Body Shop has branches all around the world but also runs an international mail order operation from two centres: the UK and USA. Both issue colour catalogues of around 40 pages, listing the now famous line of naturallv-based products said not to be tested on animals. These include sun creams, skin care products, shampoos, scents, shaving supplies, make-up and some gifts. There are also details of various campaigns in the developing world.

The Body Shop International plc
Watersmead, Littlehampton, West Sussex BN17 6LS, United Kingdom.
Tel: 0903 731500 *Fax:* 0903 726250

Catalogue:	Free
Goods:	Skin & hair care preparations
Countries sent to:	World
Methods of payment:	Visa, Mastercard, Amex, Cheque

The Body Shop has branches all round the world but also runs an international mail order operation from two centres: the UK and USA. Both issue colour catalogues of around 40 pages, listing the now famous line of naturally-based products said not to be tested on animals, These include sun creams, skin care products, shampoos, scents, shaving supplies, make-up and some gifts. There are also details of various campaigns in the developing world.

Boyds
655 Madison Avenue, New York, NY 10021, USA. *Tel:* 212 838 6558
Fax: 212 832 0972

Catalogue:	$10
Goods:	Cosmetics
Countries sent to:	World
Methods of payment:	Visa, Mastercard, Amex, Diners Club, Cheque, Bank Transfer

$10 seems rather high for this 32 page colour catalogue. The products include skin care treatments, make-up, hair brushes and various other accessories found in a chemist's shop.

Elda Originals
188 Finchley Road, Hampstead, London NW3 6DR, United Kingdom.
Tel: 071 794 828 *Fax:* 071 433 1250

Catalogue:	Free
Goods:	Health & beauty products
Countries sent to:	Europe, Africa, USA, Australasia
Methods of payment:	Cheque, Bank Transfer

A 12 page black and white catalogue with a small range of foundation garments intended to shape the body. There is also a 'vibra massager' to help reduce weight around the thighs and tummy; several skin, teeth and hair treatments, foot supports and the somewhat mysterious 'fullbloom cream'. This is said to 'beautify the bust', though quite what this means or how it is achieved is not explained.

Elora Soap Company

312 Queen St. N., Box 562, Paisley, ON N0G 2N0, Canada.
Tel: 519 353 5191

Catalogue:	Free
Goods:	Handmade soap
Countries sent to:	Asia, Europe, USA
Methods of payment:	Visa, Mastercard

This small company does not currently issue a catalogue but does
have a simple order form on which readers can request their natural,
biodegradable soap. Recommended by dermatologists, it uses only
vegetable ingredients and is available unpackaged or in wooden gift
boxes made from recycled lumber.

J. Floris

89 Jermyn Street, London, SW1Y 6JH, United Kingdom.
Tel: 071 930 2885 *Fax:* 071 930 1402

Catalogue:	Free
Goods:	Perfumes & toiletries
Countries sent to:	World
Methods of payment:	Visa, Mastercard, Amex, Diners Club, Cheque, Bank Transfer

Floris has been run by the same family for eight generations and is 'purveyor
of the finest flower perfumes and toiletries to the court of St James since
the year 1730'. Currently they hold two Royal Warrants, from the Queen
and the Prince of Wales. The wonderful atmosphere in their London shop
is reflected in this 16 page colour catalogue, featuring perfumes, toilet
waters, bath essences and a range of men's toiletries.

The shaving supplies are particularly attractive and include a
delightful wooden bowl containing shaving soap. Everything is
beautifully packaged and the perfumes suitably discreet (this writer
has been a fan for many years!). 100ml of toilet water is £23.25, 30ml
of bath essence £9.50 and the wooden shaving bowl £47.50 (£23.50
for soap refills).

Freddy
10 Rue Auber, Paris, 75009, France. *Tel:* 1 47 42 63 41
Fax: 1 48 45 00 41

Catalogue:	n/a
Goods:	Perfume & cosmetics
Countries sent to:	Europe, Australasia, USA
Methods of payment:	Cheque

Freddy of Paris do not publish a catalogue but will respond to requests to send goods overseas. They stock a good range of perfumes, cosmetics and beauty products although you need to know what you want before getting in touch.

Heleesun B.V.B.A.
St Bernardsestwe 493, 2660 Hoboken, Belgium. *Tel:* 03 830 40 47
Fax: 03 830 61 42

Catalogue:	Free
Goods:	Beauty care products
Countries sent to:	Europe
Methods of payment:	Cheque, Bank Transfer

Although this catalogue is printed in Flemish and French both are pretty easy to follow for non-speakers. The 40 colour pages feature natural beauty care products and food supplements, along with some slimming items. Prices, in Belgian francs, seem reasonable.

Penhaligon's

Crusader Estate, Hermitage Road, London N4 1LZ, United Kingdom.
Tel: 081 809 7799/081 880 2050 (International orders)
Fax: 081 800 5789

Catalogue:	Free
Goods:	Fragrance & gifts
Countries sent to:	Asia, Europe, USA, Australasia
Methods of payment:	Visa, Mastercard, Amex, Cheque

Penhaligon's have been supplying up-market fragrances for men since 1870 and hold two Royal Warrants. All their products are beautifully presented and this lavish 26 page, colour catalogue sets them off to advantage.

A 100ml bottle of After Shave Balm is £28, Eau de Toilette £32 for the same size. Lord's aftershave is £27, a bottle of shampoo £10. They also sell some exquisite accessories and gifts. A silver plate shaving stand complete with brush and razor is £95, a pair of silver cufflinks £120 and a leather tie case £60. All are very discreet, very English. There is also a range of silver scent bottles and some 'grooming' accessories for women.

Yves Rocher (London) Ltd

664 Victoria Road, South Ruislip, Middlesex HA4 0NY, United Kingdom. *Tel:* 081 842 4600 *Fax:* 081 845 1023

Catalogue:	Free
Goods:	Natural beauty products
Countries sent to:	World
Methods of payment:	Visa, Mastercard

Yves Rocher have mail order operations all over Europe but only the UK-based one seems to be interested in sending goods overseas (and I hope they clean up as a result!). The 72 page colour catalogue has sections on skin and hair care as well as perfumes, make-up and even products for men. The philosophy of the company is to produce 'green, ecologically-friendly' products using the latest scientific research.

HI-FI

The Audio Advisor
225 Oakes S.W., Grand Rapids, MI 49503, USA. *Tel:* 616 451 3868
Fax: 616 451 0709

Catalogue:	$1
Goods:	High-end audio equipment
Countries sent to:	World
Methods of payment:	Visa, Mastercard, Amex, Bank Transfer, Bank Draft

The Audio Advisor sells high-end stereo equipment, such as state-of-the-art turntables, amplifiers and CD players. Mostly these are makes which are not to be found in ordinary shops, such as PS Audio, Dynaco and Audio Alchemy. The lavishly illustrated 40 page colour catalogue also has products within the range of the average 'listener' along with helpful, unbiased descriptions. They also send out 'sale' catalogues where you can pick up genuine bargains.

A Sota Comet turntable, suitable only for enthusiasts, costs $550, while the cartridge to go with it comes in at $600. A Philips CD950 Bitstream player is $500.

Audio By Van Alstine

2202 River Hills Drive, Burnsville, MN 55337, USA.
Tel: 612 890 3517 *Fax:* 612 894 3675

Catalogue:	Free
Goods:	Custom, high-end audio equipment
Countries sent to:	World
Methods of payment:	Bank Transfer, International Money Order

Van Alstine make and sell very superior hi-fi equipment for the discerning listener. This is true state-of-the-art equipment with corresponding prices. Their excellent 32 page catalogue features amplifiers, pre-amps, tuners and CD players. They will also up-grade old equipment. All products are given full, informative descriptions. They also issue a monthly newsletter, called Audio Basics, which keeps readers up-to-date on the latest developments and products. This costs $16 per year, with $8 for airmail postage to overseas customers.

An A.V.A. Fet-Valve pre-amp costs $1,195, a CD player about the same and a tuner from $400 up to $1,200.

Cleartone Hi-Fi & Video

235 Blackburn Road, Bolton, Lancs BL1 8HB, United Kingdom.
Tel: 0204 31423 *Fax:* 0204 389214

Catalogue:	n/a
Goods:	Hi-fi, photographic & video equipment
Countries sent to:	World
Methods of payment:	Visa, Mastercard, Amex, Diners Club, Cheque, Bank Transfer

Cleartone do not publish a catalogue but you can contact them directly for information on a wide selection of hi-fi, video and photographic equipment. They also sell security systems.

Japan Audio Trading Co. Ltd
Saikaen Building, 4 33 21 Kamimeguro, Meguro-ku, Tokyo 153, Japan. *Tel:* 3715 0533 *Fax:* 3715 0533

Catalogue:	Free
Goods:	Phonograph parts
Countries sent to:	World
Methods of payment:	Bank Draft, International Money Order

This company specializes in cartridges and step-up devices for record players. They only sell the best and will ship anywhere in the world. Makes include Denon, Dynavector, Highphonic, Lyra and Ikeda. They send out an introductory letter and price list with full specifications in English, though the prices themselves are in Yen. Note that their phone number changes to a fax during the night i.e., 9pm – 9am Tokyo time.

Audiocraft cartridges are Y60,000–85,000, Audio-Technica Y16,000–72,000, while the superb Ikeda range are Y64,000–240,000.

HOBBIES

Adventures Company
435 Main Street, Johnson City, N 13790, USA. *Tel:* 607 729 6512
Fax: 607 729 4820

Catalogue:	$5
Goods:	Tools & lab-ware
Countries sent to:	World
Methods of payment:	Visa, Mastercard, Cheque, Bank Transfer, Bank Draft

Adventures' 1994 catalogue was not ready as we went to press, but we understand they sell tools, hardware and science lab equipment.

America's Hobby Center Inc.
146 W. 22nd Street, New York, NY 10011, USA. *Tel:* 212 675 8922
Fax: 212 633 2754

Catalogue:	$12 for 3 year subscription
Goods:	Radio controlled models
Countries sent to:	World
Methods of payment:	Visa, Mastercard, Bank Transfer, Cheque

Although we had not received this catalogue at the time of going to press, we gather it features a wide selection of radio controlled boats, cars, planes and helicopters as well as model trains in all gauges.

Bangkok Dolls

85 Rajatapan Lane, Maddasan, Bangkok 10400, Thailand.
Tel: 245 3008 *Fax:* 245 2512

Catalogue:	Free
Goods:	Handmade classical Thai dolls
Countries sent to:	World
Methods of payment:	Cheque, Bank Draft

This company makes, as one might expect, Thai dolls. The large 1 page, colour foldout brochure features many different types of figures, from traditional theatrical dolls through representations of hill tribes people to dolls for children. All are meticulously researched to ensure every detail is correct and carefully made by hand. The text is in English with brief descriptions of each item and clear ordering instructions. There is also a useful sheet on the history of the Ramakien, or Masked Play, from which many of the figures are drawn. Prices, in US$, start at around $10 and go up to $90 for the most elaborate. The majority, however, are under $20.

Campbell Paterson Ltd

PO Box 5555, Auckland, New Zealand. *Tel:* 379 3086 *Fax:* 379 3087

Catalogue:	NZ$111.95 + p
Goods:	New Zealand stamps
Countries sent to:	World
Methods of payment:	Visa, Mastercard, Amex, Cheque, Bank Draft

Since this catalogue costs over New Zealand $100, the company was, understandably, unwilling to send us a sample copy. However, from what we can gather it is a large, comprehensive guide to NZ stamps for the serious collector. They also publish the CP Newsletter which covers the same area.

Canadian Railway Modeller

28103 – 1453 Henderson Highway, Winnipeg MB R2G 4E9, Canada.
Tel: 204 668 0168 *Fax:* 204 668 0168

Catalogue:	Free
Goods:	Canadian railway model supplies
Countries sent to:	World
Methods of payment:	Visa, Mastercard, Cheque, Bank Transfer

Apart from the magazine *Canadian Railway Modeller* (Canadian $30 for 6 issues), this company also publishes a number of books on the same subject as well as train cards, sweatshirts, mugs etc. There is no catalogue but several information sheets.

Coles' Power Models

839 E. Front Street, PO Box 788, Ventura, CA 93002, USA.
Tel: 805 643 7065 *Fax:* 805 643 5160

Catalogue:	$7
Goods:	Model steam & gasoline engines
Countries sent to:	World
Methods of payment:	Mastercard, Cheque, Bank Draft

Established for over 65 years, Coles specialize in steam and gasoline models. Their 98 page A5 catalogue features kits to make a wide variety of engines, including highly detailed traction engines in various scales. These are available in several sections, such as drawings and castings for the boiler, front wheels, engine and clutch and so on.

They also sell a number of stationary engines as well as a large range of parts and accessories. There is even an ingenious steam engine which will attach to the front of any bicycle to power it up to 16mph! A well-produced, excellent resource for the enthusiast.

Con-Cor International Ltd

1025 Industrial Drive, Bensenville, IL 60106, USA.
Tel: 708 595 0210 *Fax:* 708 595 0924

Catalogue:	$3.50
Goods:	Model trucks
Countries sent to:	World
Methods of payment:	Visa, Mastercard, Bank Transfer

Con-Cor make 'Precise Route 66 Vehicles', which means trucks. Each one is beautifully made and detailed in HO 1/87 and 1/43 scale. The 24 page colour catalogue has clear photographs of the wide range, which also includes some cars. Prices are from around $7 to $17.

DIY Plastics UK Ltd

Regal Way, Faringdon, Oxfordshire SN7 7XD, United Kingdom.
Tel: 0367 242932 *Fax:* 0367 242200

Catalogue:	Free
Goods:	Plastics for roofing & glazing
Countries sent to:	World
Methods of payment:	Visa, Mastercard, Cheque, Bank Transfer

DIY Plastics publish a straightforward no-nonsense catalogue, with 23 colour pages featuring plastic sheets to replace glass. Each item is fully described with plenty of hints on where to use it and how to fit it. They have shipped goods to many countries and will quote for all size of consignments.

In the gardening section 2m polythene rolls are £42.50 while replacement plastic 'glass' is £12 for a 914mm x 762mm sheet.

Goss and Crested China
62 Murray Road, Horndean, Hampshire, United Kingdom.
Tel: 0705 597 440 *Fax:* 0705 591975

Catalogue:	£1.50
Goods:	Antique heraldic porcelain
Countries sent to:	Europe, USA, Australasia
Methods of payment:	Visa, Amex, Diners Club, Cheque, Bank Transfer

This highly specialized 36 page catalogue sells antique Goss and crested china (as the name might suggest). Each page has a large black and white photograph of a number of items arranged in rows. Opposite are brief descriptions and prices. These vary enormously according to the quality of the piece. Prices start around £10 but can reach several hundred.

Homebrew Mail Order
67/69 Park Lane, Hornchurch, Essex RM11 1BH, United Kingdom.
Tel: 0708 745943 *Fax:* 0708 743699

Catalogue:	Free
Goods:	Home wine and beermaking equipment
Countries sent to:	Europe, Africa
Methods of payment:	Visa, Mastercard, Cheque

The simple 12 page brochure lists a wide variety of kits for making your own wine, beer and even liqueurs at home. As well as complete kits, accessories and concentrates are sold separately.

A typical wine kit sells for £16.99 while a kit to make 40 pints of lager or British bitter is around £6.

Peter Horne Dolls

Fisher's Mill, Bridge Hill, Topsham, Exeter, Devon EX3 0QQ, United Kingdom. *Tel:* 0392 877600 *Fax:* 0392 877600

Catalogue:	Free
Goods:	Handmade dolls, dollhouses & collectors' toys
Countries sent to:	Europe, USA
Methods of payment:	Visa, Mastercard, Amex, Cheque, Bank Transfer

Peter Horne makes Dutch dolls in the picturesque Fisher's Mill. His small, 8 page catalogue shows both these traditional models as well as miniature 'dolls in eggs', which come in various sizes from a quarter inch up to two inches. They also have a large selection of twelfth scale dollhouses, for which a price list is available on request, as well as dollhouse miniatures and collectors' toys. All are handcrafted.

Dutch dolls start at around £10 rising to £78, while the dolls in eggs are £16 to £75 depending on size.

International Hobby Supply

Box 426, Woodland Hills CA 91365, USA. *Tel:* 818 886 0423 *Fax:* 818 886 2551

Catalogue:	$20 (inc. year's subscription and newsletter)
Goods:	Hobby supplies
Countries sent to:	World
Methods of payment:	Visa, Mastercard, International Money Order

This nicely produced 200 page catalogue carries a comprehensive stock of models made by manufacturers from around the world. Strictly for the serious hobbyist, there are no illustrations, just brief descriptions and prices listed by manufacturer. They also carry a line of model accessories and books.

Jarmac Inc.
Box 2785, Springfield, IL 62708, USA. *Tel:* 217 789 7290
Fax: 217 789 7290

Catalogue:	Free
Goods:	Modeller's tools
Countries sent to:	World
Methods of payment:	Visa, Mastercard, Cheque

Jarmac is a highly specialized company concentrating on precision power tools for model makers. These include table saws and sanders in suitably small sizes. Their 2 page fact sheet comes with a price list and order form.

The Little Dollhouse Company
617 Mt. Pleasant Road, Toronto, ON M4S 2M5, Canada.
Tel: 416 489 7180

Catalogue:	$9.98 refundable plus postage
Goods:	Dollhouse miniatures
Countries sent to:	World
Methods of payment:	Visa, Mastercard, Amex, Bank Transfer

Although simply printed and stapled together this 114 page brochure cannot fail to delight. Now in its 21st edition, the miniatures catalogue contains everything from the houses themselves to tiny figurines of Charles and Diana à la Royal Doulton. Aimed more at the adult hobbyist than the child, the catalogue contains useful features on subjects such as wiring dollhouses and what tools to use for what task.

The catalogue contains long descriptions of the actual houses, which can be bought pre-assembled or in kit form. These range from the sumptuous Windcrest Manor (Canadian $1,388 assembled) to a simple roombox kit ($19.98). They also have an extensive range of period furniture and even reproduction oriental rugs from Keshishian and Tidewater.

Jean McIntosh Ltd

1115 Empress Street, Winnipeg, MB R3E 3H1, Canada.
Tel: 204 786 1634 *Fax:* 204 774 4159

Catalogue:	Free
Goods:	Needlepoint & cross stitch supplies & kits
Countries sent to:	World
Methods of payment:	Visa, Mastercard, Cheque, Bank Transfer

Jean McIntosh began her needlework company in the 1950s with a small range of petit point kits available only by mail order. The company has gone from strength to strength and its current catalogue boasts an impressive number of designs illustrated in full colour. At 36 pages there are certainly enough to choose from for both the beginner and old hand. Designed for both gros point and petit point, the designs cover landscapes, still-lifes, portraits and decorative details.

All the kits come complete with white or ecru canvas and there is a small range of accessories including frames, magnifying glasses and doll kits. Single charts start at Canadian $4.25 and Woollen Needlepoint Kits go up to $149.95.

Malvern Kites

Unicorn Yard, Great Malvern, Worcestershire WR14 4PZ, United Kingdom. *Tel:* 0684 565504 *Fax:* 0684 566695

Catalogue:	£1
Goods:	Kites
Countries sent to:	World
Methods of payment:	Visa, Mastercard, Amex, Cheque, Bank Transfer

Malvern Kites' 16 page colour catalogue features an extensive range of kites suitable for complete beginners as well as experts. Along with simple models, there are high performance stunt kites, multiple kites and even kites in the shape of a pair of legs and a cat's face. They also sell some juggling equipment.

A two line starter kite is around £15, while the faster, more complex variations can go up to £100.

Meads

500 London Road, Westcliffe-on-Sea, Essex SS0 9LD, United Kingdom. *Tel:* 0702 345474

Catalogue:	£1
Goods:	Brewing kits
Countries sent to:	Europe, USA, Australasia
Methods of payment:	Visa, Mastercard, Cheque, Bank Transfer

£1 seems rather a lot for what is little more than 7 pages of computer printout listing products and prices, but no doubt this is to put off the simply curious. Meads carry a wide range of brewing kits and accessories for making your own beer, wine and liqueurs, but with no proper descriptions or illustrations you need to know exactly what you want beforehand.

Model Builders Supply

40 Engelhard Drive, Unit 11, Aurora, ON L4G 3V2, Canada. *Tel:* 905 841 8392 *Fax:* 905 841 8399

Catalogue:	Free
Goods:	Model parts & accessories
Countries sent to:	World
Methods of payment:	Visa, Mastercard, Bank Transfer

This 160 page catalogue is aimed mostly at architects and engineers to build models but may also be useful for theatre designers, modellers and even war game enthusiasts. There is a comprehensive range of finished pieces, such as trees, furniture, cookers, lampposts and so on, as well as general supplies and tools. Although in black and white, the catalogue is well presented and illustrated throughout with photographs. An excellent resource.

The Mouse Hole Workshop
PO Box 254, Brooks, ME 04921–254, USA. *Tel:* 207 722 3760

Catalogue:	Free
Goods:	Miniatures
Countries sent to:	Europe, USA
Methods of payment:	Cheque, Bank Transfer

The Mouse Hole Workshop produces 4" high mice made by hand from felt, papier mâché and florist's wire. They currently have 87 varieties which, as they point out, is more than Heinz soup. Customers range from the Rockefellers to the National Trust. The collection includes characters from *The Wind in the Willows*, a Britannia group including a London Bobby, Robin Hood and Elizabeth I, and a Nursery group with Bo-Peep, Red Riding Hood and Goldilocks.

The Mouse Hole Workshop flyer is little more than a standard piece of paper folded in three but it does have a colour photo of a cute little mouse on the front. The Workshop is an Award Member of the British Toymakers Guild and is particularly keen to sell by mail order. The usual cost of a Mouse Hole mouse is $9.95.

Murray Clock Craft Ltd
510 McNicoll Avenue, Willowdale, ON M2H 2E1, Canada.
Tel: 416 499 4531 *Fax:* 416 499 3686

Catalogue:	$2
Goods:	Clock kits & parts
Countries sent to:	World
Methods of payment:	Visa, Mastercard, Cheque, Bank Transfer

This fascinating 72 page catalogue stocks everything you need to make traditional clocks of all sorts, from full-sized grandfathers down to small shelf clocks. There are cases, plans, faces, dials, hands and movements, both electric and clockwork. There are also books on how to build clocks and the catalogue itself contains a wealth of information. There are even kits for barometers and musical boxes.

A grandfather clock case is Canadian $815, though there are cheaper versions. A walnut shelf clock kit is $55 while movements start at around $48 and go up to several hundred dollars for the larger, chiming varieties.

Ross Treasure House Ltd

823 West 1st Street, North Vancouver, BC V7P 1A4, Canada.
Tel: 604 980 2715 *Fax:* 604 980 2717

Catalogue:	See below
Goods:	Dolls, dollhouses & miniatures
Countries sent to:	World
Methods of payment:	Visa, Mastercard, Amex, Cheque, Bank Transfer

Apparently 'the world's largest miniature catalog', if that isn't an oxymoron. At over 800 pages with 28,000 items it certainly seems comprehensive. There's everything here for anyone interested in dolls, dollhouses or miniatures. All the major manufacturers are represented along with many 'cottage-craftspeople' not found anywhere else.

Weighing the same as a small baby (6lb) it is hardly surprising that there is a charge for this tome. It is Canadian $50 for the whole thing, including price list (itself some 192 pages), or $45 without.

Scope City

679 Easy Street, Simi Valley, CA 93065, USA. *Tel:* 805 522 6646
Fax: 805 582 0292

Catalogue:	Free
Goods:	Telescopes, binoculars, rifle sights, microscopes
Countries sent to:	World
Methods of payment:	Visa, Mastercard, Amex, Cheque, Bank Draft

A 14 page black and white catalogue with no illustrations but helpful and detailed descriptions of a wide range of their own make of optical goods. These include telescopes, spotting scopes, binoculars and accessories. They also sell components for making your own telescopes.

Prices are high but not unreasonable for the quality of the equipment. Newtonian telescopes start at $800 rising to $30,000 for an observatory system. Binoculars start at a more affordable $99.

Stanley Gibbons Limited

399 Strand, London WC2R 0LX, United Kingdom. *Tel:* 071 836 8444
Fax: 071 836 7342

Catalogue:	See below
Goods:	Stamps & reference books
Countries sent to:	World
Methods of payment:	Visa, Mastercard, Diners Club, Amex, Bank Transfer

Established in 1856, Stanley Gibbons is THE stamp shop. Aside from their world famous works of reference (see below) they publish two 'listings' a year, for a subscription of £10 (redeemable against purchase). In fact these are more like catalogues in their own right, with full colour illustrations of their latest acquisitions.

They also issue two smaller, free catalogues with details of their other products. These include the famous Stamp Catalogues, other works of reference, and a large range of accessories including albums, magnifiers, stockbooks and so on. And of course they sell selections of stamps.

Strike One (Islington) Ltd

33 Balcombe Street, London NW1 6HH, United Kingdom.
Tel: 071 224 9719 *Fax:* 071 354 2790

Catalogue:	Free
Goods:	Antique clocks
Countries sent to:	World
Methods of payment:	Cheque, Bank Draft

Strike One sell antique clocks, barometers and music boxes. Obviously their stock changes continually but they do produce a glossy fold-out brochure with colour photographs of typical items. These include a beautiful grandfather clock c1775, a delightful lantern clock and a two day marine chronometer in a wooden box.

Prices vary and interested readers should contact the company direct for an up-to-date price list.

Tower Hobbies
1608 Interstate Drive, Champaign, IL 61821, USA. *Tel:* 217 398 3636
Fax: 217 356 6608

Catalogue:	$3
Goods:	Radio controlled models
Countries sent to:	World
Methods of payment:	Visa, Mastercard, Cheque

Another catalogue featuring radio controlled models but once again it
was not available as we went to press.

Walthers
5601 West Florist Avenue, Box 18676, Milwaukee, WI 53218, USA.
Tel: 414 527 0770 *Fax:* 414 527 4423

Catalogue:	$10
Goods:	Model trains & accessories
Countries sent to:	World
Methods of payment:	Visa, Mastercard, Amex, Cheque, Bank Transfer

This is a massive catalogue, running to 928 pages, many in colour,
featuring everything the model train enthusiast could possibly want. It
stocks products from so many manufacturers that the index of them
takes 10 pages. The catalogue is very well laid out and extensively
cross referenced. Products include locomotives, freight cars, passenger
cars, scenery, buildings, bridges, figures, vehicles, lighting, electrical
components, paint, tools, detailing parts, books, videos and what they
call railroadiana. Altogether an excellent range.

The catalogue itself is available both to individuals and dealers.
Consumers can order direct through Walthers' mail order arm, called
The Terminal Hobby Shop.

Wells Models

Old Chapel Bakery, Union Street, Wells, Somerset BA5 2PU, United Kingdom. *Tel:* 0749 675262

Catalogue:	n/a
Goods:	Models
Countries sent to:	World
Methods of payment:	Visa, Mastercard, Amex, Cheque, Bank Transfer, Bank Draft

Wells do not publish a catalogue but sell die cast models of cars, trucks, ships, and aircraft. They also stock model kits and 'classic' toys. Readers should contact them direct to discuss their requirements.

Woodfit

Kem Mill, Chorley, Lancs PR6 7EA, United Kingdom. *Tel:* 02572 66421 *Fax:* 02572 64271

Catalogue:	£1 refundable
Goods:	Furniture fittings, DIY, hardware
Countries sent to:	World
Methods of payment:	Visa, Mastercard, Cheque

A 120 page catalogue with over 3,000 items of furniture fittings, accessories and general hardware. At least this is what they tell us – we did not receive a catalogue despite two requests.

HOUSEHOLD

Almost Heaven Hot Tubs
Route ICS, Renick, WV 24966, USA. *Tel:* 304 497 3163
Fax: 304 497 2698

Catalogue:	$3
Goods:	Hot tubs, spas, saunas, steam rooms
Countries sent to:	World
Methods of payment:	Visa, Mastercard, Amex, Diners Club, Bank Transfer, Cheque

Almost Heaven issue a splendid 28 page colour catalogue with details of their saunas, steam rooms, whirlpool baths and hot tubs. For those not in the know, these are large wooden baths filled with hot water and Californians and usually situated outside on 'the deck', or veranda as we might call it.

But you don't need to live on the West Coast to have one – the company will ship anywhere and custom make items to your own specification. They don't just sell the tubs, either, but all the pumps and heaters that go with them, and any additional equipment to make them compatible with European power sources. Hot tubs start at around $3,000, portable spas at $2,000 and whirlpool baths $1,500.

Appliances Overseas
276 5th Avenue & 30th Street, Suite 407, New York, NY 10001–4509,
USA. *Tel:* 212 545 8001 *Fax:* 212 545 8005

Catalogue:	$
Goods:	All appliances & electronics, 240v a speciality
Countries sent to:	World
Methods of payment:	Cheque, Bank Draft, International Money Order

Appliances Overseas is THE source for electronics and appliances in
the US. Established over 35 years ago, it was set up to serve the needs
of ex-pat Americans who wanted machines that worked overseas. Their
speciality is making sure the appliances are compatible with local
conditions, are covered by international guarantees and even have
agents in the area.

They sell virtually every conceivable appliance and piece of
electronics, from fridges to hi-fis, from mixers to videos. All are from
well-known names and to American specifications. So if you want
one of those giant US fridges or washing machines this is the place.
Most are dual voltage and those that are not are adapted specifically.
Indeed, the company will even advise you which machines will need
changing for a specific area. For Americans moving abroad, the goods
are tax free and attract no duty as they enter the new country either.
Even without this advantage, the prices are very competitive and many
of the goods simply unavailable outside the US. All in all, thoroughly
recommended.

The Barn People
Box 4, South Woodstock, VT 05071, USA. *Tel:* 802 457 3356

Catalogue:	n/a
Goods:	Barn frames
Countries sent to:	World
Methods of payment:	Cheque, Bank Transfer, Bank Draft

This unusual company does not issue a catalogue as its inventory changes too quickly. They sell re-assembled antique post and beam Vermont Barn frames for re-use residentially and commercially. Not for everybody, but useful to know if you DO need a barn post or two.

Bo-Peep's Wools
Box 188, Enilda, AB T0G 0W0, Canada. *Tel:* 403 523 2813
Fax: 403 523 4033

Catalogue:	$2
Goods:	Duvets & quilts
Countries sent to:	USA
Methods of payment:	Cheque, Bank Draft

Bo-Peep's catalogue was not ready when we went to press, but we understand they sell wool quilts, duvets, mattress-pads and sleeping bags. All are 100% wool with cotton covers and 'environmentally conscious' (sic).

Caeran
25 Penny Lane (Dept. R), Brantford, ON N3R 5Y5, Canada.
Tel: 519 751 0513 *Fax:* 519 751 3976

Catalogue:	$2
Goods:	Personal hygiene products & household cleaners
Countries sent to:	USA
Methods of payment:	Visa, Mastercard, Cheque, Bank Transfer

Caeran was founded to provide environmentally acceptable products for the house and home. They take great pains to fulfil this brief and all the items are made from naturally derived ingredients, packaged with minimum waste and will bio-degrade according to OECD guidelines.

The products themselves include shampoos, conditioners, cleansers, lotions and creams as well as stain removers, soap, dishwasher liquid, washing-up liquid and so on.

Casa Quintão
30 Rua Ivens, Lisbon 1200, Portugal. *Tel:* 1 346 5837
Fax: 1 346 3686

Catalogue:	Free
Goods:	Handmade wool rugs
Countries sent to:	World
Methods of payment:	Visa, Mastercard, Amex, Diners Club, Cheque, Bank Draft

Casa Quintão's 4 page colour catalogue has photographs of a selection of its beautiful handmade Arraiolos rugs. These are of Arabic origin and came to the Iberian Peninsula in the 16th century. There are around 20 very attractive designs but many more are available on request. The very brief text is in English and although there is no price list, order form or indeed any indication of how to order, the company assures us that they will respond to enquiries from anywhere in the world.

Joan Cook
119 Foster Street, PO Box 6038, Peabody, MA 01961–6038, USA.
Tel: 508 532 6523

Catalogue:	Free
Goods:	Housewares, home furnishings, gifts
Countries sent to:	World
Methods of payment:	Visa, Mastercard, Amex

Joan Cook's 52 page colour catalogue has all sorts of goods which could loosely be called 'household'. There are gadgets and accessories for the kitchen and bathroom, a few clothes, a number of decorative gifts, books on such esoteric secrets as 'How to Strip for your Man' and 'Foods for Fabulous Sex', along with scissors that will cut metal, a specially designed bike seat which supports both cheeks and the ubiquitous 100 year light bulb. In short, an interesting read.

Cynosure Ltd

Estate Office, Ipsden, Oxfordshire OX10 6AJ, United Kingdom.
Tel: 0491 680231 *Fax:* 0491 680438

Catalogue:	Free
Goods:	Silver & silver plate, particularly Sheffield cutlery
Countries sent to:	World
Methods of payment:	Visa, Mastercard, Diners Club, Cheque, Bank Transfer

Cynosure offer a wide range of both services and goods. They produce their own selection of silverware and silver plate and also have a stock of antique items. They provide new cutlery and will match existing sets – useful if you need to replace a lost knife or spoon. They will also repair silver, replace or repair glass liners and replate objects which have become worn. They will even hand-engrave silver boxes from photographs or drawings.

The 8 page catalogue was not available at the time of going to press, but from the flyer they did send us it is apparent that the goods are of a high quality while the prices seem very reasonable. An intricate cast silver bangle is £66, a delightful silver corkscrew which screws into its own handle is £55 and a pair of silver cufflinks in the shape of cricket bats £32.50.

E. Dehillerin

18–20 Rue Coquilliere, 75001 Paris, France. *Tel:* 1 42 36 53 13
Fax: 1 45 08 86 83

Catalogue:	Free
Goods:	Kitchen equipment
Countries sent to:	World
Methods of payment:	Visa, Mastercard, Bank Draft

All we know about this company is that they sell kitchen equipment worldwide. At the time of writing we had not received their catalogue.

Gallery 27

140 Westhampton Drive, Thornhill, ON L4J 7X2, Canada.
Tel: 905 669 6624

Catalogue:	Free
Goods:	Safety products for the over-50s
Countries sent to:	World
Methods of payment:	Cheque, Bank Transfer

This catalogue is neither glossy nor very professional – in fact it is little more than 22 photocopied pages – however, it does contain some genuinely interesting products, all illustrated. Most are aimed at the over-50s to 'make life easier'. These include ice-spikes which slip on to any shoe to stop slipping on ice, a specially designed pen for 'rheumatics', an instrument to help you dress, another to pull up zips. There are various ingenious gadgets to open jars, put on shoes and cut bread. All in all an interesting read.

The Gazebo of New York

127 East 57th Street, New York, NY 10022, USA. *Tel:* 212 832 7077
Fax: 212 754 0571

Catalogue:	$6
Goods:	American country home furnishings
Countries sent to:	World
Methods of payment:	Visa, Mastercard, Amex, Diners Club

The Gazebo publishes a lavish 60 page colour catalogue featuring high quality American country home furnishings. These include rugs, pillows and folk-art. They have a particularly impressive range of quilts, that American contribution to bedtime, which they claim to be the 'largest anywhere', that American contribution to salespeak.

The General Trading Company
144 Sloane Street, Sloane Square, London SW1, United Kingdom. *Tel:* 071 730 0411 *Fax:* 071 823 4624

Catalogue:	£1.50 + p
Goods:	Traditional household furnishings & unusual gifts
Countries sent to:	World
Methods of payment:	Visa, Mastercard, Amex, Diners Club, Cheque, Bank Transfer

A renowned London store in Chelsea, The General Trading Company boasts four Royal Warrants. The glossy 20 page catalogue displays unusual gifts, toys, kitchenware and books. It is a tiny selection of the store's stock but is of the same high quality.

An attractively engraved glass goblet is £12.50, a hand-painted French platter by Gien £38. The Rolls-Royce of corkscrews, the Lever-model Screwpull, is £97.50 while a teddy bear door stop is £72.

Gumps
Box 629, DeSotto, TX 75123–0629, USA. *Tel:* 214 224 8677 *Fax:* 214 228 0397

Catalogue:	$20
Goods:	Luxury home furnishings, decorations & gifts
Countries sent to:	Europe, USA
Methods of payment:	Visa, Mastercard, Amex, Diners Club

Gump's expensive but lavishly produced catalogues are subtitled 'The Rare, the Unique, The Imaginative since 1861' and certainly the merchandise is high quality and interesting. Plenty of things for the house, such as vases, cushions, lamps, occasional tables and candlesticks. There are also women's clothes and jewellery along with ornaments for the garden.

A set of 6 champagne flutes are $48, an oxblood-glaze porcelain 'mini-vase' is $22, while a two-piece Jacquard suit by Castleberry is around $200.

Handart Embroideries

Room 106, 1st Floor, Hing Wai Building, 36 Queen's Road Central, Hong Kong. *Tel:* 523 5744 *Fax:* 845 5174

Catalogue:	Free
Goods:	Embroidered goods
Countries sent to:	World
Methods of payment:	Visa, Mastercard, Amex, Diners Club

Handart do not publish a glossy colour catalogue but instead send out 18 photocopied pages with photographs and descriptions. This is to cut costs and enable them to maintain their very reasonable prices. They sell a very large range of hand-embroidered table-cloths, place mats, handkerchiefs, silk and cotton sheets, scarves, kimonos, smoking jackets, blouses, pyjamas, silk shirts, ties and so on. Only a fraction of their stock is shown and readers can contact them directly for further information. They also sell jade jewellery and offer a custom tailoring service for a small extra fee.

Cotton, hand-crocheted tablecloths start at US$10 and come in oval, square and oblong shapes. A lace parasol is $22, a baby's christening gown $35, a lady's silk nightshirt $30 and men's silk shirts $50 – custom made for $10 extra.

Horchow Collection
PO Box 620048, Dallas, TX 75262, USA. *Tel:* 214 556 6000
Fax: 214 401 6414

Catalogue:	Free
Goods:	Furniture, gifts & women's clothes
Countries sent to:	World
Methods of payment:	Visa, Mastercard, Amex, Cheque

Horchow's attractive 68 page colour catalogue carries a wide range of items for the house, all characterized by good taste. The clothes, for women only, are contemporary and stylish designs for the 20–40 age group. There's an interesting selection of furniture, from footstools through chairs to tables and sofas. They also stock porcelain, cutlery, silverware, luggage, glassware and general gifts. In fact virtually everything in this excellent catalogue is tempting.

A pewter tea set, complete with tray, is $400, a set of six Venetian glass cordials in different colours $179, Persian rugs from $129 and a jet-black cotton dress $152.

Jacaranda Tree Mail Order
60 Greenlane Drive, Unit 17, Thornhill, ON L3T 7P5, Canada.
Tel: 416 882 6696 *Fax:* 416 882 6458

Catalogue:	Free
Goods:	Gifts & household items
Countries sent to:	World
Methods of payment:	Visa, Mastercard, Cheque, Bank Transfer

Jacaranda produce an attractive 32 page colour catalogue for general household goods and gifts. All are of high quality and include bed-linen, china, glassware, curtains, lamps, some children's items and a range of practical devices for the kitchen.

Het Kantenhuis
Kalverstraat 124, Amsterdam, The Netherlands. *Tel:* 20 6248618
Fax: 20 6392768

Catalogue:	n/a
Goods:	Fabrics & gifts
Countries sent to:	World
Methods of payment:	Visa, Mastercard, Amex, Diners Club

Kantenhuis do not produce a catalogue because their product range
and prices change so often, but full details, along with photographs,
will be sent on request. They sell luxury textiles, table sets, curtain
materials, Dutch style clocks and gifts. Goods sent outside Europe are
tax free.

King's Chandelier Company
Highway 14, PO Box 667, Eden, NC 27288, USA. *Tel:* 919 623 6188
Fax: 919 627 9935

Catalogue:	$4
Goods:	Chandeliers, sconces, candelabra
Countries sent to:	World
Methods of payment:	Visa, Mastercard, Cheque, Bank Transfer

This splendid 84 page catalogue contains spectacular chandeliers of
all sorts. The company has been in business for over 60 years and is
an expert in the field.

Prices vary with the complexity of the chandelier, starting at a couple
of hundred dollars and going up to $27,000 for the stunning 'Strass
Magnum Opus'.

Lakeland Plastics Ltd
Alexandra Buildings, Windermere, Cumbria. LA23 1BQ, United Kingdom *Tel:* 05394 88100 *Fax:* 05394 88300

Catalogue:	Free
Goods:	Kitchen equipment
Countries sent to:	World
Methods of payment:	Visa, Mastercard

Lakeland Plastics calls itself 'the creative kitchenware company' and seems to live up to its name. The 78 page A5 colour catalogue is stuffed with all sorts of products for the kitchen, from saucepans, trays and storage jars to knives, scissors and gadgets. They also stock a good range of other household items, including space savers, stain removers and even some furniture. Overall an excellent catalogue.

A hand-operated pasta machine costs £30, a nutmeg grinder £4.45 and a mortar and pestle £11.

Larsen Wines (UK) Ltd
2 Belle Vue Enterprise Centre, Ivy Road, Aldershot, Hampshire GU12 4QW, United Kingdom. *Tel:* 0252 334499 *Fax:* 0252 334490

Catalogue:	Free
Goods:	Porcelain figures
Countries sent to:	World
Methods of payment:	Visa, Mastercard, Cheque

Larsen publish a 20 page colour catalogue featuring products by Royal Copenhagen Porcelain and other high-class Danish manufacturers. There is a line of porcelain plates and figures along with some jewellery and cutlery by Georg Jensen and glassware by Holme Gaard.

Lehman Hardware and Appliances

Box 41, Kidron, OH 44636–0041, USA. *Tel:* 216 857 5757
Fax: 216 857 5785

Catalogue:	$2
Goods:	Items for simple living
Countries sent to:	World
Methods of payment:	Visa, Mastercard

This terrific 132 page catalogue stocks over 2,000 items for 'simple living' used by the Amish people in the USA. This insular community continues a way of life little changed for hundreds of years, since they first arrived in America from Europe. They eschew the use of electricity and live a simple, country life (as in the film 'Witness').

It is crammed with fascinating products such as butter churns, yoghurt incubators, cast iron kitchenware, hand-powered cooking gadgets, tools, gardening gear, books on the Amish, woodburning stoves, fruit presses, wooden washboards and so on. In the way of American companies, they are keen to describe various items as 'the world's best', and may be right. These global winners include 'The World's Most Effective Strainer' and 'The World's Best $10 Bucket' (how much competition is there?).

There are too many items to pick out any prices but they seem reasonable and the catalogue itself is a delightful read for $2.

Limoges-Unic

Ventes par Correspondence, 12 Rue de Paradis, 75010 Paris, France.
Tel: 1 47 70 54 49 *Fax:* 1 45 23 18 56

Catalogue:	Free
Goods:	Porcelain
Countries sent to:	Asia, Europe, USA
Methods of payment:	Visa, Mastercard, Amex, Diners Club, Cheque, Bank Draft

Limoges produce an attractive 36 page colour catalogue with French text. They sell an extensive range of porcelain by a variety of manufacturers, including Bernardaud, Ceralene-Reynaud, Haviland & Company and Robert Haviland & C. Pardon. They also sell stylish articles for the kitchen, such as Dualit toasters (though these are made in South London, so may be cheaper in the UK), Magimix appliances, cutlery, glasses, saucepans and teapots. Well worth a look.

McCall's School

3810 Bloor Street West, Etobicoke, ON M9B 6C2, Canada.
Tel: 416 231 8040 *Fax:* 416 231 9956

Catalogue:	$15 + p
Goods:	Baking accessories
Countries sent to:	World
Methods of payment:	Visa, Mastercard, Cheque, Bank Draft

McCall's catalogue features over 8,000 items and costs Canadian $15 to send overseas, which may explain why they were reluctant to send us a review copy. However, we gather it sells cake decorating equipment, baking supplies, gadgets and novelties.

Maison F. Rubbrecht
23 Grand Place, Brussels B-1000, Belgium. *Tel:* 2 5120218
Fax: 2 5020681

Catalogue:	$5
Goods:	Lace
Countries sent to:	Europe
Methods of payment:	Visa, Mastercard, Amex, Diners Club

How exciting to find a catalogue featuring truly excellent handiwork. This 13 page colour publication specializes in Belgian lace and although the company is in Brussels, the text is in English. Goods vary from tablecloths to christening slippers and are of the finest quality. As one might expect prices are on the high side but are still excellent value for money.

Prices are in Belgian francs and US$, with a Princess lace pillowcase $85, silk-lined booties $48 and handkerchiefs $29.

Manufactum Hoof & Partner Kommanditgesellschaft

Otto Burrneisterll 24 Moltkestr. 10, 45657 Recklinghausen, Nordrhein-Westfalen, Germany. *Tel:* 02361 15229 *Fax:* 02361 914329

Catalogue:	Free
Goods:	High-class household products
Countries sent to:	Europe
Methods of payment:	Cheque, Bank Transfer

Manufactum's German-language catalogue is 112 pages of pure delight. Heals meets Divertimenti by way of the Conran Shop. In other words it sells goods for the stylish home. The kitchen section has everything the well-dressed kitchen is wearing this decade. Elegant 24 piece stainless steel cutlery sets range from German M129 to DM325. Copper kettles start at DM148 and a good collection of corkscrews from DM16. The glassware and crockery are limited but exquisite.

There is an impressive range of gift foods from good olive oils and pasta sauces to dried mushrooms. Home accessories include writing sets, lamps and tablecloths. Leather belts start at DM29 and you can even buy mother-of-pearl buttons at DM3.80 for packs of eight. Luggage, grooming products and classic sweaters take you through to a range of gardening implements that Marie Antoinette would have been proud of. And even the catalogue itself is a work of beauty – order one now!

L. V. Martin & Sons Ltd

Corner Glover Street & Melvern Road, Ngauranga Gorge, Wellington, New Zealand. *Tel:* 4 4724 503 *Fax:* 4 473 8476

Catalogue:	Free
Goods:	Gifts, toys, household items
Countries sent to:	World
Methods of payment:	Visa, Mastercard, Cheque, Bank Draft

This 72 page colour catalogue from New Zealand contains a very diverse range of products for the house and home. It features clothes, kitchen equipment, linens, toys, jewellery, gardening tools, gifts, hardware, exercise gear and gadgets. Although there is nothing specifically antipodean, the selection is nevertheless interesting and the catalogue well produced.

Maria's Versand Handelsgesellschaft m.b.H.
Modelham 17 A-5201 Seekirchen, Salzburg, Austria. *Tel:* 06212 6155
Fax: 06212

Catalogue:	SH35
Goods:	Gadgets & gifts
Countries sent to:	Europe
Methods of payment:	Cheque, Bank Transfer

This German-language, 32 page colour catalogue is printed on rather flimsy paper and features a range of gadgets at the cheaper end of the market. There are a few clothes for women, various slimming aids and exercise machines, along with the usual devices for whitening teeth, polishing nails and improving your bust (the latter comes in a small jar accompanied by impressive before and after diagrams). There are also kitchen and DIY gadgets.

David Mellor
4 Sloane Square, London SW1W 8EE, United Kingdom.
Tel: 071 730 4259

Catalogue:	£2
Goods:	Kitchenware & cutlery
Countries sent to:	World
Methods of payment:	Visa, Mastercard, Cheque, Bank Transfer

David Mellor is well known in Britain for his beautifully designed cutlery. He also has a couple of wonderful retail outlets selling a wide selection of kitchen equipment. This 55 page colour catalogue very much reflects the elegant simplicity of those stores. Subtitled 'The Complete Cook's Catalogue', it certainly lives up to its name with a terrific range of goods. Anyone interested in cooking should order a copy now.

A Le Creuset medium saucepan is £36, a salad basket £5.74, a waffle iron £30.

National Welfare Organisation
Handicraft Department, PO Box 1094, 6 Ipatias Street, Athens 101
10 Greece. *Tel:* 3211761 Ext 194 *Fax:* 3233650

Catalogue:	Free
Goods:	Rugs, carpets, cushion covers, bags, tablecloths etc.
Countries sent to:	Europe, USA, Australasia
Methods of payment:	Cheque

The National Welfare Organisation is dedicated to conserving and expanding traditional craft skills in Greece. Their glossy colour catalogue is in English and has splendid photographs of beautiful rugs and carpets.

All are handmade by Greek women working in the provinces and follow traditional designs. Prices vary according to size and quality – measured in knots per square metre. The cheapest, with 36,000 knots, works out at DR38.984, while the most expensive is DR177.966. These are high-quality, unusual items.

Nordiska Kristall
Kungsgatan 9, S-111 43 Stockholm, Sweden. *Tel:* 08 10 43 72
Fax: 08 21 68 45

Catalogue:	Free
Goods:	Crystal glassware
Countries sent to:	World
Methods of payment:	Visa, Mastercard, Amex

Nordiska has been selling fine Swedish crystal since 1918 and have built up an extensive international mail order business. Although their complete catalogue was not ready as we went to press, they did send us several brochures showing their goods. These include bowls, glasses, jugs, candlesticks, ashtrays and so on, all in stunning contemporary designs. Most glassware companies tend to sell rather conventional pieces, this collection is therefore particularly refreshing. The brochures are in English, with prices in US$, but they also speak French, German and Japanese.

Phillips Lamp Shades Ltd

172 Main Street, Toronto, ON M4E 2W1, Canada. *Tel:* 416 691 7372
Fax: 416 691 7360

Catalogue:	$5.50
Goods:	Kerosene lighting products
Countries sent to:	World
Methods of payment:	Visa, Mastercard

Not to be confused with the Dutch electrical giant, this Phillips specializes in kerosene lights, especially the Aladdin range. The 70 page black and white catalogue features not only complete lamps but a very extensive range of parts and accessories to keep them going, including parts for older models. And if you think kerosene lamps are restricted to 'Tilly' lamps for camping, think again. Here you can buy very ornate and beautiful fixtures in dozens of different styles: free standing, floor, wall mounted and so on. The catalogue also includes many useful tips and suggestions for getting the best out of the Aladdin range.

Porsgrunn Butikk Oslo A/S

Karl Johansgate 14, Oslo 1, Norway. *Tel:* 22 42 74 83
Fax: 22 42 50 69

Catalogue:	n/a
Goods:	Porcelain
Countries sent to:	Europe, USA
Methods of payment:	Visa

Porsgruun sell porcelain tableware and collectables along with gifts. However, they do not issue a catalogue so interested readers have to contact them direct.

Renolds Global Productions
628 St Kilda Road, Melbourne, Australia. *Tel:* 03 510 1525
Fax: 03 510 1045

Catalogue:	n/a
Goods:	Cook book videos
Countries sent to:	World
Methods of payment:	Visa, Mastercard, Cheque, Bank Draft

Renolds sell a number of cook book videos but do not produce a catalogue. Interested readers should contact them direct stating their requirements.

Shear Comfort Ltd
2409 Burrard Street, Vancouver, BC V6J 3J3, Canada.
Tel: 604 732 3337 *Fax:* 604 732 4743

Catalogue:	Free
Goods:	Wool, leather & sheepskin products
Countries sent to:	World
Methods of payment:	Visa, Mastercard, Cheque, Bank Transfer, Bank Draft

Shear Comfort's 10 page catalogue has a variety of products all made from sheepskin and wool. For example, a pair of fleece-lined slippers are Canadian $60, a car cover $110. They also produce traditional sheepskin rugs, golf headcovers ($50 for four) and pure new wool 'sleepers' which seem to be a sort of blanket ($170 for a double bed, $150 single).

Skandinavisk Glas
4 Ny Ostergrade, 1101 Copenhagen, Denmark. *Tel:* 33 13 80 95
Fax: 33 32 33 35

Catalogue:	$3
Goods:	Porcelain
Countries sent to:	World
Methods of payment:	Visa, Mastercard, Amex, Diners Club, Cheque, Bank Transfer, International Money Order

This Danish company produces several colour catalogues in English, featuring a range of porcelain priced in US$. The well-known names are all here, including Wedgwood, Waterford and Spode. Along with dinner plates, tea sets and other practical items, there are decorative gifts such as porcelain figures. Some of these are attractive, others are a little twee. There is also a small selection of glassware.

An Adele Melikoff goblet is $75, a Wedgwood three-piece nursery set $32 and a Spode dinner plate $19.

Sotainvalidien Veljesliiton Naisjarjesto r.y.n.
Ryijpalvelu, Kasarmikatu 34, 00130 Helsinki, Finland. *Tel:* 90 660615
Fax: 90 176503

Catalogue:	$10
Goods:	Rugs
Countries sent to:	World
Methods of payment:	Visa, Mastercard, Amex, Diners Club, Cheque

In English this company translates as the 'Women's Organization of the Disabled War Veterans'. The large, glossy catalogue has colour photographs of Finnish wool rugs and ryijys (wall rugs). They can either be ordered as completed items or as kits for you to make. Most of them are contemporary in design and although the catalogue itself is in Finnish, the accompanying order form, price list and fact sheet are in English.

A typical 48" x 64" rug is Finnish M6,100 or M1,950 as a kit.

Steuben Glass

Fifth Avenue at 56th Street, New York, NY 10022, USA.
Tel: 212 752 1441 *Fax:* 212 371 5798

Catalogue:	$8 + p
Goods:	Glassware
Countries sent to:	World
Methods of payment:	Visa, Mastercard, Amex, Diners Club, Cheque

A beautifully produced 108 page catalogue which comes in its own special sleeve. Lavishly illustrated, it does justice to the wide selection of beautiful designer glass objects. These include crystal vases, bowls, tableware, barware, animals, sculptures and paperweights. All are from original designs.

Prices are not low but these are impressive works of art. A simple paperweight can be over $300, a bowl nearly $800 and the stunning 'Archaic Vase', based on an ancient Etruscan design, $2,375.

Stockwell China Bazaar

67 Glassford Street, Glasgow, G1 1UB, United Kingdom.
Tel: 041 552 1906 *Fax:* 041 553 1925

Catalogue:	Free
Goods:	China
Countries sent to:	World
Methods of payment:	Cheque, Bank Draft

This company offers an excellent selection of china and glass for both the home and office. They stock all the major manufacturers, including Wedgwood, Aynsley, Villeroy & Boch, Spode, Royal Worcester, Royal Albert, Denby, Portmerion, Royal Doulton, Royal Crown Derby, Minton, Duchess, Royal Grafton, Guy Degrenne, Dartington, Thomas and Robbe & Berking. They also sell a small range of cutlery.

The company will ship anywhere in the world and offers a wedding list service. A Waterford wine decanter is around £140, a Wedgwood 10" plate from £10 and a Portmerion teapot £31.

Tibetan Self-Help Refugee Centre
65 Ghandi Road, Darjeeling, India. *Tel:* 0354 2346

Catalogue:	$1.50
Goods:	Rugs
Countries sent to:	Europe, USA, Australasia
Methods of payment:	Visa, Amex, Cheque, Bank Transfer

Set up in 1959, this refuge gives work to Tibetans fleeing after the Chinese invasion of their country. The 32 page English-language catalogue has full colour photographs of a wide selection of hand-knotted woollen rugs as well as some leather items, bags, purses, sweaters and toys. The rugs in particular look extremely attractive and the prices seem reasonable.

3' x 6' rugs start at US$162, rising to around $200. Cushion covers are $25 while a hand-knitted sweater is $28. Obviously postage is extra but is manageable if by surface. The Centre regularly exports all round the world.

Tropicrafts Island Mats (1990) Ltd
Turkey Lane, Roseau, Dominica, West Indies. *Tel:* 448 2747
Fax: 448 7126

Catalogue:	Free
Goods:	Handcrafted straw goods
Countries sent to:	World
Methods of payment:	Visa, Mastercard, Cheque, Bank Draft

We did not receive this catalogue in time to look at, but understand it features a number of products made out of straw, such as mats.

United Cutlers of Sheffield
Petre Street, Sheffield S4 8LL, United Kingdom. *Tel:* 0742 433984
Fax: 0742 437128

Catalogue:	Free
Goods:	High quality table cutlery and kitchen knives
Countries sent to:	World
Methods of payment:	Visa, Mastercard, Amex, Diners Club, Cheque, Bank Transfer

United Cutlers is a member of the Guild of Master Craftsmen and makes high quality cutlery in silver, silver plate and stainless steel. Each item is individually crafted and hand polished. Prices are kept down by selling direct to the public.

The range is traditional, both in terms of look and finish. Prices vary but a table knife is around £12.50 in stainless steel, £17.50 in silver plate and £35 in silver. A white handled version is just £8.50. These prices compare very favourably with similar quality items in a shop.

Rowland Ward
PO Box 40991, Nairobi, Kenya. *Tel:* 25509 *Fax:* 218154

Catalogue:	Free
Goods:	Hand-engraved crystal
Countries sent to:	World
Methods of payment:	Visa, Mastercard, Amex, Cheque, Bank Transfer

The simple 4 page brochure has black and white photographs of a number of hand-engraved crystal glasses. There are glasses of all different styles along with decanters, bowls, jugs and paperweights. All are engraved with big game and fish. The glass itself is mouth-blown in Bavaria. The company also told us it makes hand-woven goods such as carpets, bedcovers, tablecloths and cushions but that catalogue was not ready as we went to press. Prices on request.

Waterford Crystal Ltd
Kilbarry, Waterford, Ireland. *Tel:* 051 73311 *Fax:* 051 79321

Catalogue:	£3.50
Goods:	Cut glassware
Countries sent to:	World
Methods of payment:	Visa, Mastercard, Amex, Diners Club, Cheque, Bank Draft

World famous for its crystal, Waterford's produce a glossy, 92 page colour catalogue beautifully displaying their entire range. This includes not just the normal glasses and decanters, but also vases, trophies, candlesticks, ornaments and even chandeliers.

Willi Geck
Postfach 48, 65337 Eltville 2, Germany. *Tel:* 06123 607 18
Fax: 06123 1682

Catalogue:	Free
Goods:	China, crystal, glassware & gifts
Countries sent to:	World
Methods of payment:	Visa, Mastercard, Amex, Diners Club, Cheque, Bank Draft

Willi Geck have a number of retail outlets in Germany selling an excellent range of porcelain, cutlery, silver, glassware and gifts by major manufacturers. They also have a thriving international mail order business and issue catalogues in English and Japanese as well as German.

Their English version runs to 60 colour pages featuring porcelain dinner services by KPM, Fürstenberg, Rosenthal, Villeroy & Boch©, Meissen and others. They also sell silver candelabra, trays, bowls and cutlery along with porcelain figurines, dolls and gifts. They even have a range of crystal chandeliers. Prices are in US$ and include shipping by surface mail.

JEWELLERY

Cairncross of Perth
18 St John Street, Perth, Scotland, United Kingdom. *Tel:* 0738 24367
Fax: 0738 43913

Catalogue:	Free
Goods:	Quality jewellery, silver, watches
Countries sent to:	Europe, USA
Methods of payment:	Visa, Mastercard, Amex, Cheque, Bank Transfer

A beautifully produced if slim colour catalogue (12 pages) shows a unique range of pearl jewellery. Cairncross is the 'home' of Scottish freshwater pearls, fished out of the River Spey amongst others.

The handmade settings are traditional in design, using gold and silver. As you might expect with items of this quality prices are hardly low. The cheapest is £63, for a Baroque cage charm, but the average price is in the hundreds. Indeed there are several pieces in the thousands, one at £5,000, and others simply have a discreet 'Price on request'.

Garrard, the Crown Jewellers

112 Regent Street, London W1A 2JJ, United Kingdom.
Tel: 071 734 7020 *Fax:* 071 439 9197

Catalogue:	£4
Goods:	Antique & modern jewellery
Countries sent to:	World
Methods of payment:	Visa, Mastercard, Amex, Diners Club, Cheque, Bank Transfer

Garrard's are THE Crown Jewellers and hold no less than three Royal Warrants. They produce two catalogues, one for jewellery and gifts, the other for watches. Both are stunning. The larger of the two has beautiful photographs of truly exquisite jewellery, clocks, antique silver and gold, ornaments and tableware. Prices are the sort that if you're asking you probably can't afford – there can't be many mail order catalogues with items at £175,000 (emerald and diamond necklace with earrings), though to be fair prices do start in the low hundreds.

As far as the watches go, there isn't much here for under £1,000, with many around £20,000 rising to £225,000 which even by Garrard's standards seems a touch on the pricey side. All the great makes are represented here, along with many obscure but exclusive ones.

Itraco Watch Co.

Fachstrasse 28A, CH–8942 Oberrieden, Switzerland.
Tel: 01 720 04 97 *Fax:* 01 720 04 45

Catalogue:	$5
Goods:	Swiss watches
Countries sent to:	Europe
Methods of payment:	Visa, Mastercard, Amex

Itraco make a large selection of watches in different styles for both men and women. They range from half-hunters through chunky sports models to elegant dress watches. The 32 page catalogue has large colour photographs of the watches and all seem well made. However, there was no price list with ours so we cannot comment on value for money.

Rama Jewellery
987 Silom Road, Bangkok, Thailand. *Tel:* 266 8654 7 *Fax:* 266 8417

Catalogue:	Free
Goods:	Earrings, bracelets, some silverware
Countries sent to:	World
Methods of payment:	Visa, Mastercard, Amex, Diners Club, Bank Draft

Rama have been producing jewellery since 1960 and have built up a large international mail order business as well. All the items are handmade in their own workshops and include pieces using gold and silver with gems such as emeralds, diamonds, rubies, sapphires and opals as well as many local stones. Their two foldout colour brochures have clear photographs of earrings, bracelets, necklaces and rings. They also sell silver cutlery, candlesticks, trays, goblets and so on, all attractively designed and well produced. The text is in English but there was no price list with our brochure so we cannot comment on value for money.

Shetland Jewellery
Soundside, Weisdale, Shetland, Scotland ZE2 9LQ, United Kingdom. *Tel:* 0595 72 275 *Fax:* 0595 72 352

Catalogue:	Free
Goods:	Silver and gold jewellery
Countries sent to:	Europe, USA
Methods of payment:	Visa, Mastercard, Cheque, Bank Transfer

This unusual catalogue consists of a large folder with A4 colour photos of selected jewellery and an extensive price list. The items themselves come in 'collections', each featuring earrings, pendants, brooches, necklaces and bracelets as well as some cufflinks and other pieces. The collections are 'Scottish', 'Celtic', 'Nordic', 'Wildlife' and 'Robert Welch' and come in gold and silver.

Venus Jewellery

167/1–2 Vithayu Road, Bangkok, Thailand. *Tel:* 251 3227
Fax: 254 3488

Catalogue:	Free
Goods:	Rings
Countries sent to:	World
Methods of payment:	Amex, Cheque

Venus have been in business for over 28 years, selling their quality jewellery both in Bangkok and by mail. The 16 page, colour brochure folds out to show clear photographs of their excellent selection of women's rings. The text is in English and the price list in $. They also provide a cardboard template to check finger size.

Prices depend on setting and stones, but start at around $75 rising to a hefty $1,600 for a diamond ring. They also sell bracelets and necklaces.

Kays

Kays Overseas Division, Northwick Avenue, Barbourne, Worcester WR99 1GA, United Kingdom. *Tel:* 0905 23411 *Fax:* 0905 615233

Catalogue:	£6–£7
Goods:	Virtually everything
Countries sent to:	World
Methods of payment:	Visa, Mastercard, Amex, Diners Club, Cheque, Bank Draft, International Money Order

Kays is one of the UK's oldest and largest mail order companies. The catalogue is enormous, the size of a phone book, and runs to over 1000 pages. As you might expect it sells virtually everything; clothes, shoes, sports goods, garden equipment, tools, electronics, TVs, videos, car accessories, kitchen equipment, toys . . . in short it is the mail order equivalent of the department store.

While some of the merchandise is a little on the tasteless side, all the well-known brand names are there too: Sony, Nikon, Reebock, Black & Decker and so on, so there is genuinely something for everybody. Prices seem reasonable though not spectacularly cheap: Reebock running shoes at £49, the latest Toshiba TV at £369, a set of Le Creuset for £109. Kays are well set up for international customers and have a history of sending goods to overseas embassies. The catalogue is printed especially for an international market and the postal charges have been simplified: £10 for goods up to £100, £20 for goods between £100 – £200 and 10% of the value thereafter. Insurance is included in these prices.

Oy Stockmann AB
Export Service, PO Box 220, 00100 Helsinki, Finland. *Tel:* 121 3606
Fax: 121 3781

Catalogue:	Free
Goods:	Household & office goods
Countries sent to:	World
Methods of payment:	Visa, Mastercard, Amex, Diners Club, Cheque

Stockmann is the largest store in Scandinavia and has been established for over 130 years. As one might expect of a shop this size they sell virtually everything and issue an excellent 'Export Catalogue' featuring a selection of goods.

The 110 colour pages have text in English, French, German, Spanish and Russian. Goods include household furniture, lighting, glassware, kitchen equipment, cutlery, rugs, textiles, house electronics, appliances, office furniture and machines and even cars.

Stockmann's have many years of experience in sending goods overseas, both to individuals and businesses (for whom they have a special 'Business to Business Export Service'). They can also quote on items not included in their catalogue.

Redoute Catalogue
57 rue de Blanchemaille, 59082 Roubaix Cedex, France.
Tel: 20 69 60 00 *Fax:* 20 36 99 37

Catalogue:	FF
Goods:	Large range
Countries sent to:	Asia, Europe
Methods of payment:	Cheque, Visa

A massive 1,208 pages makes this big even by giant catalogue standards. As you might expect it sells virtually everything, although about two-thirds is devoted to clothes. The text is in French but easy to follow and you may find here the sort of clothes not normally associated with such catalogues. There are some very stylish designs and a good range of ski clothes.

3 Suisses

12 Rue de la Centenaire, 59170, Croix, France. *Tel:* 20 72 59 60
Fax: 20 72 04 06

Catalogue:	39FF
Goods:	Virtually everything
Countries sent to:	Europe
Methods of payment:	Visa, Cheque

3 Suisses have mail order operations throughout continental Europe but this is the only one we found which would export. Their 930 page catalogue contains a huge range of goods, many of which display typical French style. Prices seem reasonable and although the text is in French the symbol system works well and is easy to follow.

Wehkamp B.V.

75 Industriepark-West, 9100-St-Niklaas, Belgium. *Tel:* 038 264 264
Fax: 038 264 730

Catalogue:	Free
Goods:	Virtually everything
Countries sent to:	Europe
Methods of payment:	Cheque, Bank Transfer

Another giant catalogue in the department store mould, selling virtually everything. This one has around 750 pages and is in Dutch, which is surprisingly easy to follow for English-speakers. The products may be fairly middle of the road but there are many well-known brand-names and the quality is as you would expect from this kind of operation. Note: they only send goods to the Netherlands and the Flemish part of Belgium.

MARINE

Boat Plans International
Box 1073 GS, Whistler, BC V0N 1B0, Canada. *Tel:* 604 932 6874
Fax: 604 938 1186

Catalogue:	$10
Goods:	Boat plans & equipment for DIY boats
Countries sent to:	World
Methods of payment:	Visa, Mastercard, Cheque, Bank Transfer

Boat Plans lives up to its name and sells . . . boatplans. Thousands of them. In fact so many that they have a rather ingenious customized catalogue which is produced specifically for each client's needs. You simply let them know what sort of boat you are interested in – type, size, approximate specification – and they will make up a 60 page catalogue just for you, featuring plans for that sort of boat.

They also stock 'bare' hulls to get you started along with engines, winches and the hundreds of other bits and pieces you will need. In addition they have 800 videos and 1,500 books on marine subjects.

Classical Airboaters Catalog
Classic Airboats, 306 Shearer Boulevard, Cocoa, FL 32922, USA.
Tel: 407 633 4026 *Fax:* 407 632 6043

Catalogue:	$5
Goods:	Powered skiffs
Countries sent to:	World
Methods of payment:	Visa, Mastercard, Diners Club, Cheque, Bank Transfer

Airboats are not inflatables, as one might expect, but flat-bottomed skiffs powered by aeroplane propellers attached to a large engine on the back. Suitable for skimming across flat water at high speed (up to 60mph) they are popular in the Florida Everglades, where this company is based.

The 64 page colour catalogue, printed like a tabloid newspaper, shows many variations on this theme. One headline stands out: 'Classic airboats best illustrates the American dream. It's about freedom. Go where others can't'. Eat your heart out Arthur Miller.

The company sells complete boats as well as kits to make your own. They also stock a huge range of parts and accessories, from bolts up to hulls, propellers and engines. Complete boats cost from $10,000 and go up to about twice that.

Davis Instruments
3465 Diablo Avenue, Hayward, CA 94545, USA. *Tel:* 510 732 9229
Fax: 510 732 9188

Catalogue:	Free
Goods:	Boating accessories & navigational equipment
Countries sent to:	World
Methods of payment:	Visa, Mastercard, Amex, Diners Club, Cheque, Bank Transfer

At a glossy 32 pages the 1993 catalogue carries in-depth descriptions of a wide range of articles for the sailing family. All the products are of good quality and provide great value for money. From wind speed indicators ($42.95) and sextants (from $45.95) through range finders, navigation kits and boarding ladders to boating gloves, anchor holders, dock grabbers and deck mops, the catalogue contains a host of invaluable on-board tools.

Defender Industries
255 Main Street, Box 820, New Rochelle, NY 10801, USA.
Tel: 914 632 3001 *Fax:* 914 632 6544

Catalogue:	$15
Goods:	Boating supplies
Countries sent to:	World
Methods of payment:	Visa, Mastercard

This 282 page catalogue is mostly in black and white with the occasional colour page. Founded in 1938, Defender carries virtually everything for the boat, in fact it even sells boats themselves – a range of inflatables. There are pumps, compasses, binoculars, marine electronics, engines, flags, flares, winches, fishing accessories – the list goes on and on. An excellent, comprehensive catalogue.

E & B Discount Marine

201 Meadow Road, Edison, NJ 08818, USA. *Tel:* 908 819 4600
Fax: 908 819 9222

Catalogue:	$
Goods:	Recreational marine accessories & clothing
Countries sent to:	World
Methods of payment:	Visa, Mastercard, Amex, Bank Transfer

E & B Discount Marine claim never to be knowingly undersold. If
you can find a lower advertised price for any product in the 1993
catalogue within 30 days the difference will be refunded.

The excellent catalogue runs to 283 pages in a variety of black and
white and colour pages. It comes packed with thousands of items for
use on board ship, on the water or at the quayside. Just about anything
you need can be found here, from the smallest accessory up to the
latest radar. E & B also boast their own range of equipment under the
trade names Seafit, Bow t'Stern, SeaRanger and North Atlantic Trading
Co.

M & E Supply Company

US Route 130 South, Collingswood, NJ 08107, USA.
Tel: 609 541 6500 *Fax:* 609 858 3117

Catalogue:	$2
Goods:	Marine supplies & equipment
Countries sent to:	World
Methods of payment:	Visa, Mastercard, Amex, Diners Club, Cheque, Bank Transfer

$2 buys you M & E's comprehensive, 330 page catalogue listing an
enormous stock of marine supplies. These range from electronic goods
– such as radar, satellite position finders and radios – through
compasses and boat accessories, to binoculars, engines and even
inflatable boats. There is everything here, from the tiniest nut and bolt
up to large pumps and motors. They also occasionally send out a 64
page colour supplement of sale items.

Panther Airboat Corp.
300 N. Wilson Avenue, Cocoa, FL 32922, USA. *Tel:* 305 632 1722

Catalogue:	Free
Goods:	Airboats
Countries sent to:	World
Methods of payment:	Cheque, International Money Order

A sister company to Classic Airboats (see above), they also sell a range of boats. These tend to be smaller, but very powerful.

Skipper Marine Electronics
3170 Commercial Avenue, Northbrook, IL 60062, USA.
Tel: 708 272 4700 *Fax:* 708 291 0244

Catalogue:	Free
Goods:	Marine electronics
Countries sent to:	World
Methods of payment:	Visa, Mastercard, Bank Transfer

Skipper claims to be the world's largest marine and fishing electronics dealer. The 120 page colour catalogue sells virtually every electronic device you could need on a boat. Aside from radar and global positioning equipment, there are fish finders, digital sounders, radios, sonars, speed and depth instruments and so on. They also sell watches, hi-fi and even TV systems for the boat. Each product is described in depth and there are useful articles scattered throughout. A thoroughly professional publication.

The Tender Craft Boat Shop Inc.
284 Brock Avenue, Toronto, ON M6K 2M4, Canada.
Tel: 416 531 2941 *Fax:* 416 323 0992

Catalogue:	Free
Goods:	Boats
Countries sent to:	Asia, Europe, USA
Methods of payment:	Visa, Mastercard, Cheque, Bank Transfer, Bank Draft

This company is a fully-fledged boatbuilder in its own right and has produced this attractive 34 page catalogue to sell both complete boats and kits, as well as an extensive range of supplies needed to build a boat. Here you can find all the special resins, paints and hardware that can be difficult to track down.

As the name suggests, the boats are mostly small tenders, although some do have sails and they also sell traditional canoes. A simple boat, complete, costs around Canadian $1,800 while the most expensive is $6,500.

Windsurfing Express
6043 N.W. 167 Street, Hialeah, FL 33015 9932, USA.
Tel: 305 557 5217 *Fax:* 305 822 2839

Catalogue:	Free
Goods:	Windsurfing equipment
Countries sent to:	World
Methods of payment:	Visa, Mastercard, Amex, Diners Club, Cheque

Windsurfing Express's glossy 36 page colour catalogue features a good selection of boards from the Genesis range (complete with lifetime guarantee) which start at $499. They also stock boards from Seatrend, Racetec and Acetec all at reduced prices, as well as a large collection of harnesses, footstraps, car-racks, fins, footwear and wetsuits by Hood River, O'Neill and Ronny.

MISCELLANEOUS

Australian Lottery Systems P/L
GPO Box 7-A, Melbourne, 3001, Australia. *Tel:* 61 3 527 6922
Fax: 61 3 527 2088

Catalogue:	Free
Goods:	Lottery games
Countries sent to:	World
Methods of payment:	Visa, Mastercard, Amex, Diners Club, Cheque, Bank Transfer

This is not so much a catalogue as a series of leaflets from Australia's largest lottery company. With nearly 300,000 prizes a week it certainly seems tempting, especially since the first prize can be Australian $150 million.

International subscribers pay by credit card and circle a series of numbers. There is a draw on Australian TV every Saturday, while overseas customers are kept in touch by air mail. The cost of a 100 week ticket which enters you in 500 draws is US$1095, but you can enter for much less. 50 weeks comes to $598; 25 weeks $425 and 15 weeks $285. They have many international customers and accept payment in sterling, US dollars and yen.

Better Yield Insects
R.R. 3, Site 4, Box 48, Belle River, ON N0R 1A0, Canada.
Tel: 519 727 6108 *Fax:* 519 727 5989

Catalogue:	Free
Goods:	Insect control
Countries sent to:	World
Methods of payment:	Visa, Mastercard, Cheque

This unusual company sells insects which control other pests – presumably by eating them. Their simple, 5 page brochure gives details of a number of species and the pests they control. They cater for about 40 predators and also have a garden pack which should help terminate and control most common pests. But bear in mind that some countries may have import restrictions on these 'products'.

Bianchi International

100 Calle Cortez, Temecula, CA 92590, USA. *Tel:* 714 676 5621
Fax: 909 676 6777

Catalogue:	$5
Goods:	Law enforcement products
Countries sent to:	World
Methods of payment:	Visa, Mastercard

For non-American readers this 50 page, glossy colour catalogue is
quite an eye-opener. It sells a comprehensive if at times bewildering
range of gun holsters made in leather, 'combat nylon' and other
materials. Here you can find a snug home for your automatic under
your armpit, slung by your hip or ingeniously hidden in a bum-bag.
They also sell a good range of leather belts, batons, handcuff pouches
and other paraphernalia. All the equipment is very well designed and
made – a thoroughly professional outfit.

Cohasset Colonials by Hagerty

38 Parker Avenue, Cohasset, MA 02025–2096, USA.
Tel: 617 383 0110 *Fax:* 617 383 9862

Catalogue:	$3
Goods:	Sundials
Countries sent to:	Asia, Europe, USA
Methods of payment:	Cheque, International Money Order

This company manufactures quality brass sundials and compass
indicators, along with cast name plates in bronze, brass and aluminium.
Three slim brochures describe the products but there is no price list.
The company also wishes us to point out that the weight of the items
means postage can be excessive.

Commetrics Ltd (Ultravision)

680 Victoria, Suite 111, St Lambert, PQ J4P 3S1, Canada.
Tel: 514 672 4534 *Fax:* 514 672 1880

Catalogue:	$
Goods:	Optical goods
Countries sent to:	World
Methods of payment:	Visa, Mastercard, Amex, Cheque, Bank Draft

This company produces a fascinating catalogue of visual aids. Printed on A4 sheets, it runs to around 36 pages and is illustrated with black and white photographs. Along with conventional optical goods such as binoculars and sunglasses, they sell a wonderful range of glasses and aids which are simply not available elsewhere. For example there are special glasses for working in with computers, a series of lamps and magnifiers for intricate work, all sorts of magnifying glasses, many with battery powered lights, frames with 'headlights' on either side, talking watches and clocks, TV magnifiers and my favourite, a pair of bed glasses which have a prism so you can lie flat and still read or watch TV.

Del Bello Gallery

363 Queen Street West, Toronto, ON M5V 2A4, Canada.
Tel: 416 593 0884 *Fax:* 416 593 8729

Catalogue:	Free
Goods:	Prints & paintings
Countries sent to:	World
Methods of payment:	Mastercard, Cheque, Bank Draft

The 60 page catalogue features limited edition prints along with miniature paintings, sculptures, water colours and drawings. Prices start at a very reasonable Canadian $20 rising to $5,000.

Jean Paul Guisset
Z.I. de St Witz Survilliers, 95470 Fosses, Val-D'Oise, France.
Tel: 1 34 68 39 40 *Fax:* 1 34 68 41 40

Catalogue:	Free
Goods:	Office equipment
Countries sent to:	Africa, USA, Europe
Methods of payment:	Visa, Cheque

A massive 240 page colour catalogue listing a very wide range of office equipment, from envelopes through to chairs and filing cabinets. Although in French, it is easy to follow and they are very used to exporting goods all over the world.

International Police Equipment Co.
1270 Markham Street, Perris, CA 91710, USA. *Tel:* 909 943 7100
Fax: 909 943 8491

Catalogue:	$
Goods:	Police & investigation equipment
Countries sent to:	World
Methods of payment:	Visa, Mastercard, Cheque, Bank Transfer

A tall, narrow 16 page catalogue with the full title: 'Confidential Catalog of Police and Investigation Equipment'. This turns out to consist mostly of official-looking badges with inscriptions such as 'International Private Investigator' or 'Official Press Photographer' and even 'Deputy Sheriff'. These sell for around $18. Along the same lines are personal business cards establishing various identities, such as 'Special Agent'.

More interesting are the lock pick sets, which start at $19 and rise to $70 for the 'Lock Gun', said to open any pin tumbler lock. There is even a range of handcuffs and one of those blue flashing lights which you can slap on to the roof of your car to cut through traffic in the rush hour.

Kaiser & Kraft

56 Haachtsestw, 1831 Diegem, Bruxelles, Belgium.
Tel: 02 720 61 97 *Fax:* 02 720 00 16

Catalogue:	Free
Goods:	Office equipment
Countries sent to:	Asia, Europe, Africa
Methods of payment:	Cheque, Bank Transfer

This giant, 740 page French catalogue is about the size and weight of a phone book. It doesn't just contain chairs and filing cabinets, but also the sort of equipment used in industry: trolleys, hydraulic jacks, scaffolding, shelving systems and so on. Aimed at the business market, it is simple to follow despite being in French.

Kuratli Versand AG

Obermatt 3, 8905 Arni, Switzerland. *Tel:* 057 341 808
Fax: 057 342 432

Catalogue:	Free
Goods:	Products for cats & dogs
Countries sent to:	Europe
Methods of payment:	Cheque, Bank Transfer

Kuratli Versand's 32 page brochure features cat and dog products from Germany and is ideal for the pet who has everything. Baskets for the home and car, a huge array of stylish leads, and fully automated food dispensers are some of the attractions on offer. And if your love of cats goes further you can buy feline inspired glove puppets (DM48–98), jewellery, watches, tea-pots and mugs (DM33.80), duvet sets, mobiles and much more.

The company also has mail order outlets in France and Germany.

Kuratli-Versand

Gartenstr 2, D-79576 Weil a/Rh, Germany. *Tel:* 07621 78841
Fax: 07621 78842

Kuratli-Expédition

Boîte Postale 900, F-68640 Steinsoultz, France. *Tel:* 89 25 87 07

Manutan

10516 rue Amperes, Zone Industriel, 95506, Gonesse Cedex, France.
Tel: 1 43 46 12 60 *Fax:* 1 46 28 64 89

Catalogue:	Free
Goods:	Industrial goods
Countries sent to:	Europe
Methods of payment:	Cheque

Manutan Export sells industrial equipment of interest primarily to the business customer.

A large part of the 257 page catalogue comprises a range of handling, lifting and storage equipment, from automatically tilting skips, hoists and workshop cranes, to storage pallets and industrial shelving. Safety and security feature strongly (steel toe-capped safety boots from 228FF, rubber traffic cones from 53.20FF) and the measurement and guidance section contains thermohygrographs (it measures temperature and humidity), voltage testers and frequency meters.

Nova Selar SRL

Via Cigna 209, 10155 Torino, Italy. *Tel:* 011 242 4223
Fax: 011 246 5301

Catalogue:	Free
Goods:	Promotional gifts
Countries sent to:	Europe, USA
Methods of payment:	Amex, Diners Club, Cheque, Bank Transfer

Nova Selar is a collection of corporate promotional gift ideas from Italy. Logos can be overprinted on T-shirts, polo shirts, hold-alls, clocks, watches, specially wrapped confectionery and a host of other items. More up-market corporate gifts include 24 carat gold-plated jewellery, watches and pen sets.

The brochure is 36 pages with good colour reproduction. Prices vary from 1,690L for a frisbee to 104,000L for an elegant matt black answering machine.

Renton Management Services P/L
2–4 Stamford Avenue, Ermington, 2115, Australia. *Tel:* 02 874 0235
Fax: 02 804 6018

Catalogue:	Free
Goods:	Stickers
Countries sent to:	USA, Australasia
Methods of payment:	Cheque, Bank Draft

A catalogue devoted to stickers! Stickers for parcels, letters, Christmas cards, invoices, changes of address – stickers for every occasion in fact. There are some marvellous ones to persuade late payers to cough up. They start as 'Early Reminders', progress through 'Firm Early Approach' and end with 'Pressure to Pay' stickers. These have messages like: 'Suppose we owed you this money?' and 'Too many times we have asked for payment of this overdue account . . .'

Traveller's Checklist
335 Cornwall Bridge Road, Sharon, CT 06069, USA.
Tel: 203 364 0144 *Fax:* 203 364 0369

Catalogue:	$2
Goods:	Travel accessories
Countries sent to:	World
Methods of payment:	Visa, Mastercard, Cheque

This catalogue – not much more than a folded single sheet – is a boon to travellers. Full of hard-to-find travel accessories, it stocks the sort of thing one always wished one had packed but somehow didn't. Along with the usual folding irons and miniature hair dryers, there are a variety of voltage converters – genuine transformers, not just plugs – some useful locks, bags and first aid kits and a good deal more. One item struck me as particularly clever: a 'two-faced extension mirror'. This mirror is mounted on a telescopic arm with a suction pad on one end which can be stuck to any surface in a mirrorless bathroom.

Uncle Sam Umbrella Shop
161 West 57th Street, New York, NY 10019, USA. *Tel:* 212 582 1976

Catalogue:	Free
Goods:	Umbrellas & walking sticks
Countries sent to:	World
Methods of payment:	Visa, Mastercard, Amex, Cheque, Bank Draft

This specialist company just sells umbrellas, canes and walking sticks. The stock includes both contemporary designs and antique models. They will also custom make items to readers' own specifications. As we went to press they had not produced a catalogue but told us they intended to have one out for 1994.

MUSEUMS

Albright-Knox Art Gallery

The Shop, 1285 Elmwood Avenue, Buffalo, NY 14222, USA.
Tel: 716 882 8700 *Fax:* 716 882 1958

Catalogue:	Free
Goods:	Exhibition catalogues, posters, museum products
Countries sent to:	World
Methods of payment:	Visa, Mastercard, Amex, Cheque, Bank Transfer

This world famous museum, known for its collection of modern American art, publishes a number of fact sheets and a small brochure rather than a proper catalogue. Posters, cards and books are the main items.

British Museum Publications

British Museum Connection, 46 Bloomsbury Street, London WC1B 3QQ, United Kingdom. *Tel:* 071 323 1234 *Fax:* 071 436 7315

Catalogue:	Free
Goods:	Gifts inspired by items in the British Museum
Countries sent to:	World
Methods of payment:	Visa, Mastercard, Amex, Diners Club, Cheque

Unlike many museum catalogues, these products are genuinely based on the exhibits. For example, bronze replicas of Egyptian artefacts, Greek vases and statues, Roman medallions and spoons and so on. There is also a range of jewellery from various different periods. The goods are well made and surprisingly 'untacky'.

An Anglo-Saxon blue brooch is £35, a pair of cufflinks based on an ancient Chinese design also £35, a beautiful bronze and silver replica of the Gayer-Anderson cat from an Egyptian original dated 600BC, £350.

Canadian Warplane Heritage Museum
Aviation Shop & Art Gallery, PO Box 35, Mount Hope, ON L0R 1W0, Canada. *Tel:* 905 679 4183 *Fax:* 905 679 4186

Catalogue:	Free
Goods:	Aviation-related merchandise
Countries sent to:	World
Methods of payment:	Visa, Mastercard, Cheque, Bank Transfer

This 48 page catalogue is published by the Canadian Warplane Heritage Museum and sells an interesting variety of goods. There are large prints of Don Connoly's warplane paintings from Canadian $75–$450, T-shirts with planes on them, Ray-Ban sunglasses for $90–$160 (remember these are Canadian dollars), leather flying jackets from $775 and even Lego kits to build planes. There are numerous other gifts, a good selection of books and also videos.

Design Marketing Ltd
Hendon Road, Sunderland, SR9 9AD, United Kingdom. *Tel:* 091 514 4666 *Fax:* 091 514 4574

Catalogue:	Free
Goods:	Gifts of all sorts
Countries sent to:	World
Methods of payment:	Visa, Mastercard, Amex, Cheque

The 'Brainwaves' catalogue is produced by the world famous Science Museum in London. Its 32 pages in full colour are full of toys and gadgets, for both adults and children, although little seems to come directly from the museum itself.

An old-fashioned brass telescope is priced at £35, a pair of glasses with built-in windscreen wipers is £6.95 while a wine cooler which cools a bottle in six minutes is £6.95.

The Eleganza Collection
Eleganza Ltd, 3217 Smith Street, Seattle, WA 98199, USA.
Tel: 206 283 0609 *Fax:* 206 283 5282

Catalogue:	$20
Goods:	Museum reproduction statues, Greek vases, frescoes
Countries sent to:	World
Methods of payment:	Visa, Mastercard, Amex, Cheque, Bank Transfer

Eleganza is a unique and fascinating company selling 'Museum quality reproductions of sculptural masterpieces'. Their beautifully produced glossy 120 page catalogue features sculptures and artifacts from ancient Egypt, classical Greece and Rome, Renaissance Italy and some more modern work. Here you can find reproductions of Perseus with the Head of Medusa, a bust of Pallas Athena or Hippocrates along with Michelangelo's David, Pietá and Moses. More modern artists are represented by Houdon, Rodin and Degas. The sculptures are made of bronze or 'bonded' marble and come in a variety of sizes from miniature to virtually full-size. There is also a selection of Greek vases, bowls and jugs along with frescoes and pedestals.

Prices do not seem unreasonable, with Bernini's David $692 (23" x 10"), Rodin's Thinker $660 and copies of Michelangelo's David from a mere $120 (12" base) to a hefty $5,775 (64" base). The mask of Tutankhamun is $225 while Greek vases start at $54. Eleganza can also arrange 'custom' reproductions using genuine, hand carved Carrara marble.

Greenwich Zer0

Catalogue Centre, Ferry Lane, Shepperton-on-Thames, Middlesex
TW17 9LQ, United Kingdom. *Tel:* 0932 253333 *Fax:* 0932 241679

Catalogue:	Free
Goods:	Gifts
Countries sent to:	World
Methods of payment:	Visa, Mastercard, Cheque

Greenwich Zer0 is the mail order department of the famous maritime
museum at Greenwich, London, home of GMT and the meridian line.
Twenty-four colour pages feature clothes and gifts with a nautical or
historical bent. There are brass opera glasses next to modern Ross
binoculars, a variety of clocks and instruments along with a line of
practical clothing such as Guernsey sweaters and duffel coats.

They also sell ships' bells and an attractive line of 'cabin furniture'
including chairs and tables. One oddity is the box containing Nelson
Blazer Buttons. These are made from a mould taken from one of the
original buttons on Nelson's tunic.

The Minneapolis Institute of Arts

2400 Third Avenue South, Minneapolis, MN 55404, USA.
Tel: 612 870 3046 *Fax:* 612 870 3004

Catalogue:	Free
Goods:	Museum reproductions
Countries sent to:	World
Methods of payment:	Visa, Mastercard, Amex, Bank Transfer, Bank Draft

The museum's 16 page colour catalogue features a number of silk
goods, such as scarves, ties and shawls, with prints inspired by the
collection. They also sell books, toys and a small range of jewellery. A
silk scarf with a William Morris print is $50, a patchwork shawl based
on a Kashmir design, $45, a pair of earrings made from recycled glass
$17.

Museum & Galleries Marketing Ltd
24 St Charles Square, London W10 6EE, United Kingdom.
Tel: 081 960 1650 *Fax:* 081 959 7055

Catalogue:	Free
Goods:	Museum-inspired products
Countries sent to:	USA
Methods of payment:	Visa, Cheque, Bank Transfer

Unfortunately this catalogue was being printed as we went to press but should be available in early 1994. We gather it features gifts and stationery inspired by museum collections from a variety of institutions.

Museum of Fine Arts, Boston
Department RHI, 465 Huntington Avenue, Boston, MA 02115, USA.
Tel: 617 267 6008 *Fax:* 617 267 1734

Catalogue:	$2
Goods:	Museum reproductions & gifts
Countries sent to:	World
Methods of payment:	Visa, Mastercard, Amex, Cheque, International Money Order

This 102 page colour catalogue is full of elegant reproductions from the museum's collection, including prints, jewellery and sculpture. It also has a range of toys, gifts and even some clothes and tapestries. When ordering, ask for their International Shipping Guide.

Reproduction Egyptian necklaces in 24K goldplate start at around $98 while earrings are $30. Framed prints sell for $175, postcards for $16.

The Museum Shop
200 Eastern Parkway, Brooklyn, NY 11238, USA.
Tel: 212 638 5000 x 258 *Fax:* 718 638 3731

Catalogue:	Free
Goods:	Museum reproductions & gifts
Countries sent to:	World
Methods of payment:	Visa, Mastercard, Amex, Cheque, Bank Transfer

The museum does not publish a comprehensive catalogue although it does have an extensive mail order department. This sends out several pages detailing some of their more popular items along with information on catalogues describing the exhibits of the museum by department, many of which are available as reproductions. These catalogues cost from $10 up to $35.

In addition the museum sells jewellery, gifts, books, stationery, fashion items and some gifts for children. If you have a particular area of interest, simply call and discuss your needs – the staff are very helpful.

The National Gallery Publications Ltd
5/6 Pall Mall East, London SW1Y 5BA, United Kingdom.
Tel: 071 839 8544 *Fax:* 071 930 0108

Catalogue:	Free
Goods:	Cards, stationery, gifts, videos, diaries etc.
Countries sent to:	World
Methods of payment:	Visa, Mastercard, Amex, Cheque, Bank Transfer

The National Gallery Catalogue is a glossy 26 page brochure full of quality gifts inspired by the Gallery's collection. It contains the usual range of stationery items from notebooks (£0.80–£4.95) to paperweights (£4.95). It also stocks a superb range of Christmas cards available in sets of 5–25 which are great value and as an added bonus now has a personalization service which will overprint your name and address.

The Gallery's book collection features a broad range of titles from the modestly priced romp through the collection, More Than Meets the Eye (£5.95) to the sumptuous 2 volume edition of life-size photographs of the Sistine Chapel (£600).

Smithsonian Institution
7955 Angus Court, Springfield, VA 22153, USA. *Tel:* 703 455 1700
Fax: 202 357 4971

Catalogue:	Free
Goods:	Reproductions & gifts
Countries sent to:	World
Methods of payment:	Visa, Mastercard, Amex

This internationally famous institution has a catalogue from which all profits go towards its 'cultural mission'. They sell a number of fine reproductions, toys, home decorations and jewellery.

Tate Gallery Publications

Millbank, London SW1P 4RG, United Kingdom. *Tel:* 071 887 8869
Fax: 071 887 8878

Catalogue:	£3 for print catalogue, others free
Goods:	Prints, books, postcards, greeting cards
Countries sent to:	World
Methods of payment:	Visa, Mastercard, Cheque, Bank Transfer

The world famous Tate Gallery, with its impressive collection of modern art, publishes three separate catalogues for books, cards and prints. There is a charge only for the latter, a large format, glossy number running to 26 pages. It contains excellent reproductions of prints and exhibition posters from the Tate's collection, featuring artists such as Turner, Palmer and Matisse. The other two catalogues, both free, show a range of art books and postcards.

Prices seem very reasonable, with large colour prints and posters at around £6, smaller ones £4.

Textile Museum

2320 S Street N.W., Washington DC 20008, USA. *Tel:* 202 667 0442
Fax: 202 483 0994

Catalogue:	Free
Goods:	Textile books, clothes & cards
Countries sent to:	World
Methods of payment:	Visa, Mastercard, Amex, Cheque

A slim 16 page colour catalogue which contains mostly books on rugs and textiles. However, there are a line of scarves, ties and waistcoats for sale, all made of beautiful fabrics. A waistcoat is $82 while a scarf is $58 and ties $52.

The V & A Treasury
Freepost SU361, Dept 5316, Hendon Road, Sunderland, SR9 9AD
United Kingdom. *Tel:* 091 514 2999 *Fax:* 091 514 4574

Catalogue:	Free
Goods:	Reproductions & gifts
Countries sent to:	World
Methods of payment:	Visa, Mastercard, Amex, Cheque

The Victoria and Albert Museum is one of the most famous in London
and specializes in the decorative arts. This quality 48 page catalogue
offers a rich variety of items which have been directly inspired by
designs from their magnificent collection. Here we have glassware,
clothes, lacework, china, carpets, cushions, furniture, toys and a large
number of small gifts. All are beautifully made and, for the quality,
not too pricey.

A William Morris cushion, entirely hand-stitched, is £60, a
personalized leather-bound hip flask £40 and a delightful, classic teddy
bear £25 (this can also be embroidered with a child's name for no
extra cost).

**As we went to press this company ceased trading and will be
deleted from future editions of this Directory.**

MUSICAL INSTRUMENTS

Bronen's Enterprises Inc.

2462 Webster Avenue, Bronx, NY 10458, USA. *Tel:* 718 364 3350

Catalogue:	Free
Goods:	Instruments & sheet music
Countries sent to:	World
Methods of payment:	Visa, Mastercard, Amex, Bank Transfer

We did not receive a catalogue from this company before we went to press, but gather they sell musical instruments and sheet music.

Charles Catalog

Charles Double Reed Company, 141 West 28th Street (1203), New York, NY 10001, USA. *Tel:* 212 967 3113 *Fax:* 212 967 6706

Catalogue:	$
Goods:	Oboes & bassoons & accessories
Countries sent to:	World
Methods of payment:	Visa, Mastercard, Amex, Bank Transfer, Cheque

This nicely produced 24 page catalogue specializes in oboes and bassoons. Run and staffed by musicians, all of whom have had a conservatory training in one of the two instruments, the company sells both new and used. It also stocks over 400 rare products widely sought by students and professionals, such as tools for making and forming reeds, cases, polishing cloths, reed rushes and tools, oils, shrink tubing and so on. They also have a good range of books and offer a repair service. If you play either the oboe or the bassoon this is a must.

Discount Music Supply

Dept EG, 41 Vreeland Avenue, Totowa, NJ 07512–1120 USA.
Tel: 201 942 9411 *Fax:* 201 890 7922

Catalogue:	Free
Goods:	Guitars & accessories
Countries sent to:	World
Methods of payment:	Visa, Mastercard, Bank Transfer

A small, 40 page black and white catalogue specializing in electric guitars, amplifiers and other accessories. It also sells a small range of acoustic guitars, harmonicas and Casio keyboards.

Hondo electric guitars start at $166 with amplifiers from $80.

Elderly Instruments

1100 North Washington, PO Box 14210, Lansing, MI 48901, USA.
Tel: 517 372 7890 *Fax:* 517 372 5155

Catalogue:	$2
Goods:	CDs, records, cassettes & instruments
Countries sent to:	World
Methods of payment:	Visa, Mastercard, Diners Club, Bank Transfer

Elderly Instruments, despite its name, sells not only new instruments but also CDs, cassettes, videos and books – in fact anything connected to music. They have excellent instructional books, videos and cassettes as well as music simply for listening to. There are five different catalogues: Books & Videos; Records, Cassettes and CDs; Acoustic Instruments and Accessories; Electric Instruments & Accessories and finally a monthly Used Instrument List.

The main catalogues are around 84 pages, well laid out and comprehensive. When requesting one be sure to ask for the special international order form. Instructional cassettes start around $5.50 and are available for just about every instrument imaginable. Videos start at $16.50, but are of course in US format (see COMPATIBILITY, above, for details). CDs start at around $12. There is a $2.50 handling charge per order; surface mail is $6.55 for up to 2lb while air mail is $9.25 for 1lb (to UK, other destinations may vary).

Waltons Musical Instruments Galleries
2–5 North Frederick Street, Dublin 1, Ireland. *Tel:* 8747 805
Fax: 878 6065

Catalogue:	Free
Goods:	Irish instruments & music
Countries sent to:	World
Methods of payment:	Visa, Mastercard, Amex, Diners Club, Cheque, Bank Draft

The majority of this 14 page catalogue is taken up with books on Irish music. Some come with cassettes featuring the songs or instructing you how to play them. There is music for guitar, banjo, harmonica, tin whistle and voice. The selection of instruments themselves is a little smaller with harps, tin whistles and bodhrans (traditional goatskin hand drums).

Waltons also have a distributor in the US:
Walton Music Inc.
PO Box 1505, Westfield, MA 0108–1505. *Tel:* 413 562 0223
Fax: 413 562 5715

W. D. Music Products Inc.
4070 Mayflower Road, Fort Myers, FL 33916, USA.
Tel: 813 337 7575 *Fax:* 813 337 4585

Catalogue:	$
Goods:	Components for electric guitars
Countries sent to:	World
Methods of payment:	Visa, Mastercard, Cheque, Bank Transfer

A 30 page colour catalogue with virtually everything needed to build or repair electric guitars. This includes bodies, bridges, necks, neck plates, pickups, string, switches and so on. An excellent, informative catalogue.

OUTDOOR

Bass Pro Shops
1935 S. Campbell, Springfield, MO 65898, USA. *Tel:* 417 887 1915
Fax: 417 887 1807

Catalogue:	Free
Goods:	Outdoor gear
Countries sent to:	World
Methods of payment:	Visa, Mastercard, Amex, Cheque, Bank Transfer

This catalogue, entitled 'Outdoor World', is an impressive 215 pages containing a huge range of goods for the outdoors sportsperson. It covers camping, fishing and hunting and even sells complete speedboats (a very reasonable $9,000). They also stock guns, bows, knives, clothes, shoes, boots, tents, hammocks, watches, stoves, marine electronics – in fact you name it and they probably sell it. Indispensable for anyone who enjoys the great outdoors.

L.L. Bean Inc.
Freeport, ME 04033 0001, USA. *Tel:* 207 865 3111
Fax: 207 878 2104

Catalogue:	Free
Goods:	Clothes & much else
Countries sent to:	World
Methods of payment:	Visa, Mastercard, Amex, Cheque, Bank Transfer

L.L.Bean is virtually synonymous with American mail order. By far the most famous catalogue company in the US it now has a very large international customer base too. Their enviable reputation is based on well-designed, high-quality clothes and the amazing money-back guarantees: if products fail to satisfy in any way you can return them at ANY TIME for a full refund. They always honour this pledge but rarely have to – the quality of Bean products is legendary.

Catalogues are issued four times a year to coincide with seasons and are on average 216 pages, in colour. Apart from a wonderful range of clothes for men and women – mostly in preppy styles – they also stock luggage, sports goods, camping equipment and clothes for children. In addition there are four specialist catalogues which can be requested separately: Fly Fishing; Hunting; Home & Camp and Winter Sports. If you intend to order just one catalogue from the USA, make it Bean's.

Far too many prices to mention, but generally good value for money. Fleece jackets are $58, Gortex windproof jackets $130, a chamois cloth shirt $28, jeans $43, field boots (similar to Timberland) $95.

Brigade Quartermasters Ltd
1025 Cobb International Boulevard, Kennesaw, GA 30144, USA.
Tel: 404 428 1248 *Fax:* 404 426 7726

Catalogue:	$3
Goods:	Military surplus
Countries sent to:	World
Methods of payment:	Visa, Mastercard, Amex, Diners Club, Cheque, Bank Transfer

This catalogue is also known as 'The Outdoor Action Gear Sourcebook' and certainly lives up to its name. The emphasis is on quasi-military equipment and you could virtually equip the SAS from this one company. There is a wide range of camouflage jackets and trousers along with binoculars, nightsights, boots, camping equipment, knives, hiking gear, clothes and sunglasses. But that is to only touch on the enormous number of useful – and sometimes downright bizarre – products. You want to buy an aluminium blowpipe for firing darts? This is the place. Or perhaps a telescopic umbrella with a sword hidden inside, or an electric stun gun? Look no further. A fascinating read.

Dunn's Supp.y
1 Madison Avenue, Grand Junction, TN 38039, USA.
Tel: 901 764 6901 *Fax:* 901 764 6503

Catalogue:	Free
Goods:	Outdoor equipment
Countries sent to:	World
Methods of payment:	Visa, Mastercard, Cheque, Bank Transfer

Dunn's publish an up-market catalogue catering to the hunter and outdoor sportsperson. There's a wonderful range of practical clothing here including jackets, sweaters and trousers. They also sell Timberland boots, Barbour waterproofs and Harris tweed jackets. Some of the hardware, such as holsters and gunsights, seem unusual to British readers, but there is an excellent section for dogs which may make them feel more at home. Overall, a superior catalogue with many interesting items.

Huntsman Dual waterproof boots are $140, deerskin gloves $30, a pair of Timberland boots $90.

Le Baron Outdoor Products Ltd
8601 St Lawrence Boulevard, Montreal PQ H2P 2M9, Canada.
Tel: 514 381 4231 *Fax:* 514 381 2822

Catalogue:	$8
Goods:	Equipment for fishing, camping, hiking etc.
Countries sent to:	World
Methods of payment:	Visa, Mastercard, Bank Draft

Le Baron produce two catalogues a year, Spring and Fall, which run to about 300 colour pages each. They stock a huge selection of goods for camping, fishing, hunting and general outdoor activities plus an excellent range of clothing. You can buy guns, rifles, crossbows, sleeping bags, tents, snowshoes, shoes (including ones by Rocky), boots and jackets. All are at discount prices and because this is a Canadian company, the exchange rate may be more favourable for UK readers than similar outlets in the US. Worth the Canadian $8 for people interested in outdoor activities.

Mass Army & Navy Store
15 Fordham Road, Boston, MA 02134, USA. *Tel:* 617 783 1250
Fax: 617 254 6607

Catalogue:	Free
Goods:	US & European surplus
Countries sent to:	World
Methods of payment:	Visa, Mastercard, Cheque, Bank Transfer

Mass Army's excellent 46 page colour catalogue carries a great range of camping and outdoor gear, much of it government surplus. Here you can find tents, sleeping bags, backpacks, hats, combat dress and field supplies. They also stock Levi jeans, boots, watches and genuine military hardware such as helmets, jerrycans, knives and even gas masks.

Levi 501s are $30, Levi jackets $55. A three-man camouflaged dome tent is $95 and a pair of genuine US army combat boots, $55.

Patagonia Mail Order
1609 W. Babcock Street, PO Box 8900, Bozeman, MT 59715, USA.
Tel: 406 587 3838 *Fax:* 406 587 7078

Catalogue:	Free
Goods:	Sportswear
Countries sent to:	World
Methods of payment:	Visa, Mastercard, Cheque

Patagonia is rightly world famous for its excellent range of outdoor clothes. These are sold in high-class sports shops everywhere but they also operate a large international mail order department. Indeed they are so committed to this that they produce their catalogues in a variety of different languages, including French, German, Italian and Japanese.

The 110 page catalogue is printed on recycled paper, part of the company's commitment to the environment which it takes very seriously. Beautifully presented, it features clothes for every outdoor activity, from skiing to canoeing. All are designed and made by experts who really understand the sports. They also issue a separate children's catalogue. Thoroughly recommended.

A hiking parka sells for around $300, a fleece top $99, a canvas shirt $56.

They also have an office in Paris – *Tel:* 1 41 10 18 18 *Fax:* 1 46 05 57 22

REI

International Dept, Sumner, WA 98352–0001, USA.
Tel: 206 891 2500 *Fax:* 206 891 2523

Catalogue:	Free
Goods:	Outdoor clothes & equipment
Countries sent to:	World
Methods of payment:	Visa, Mastercard, Cheque, Bank Transfer

REI has been outfitting campers and outdoor enthusiasts over 55 years and is one of the best suppliers in the US. The current catalogue runs to a very plush 108 pages of full colour. It features a superb range of outdoor clothing and equipment and contains detailed descriptions of every item. There is a large choice of own-label and other manufacturers' tents, sleeping bags, cooking equipment, water filters, binoculars, backpacks, watches, clothing and shoes.

REI is a co-operative which anyone can join and benefit from discounts on the goods. Lifetime membership is $10. If you are interested in hiking, skiing, walking or other outdoor activities, this catalogue is a must.

S.I.R. Mail Order

1385 Ellice Avenue, Winnipeg, MB R3G 3N1, Canada.
Tel: 204 788 4867 *Fax:* 204 786 8964

Catalogue:	$6
Goods:	Hunting, fishing, camping & sporting goods
Countries sent to:	World
Methods of payment:	Visa, Mastercard, Amex, Cheque, Bank Transfer

This pocket-sized, 392 page catalogue is well worth the Canadian $6 charge. It is packed with everything for hunting, shooting and fishing and a good deal else besides. There are books, videos, knives, guns, tents, watches, clothes, fishing rods, binoculars . . . the list goes on and on. A number of items may be restricted in certain countries – for example rifles to the UK – but there is still plenty here that can be imported. Prices are too numerous to detail but seem reasonable and are of course in Canadian $, which generally has a good rate against the £.

Stephenson
R.E.D. 4, Box 145, Gilford, NH 03246, USA. *Tel:* 603 293 7016

Catalogue:	$3
Goods:	Mountaineering, hiking equipment
Countries sent to:	World
Methods of payment:	Cheque, Bank Draft

Stephenson produce a compact 10 page catalogue featuring their own range of highly specialized, innovative tents and sleeping bags. Designed for the serious hiker and expeditionist, they are lightweight, waterproof and warm. The tents are ingeniously shaped to give the maximum amount of room yet fold into a small pack. The sleeping bags work across an amazing range of temperatures (+60 to –70F) and come with built in 'mattresses'. They also sell a limited selection of clothing. As well as numerous letters of recommendation, the catalogue features various nude models demonstrating the equipment (strangely, all female), which is apparently connected to the company's philosophy of 'promoting natural living and camping'.

Prices are not low but reasonable for the quality of product – you are unlikely to get similar gear anywhere else. Tents start at $380, sleeping bags at $400.

Tilley Endurables
900 Don Mills Road, Don Mills, ON M3C 1V8, Canada.
Tel: 416 444 4465 *Fax:* 416 444 3860

Catalogue:	Free
Goods:	Travel & adventure clothing
Countries sent to:	World
Methods of payment:	Visa, Mastercard, Amex, Cheque, Bank Transfer

Tilley claim to produce 'the world's best travel and adventure clothing', which is the sort of statement one usually associates with American rather than Canadian companies. Their 68 page colour catalogue features a large range of such clothes, all made in Canada. The products are well designed and suitable for just about any outdoor activity.

U.S. Cavalry Store
2855 Centennial Avenue, Radcliff, KY 40160–9000, USA.
Tel: 502 351 1164 *Fax:* 502 352 0266

Catalogue:	$5
Goods:	Army & Navy surplus
Countries sent to:	World
Methods of payment:	Visa, Mastercard, Cheque, Bank Transfer, International Money Order

This impressive 132 page colour catalogue claims to be the source for 'the world's finest military and adventure equipment', which by and large means gear you need to go out and kill people. However, the range really is extensive, from Gortex camouflage suits for snow, desert and woodland backgrounds, through all sorts of camping equipment, to nightsights, backpacks, sunglasses, mountaineering gear and even crossbows and paint guns. There is a lethal selection of knives and swords, books on survival techniques and a good range of surveillance electronics.

They also sell some less military clothes, such as denim shirts, oilskin drover coats and leather jackets. Although mostly for the professional or military enthusiast, this well produced catalogue also has plenty for anyone interested in outdoor activities. A Japanese language version is available for $5.

Winnipeg Fur Exchange
314 Ross Avenue, Winnipeg, MB R3A 0L4, Canada.
Tel: 204 942 3333 *Fax:* 204 957 0330

Catalogue:	Free
Goods:	Clothes & hunting accessories
Countries sent to:	Asia, Europe, USA
Methods of payment:	Visa, Mastercard, Amex, Cheque, Bank Transfer

An excellent 136 page colour catalogue of Canadian clothes, boots and what might be described as hunting accessories. Most of the clothes are tough, practical and suitable for cold climates, though there are also shirts, jeans (Lee) and blouses. There are dozens of outdoor jackets, in wool, cotton, leather and fur, along with hats and shirts. They also carry a range of Australian clothing, including the long oilskin Drover coats (similar to Barbours but with the option of fur linings).

There is an interesting selection of shoes, from moccasins through cowboy boots to tough, waterproof 'hunting' boots, similar to the American Timberland look. There are even specialist cold-climate boots, which are said to keep feet warm in temperatures of –40ºC! In short too much to describe in a short entry but well worth a look. Men's down-filled jackets are priced at Canadian $155, leather versions start at $270 or so and go up to $350. Leather moccasins are between $30 – $40, while a pair of cowboy boots sell at $170. Insulated, Gortex hunting boots are $220 but there are cheaper versions for around $100.

PHOTOGRAPHY

Adorama
42 West 18th Street, New York, NY 10011, USA. *Tel:* 212 741 0052
Fax: 212 463 7223

Catalogue:	$5
Goods:	Cameras, video equipment
Countries sent to:	World
Methods of payment:	Visa, Mastercard, Amex, Cheque, Bank Transfer

Adorama regularly advertise in the US photographic press but also produce a free 32 page black and white catalogue listing a selection of products. Their $5 version is a magnificent 250 pages and contains virtually everything available in the photographic and video world.

Along with cameras, video equipment, lenses and darkroom equipment, Adorama also sell books and a range of secondhand cameras. A Nikon N5005 SLR sells for $289.95, a JVC GRM3U VHS-C video camera for $559.95.

Photographer's Catalog
Calumet Photographic Inc., 890 Supreme Drive, Bensenville, IL 60106, USA. *Tel:* 708 860 7447 *Fax:* 708 860 5168

Catalogue:	Free
Goods:	Photographic equipment & supplies
Countries sent to:	World
Methods of payment:	Visa, Mastercard, Amex, Cheque, Bank Transfer

A 232 page colour catalogue for the serious photographer. Very well produced, it features 35mm and large format cameras, lighting and darkroom equipment, films, paper, books and videos. An extensive index at the back helps keep track of the impressive stock. Prices are too numerous to mention but generally lower than in the UK or Europe.

Cambridge Camera Exchange

7th Avenue & 13th Street, New York, NY 10011, USA.
Tel: 212 675 8600 *Fax:* 212 463 0093

Catalogue:	Free
Goods:	Cameras & photographic equipment
Countries sent to:	World
Methods of payment:	Visa, Mastercard, Amex, Cheque, Bank Draft

We did not receive this catalogue in time, but are told it covers a wide range of cameras and photographic equipment at competitive prices.

Cleartone Hi-Fi & Video

235 Blackburn Road, Bolton, Lancs BL1 8HB, United Kingdom.
Tel: 0204 31423 *Fax:* 0204 389214

Catalogue:	n/a
Goods:	Photographic, video & hi-fi equipment
Countries sent to:	World
Methods of payment:	Visa, Mastercard, Amex, Diners Club, Cheque, Bank Transfer

Cleartone do not publish a catalogue but you can contact them direct for information on a wide selection of hi-fi, video and photographic equipment. They also sell security systems.

47th Street Photo

455 Smith Street, Brooklyn, NY 11231, USA. *Tel:* 718 722 4750
Fax: 718 722 3510

Catalogue:	$3
Goods:	Photographic & video equipment, TVs, computers & electronics
Countries sent to:	World
Methods of payment:	Visa, Mastercard, Amex, Cheque, Bank Draft

47th Street Photo call their 150 page black and white catalogue 'The Source' and it certainly is one of the best places to buy a huge range of goods at excellent prices. They do not just sell cameras either, but also computers (including Toshiba laptops), video equipment, TVs, personal stereos, hi-fi, radar detectors, calculators, copiers and fax machines, home appliances (irons, vacuums, microwave ovens etc.), phones, watches and a lot more. And to make things even better, they stock video and TV systems in a variety of formats, so you can buy PAL equipment here.

Prices are far too numerous to mention but you can be sure that they are amongst the most competitive in the US. This is one of those catalogues you can't really do without.

Frank's Highland Park Camera

5715 N. Figueroa Street, Los Angeles, CA 90042, USA.
Tel: 213 255 5151 *Fax:* 213 255 1036

Catalogue:	$7
Goods:	Photographic equipment
Countries sent to:	World
Methods of payment:	Visa, Amex, Bank Transfer

Again, we did not receive this catalogue in time but it is said to include cameras, photographic accessories and video equipment.

Global Cameras Ltd

233 Station Road, Harrow, Middlesex HA1 2TB, United Kingdom.
Tel: 081 427 7492 *Fax:* 081 427 1717

Catalogue:	n/a
Goods:	Photographic & video camera equipment
Countries sent to:	World
Methods of payment:	Visa, Mastercard, Cheque, Bank Transfer

Global Cameras sell a range of cameras and video equipment. They do not issue a catalogue but advertise widely in the international and domestic photographic press.

Norman Camera & Video
3602 W. Westnedge, Kalamazoo, MI 49008, USA. *Tel:* 616 343 0460
Fax: 616 343 6410

Catalogue:	Free
Goods:	Photographic equipment & supplies
Countries sent to:	World
Methods of payment:	Visa, Mastercard, Cheque, Bank Transfer

The catalogue was out of print as we went to press, but we gather this company sells a wide range of cameras, photographic accessories and video equipment, including camcorders.

Techno Retail Ltd
Unit 9, Hampton Farm Industrial Estate, Feltham, Middlesex, United Kingdom. *Tel:* 081 898 9934 *Fax:* 081 894 4652

Catalogue:	Free
Goods:	Cameras, video & electronic goods
Countries sent to:	World
Methods of payment:	Visa, Mastercard, Amex, Diners Club, Cheque, Bank Transfer

Techno is a very successful high street chain in the UK but also operate a mail order department. They carry a wide range of cameras and lenses along with accessories such as filters, film and cases. They also have an excellent selection of video equipment, from basic camcorders up to semi-professional machines, editing desks, monitors, VCRs and so on. Lastly, they stock personal hi-fis and palmtop computers such as the Psion Series 3 and Sharp ZQ machines. And of course they sell batteries, blank cassettes and videos.

A Canon EOS 1000FN 35mm SLR is £360, a Sony FX200 video camera £600 and JVC HR-D980 VCR £500.

Zone VI Studios Inc.
PO Box 219, Newfane, VT 05345, USA. *Tel:* 802 257 5161
Fax: 802 257 5165

Catalogue:	Free
Goods:	Large format cameras
Countries sent to:	World
Methods of payment:	Visa, Mastercard, Amex, Diners Club, Cheque, Bank Transfer

Zone VI is a well-known photographic specialist not just in the US but throughout the world. They sell their own brand of large format cameras, enlargers and darkroom equipment along with books and other accessories. The emphasis is on quality, something well reflected in their attractive 58 page colour catalogue. The owner, Fred Picker, is not only an expert but an enthusiast and both these qualities appear in the excellent copy. He also produces a newsletter on large format photography.

The cameras are expensive but worth the money. An 8" x 10" wooden camera with bellows and gold-plated hardware is $2,200, with lens board extra. A Zone VI enlarger comes to around $2,000 once all the extras have been added in.

RECORDINGS

Adventures in Cassettes

5353 Nathan Lane, Minneapolis, MN 55442, USA. *Tel:* 612 553 2000
Fax: 612 553 0424

Catalogue:	Free
Goods:	Cassettes & CDs
Countries sent to:	World
Methods of payment:	Visa, Mastercard, Amex, Cheque, Bank Transfer

Despite the name, this company does not only sell cassettes but also has a line of CDs. The 24 page colour catalogue is broken down into: Rock and Roll, Classical, Country, Broadway, Inspirational, Easy Listening, New Age, Nature's Magic (i.e. sounds of surf, winds etc.), Health, Children's and Foreign Language.

They also have a selection of old-time American radio programmes on tape (separate catalogue) and 'Pet Problems' (why isn't this company from California?!). These are prepared by 'a professional dog trainer' and are on such subjects as 'Stop Chewing', 'Stop Jumping' and 'Litterbox Training' – all presumably for pets rather than owners.

Cassettes start at around $3.99 and, amazingly, so do CDs, though some of the recordings are not that well known.

American Pie

PO Box 66455, Los Angeles, CA 90066, USA. *Tel:* 310 821 4005
Fax: 310 823 3389

Catalogue:	$5
Goods:	Oldies on 45s, CDs & cassettes
Countries sent to:	World
Methods of payment:	Visa, Mastercard, Bank Transfer, International Money Order

If you are after any 'oldies' this is the ideal catalogue. They sell both original 45 rpm recordings and cassettes and CDs featuring greatest hits. Forty closely typed pages display a vast stock all at very reasonable prices: CDs start at under $10 while the price of 45s depends on how rare they are. They also sell music videos and books.

Audiosonic (Gloucester) Ltd
6 College Street, Gloucester GL1 2NE, United Kingdom.
Tel: 0452 302280

Catalogue:	Free
Goods:	Classical CDs & cassettes
Countries sent to:	World
Methods of payment:	Visa, Mastercard, Cheque

Audiosonic place regular advertisements in that bible for music lovers, *Gramophone* magazine, and this is where you will find most of their prices and special offers. However, they do mail a simple computer printout of price bands according to label. These start at £5 for Naxos, Pickwick, Virgo and so on, and go up to £18 for Virgin and VCK. They also include details of their latest special offers. One advantage is that the company does not charge any postage for UK or overseas orders outside the EC. European customers are charged 50p per disc.

Bath Compact Discs
11 Broad Street, Bath, Avon BA1 5LJ, United Kingdom.
Tel: 0225 464766 *Fax:* 0225 464766

Catalogue:	n/a
Goods:	Classical CDs
Countries sent to:	World
Methods of payment:	Visa, Mastercard, Cheque, Bank Transfer

This company specializes in classical recordings. Although they do not issue a catalogue, most labels are available and they will ship anywhere. The service is therefore suitable for people who know what they want and can order using standard reference works, such as the *Gramophone* listing.

BBC Catalogue
BBC World Service Mail Order, PO Box 76, Bush House, London
WC2B 4PH, United Kingdom. *Tel:* 071 379 4479 *Fax:* 071 497 0498

Catalogue:	£2.50
Goods:	Books, videos & tapes
Countries sent to:	World
Methods of payment:	Visa, Mastercard, Amex, Diners Club, Cheque

Unfortunately this excellent 40 page catalogue selling 'the best of the
BBC by Mail Order' is available everywhere except the UK! Readers
elsewhere can buy videos from 50 years of BBC TV as well as tapes
of favourite radio programmes, a wide selection of books, CDs, some
general gifts and a range of shortwave radios to pick up the World
Service.

Videos start at around £11 and are available only on VHS PAL
format, cassettes from £8. To obtain videos in other formats you
need to order them 'locally'. Here we give contacts for Australia
and the US.

Australia: Head of Marketing, Polygram, Unit A, 122 McEvoy
Street, Alexandria, NSW 2015, Australia. *Tel:* 612 318 8666

Canada & USA: Head of Marketing, CBS Fox, 1330 Avenue of
the Americas, 5th Floor, New York, NY 10019, USA.
Tel: 212 373 4803 *Fax:* 212 373 4800

Berkshire Record Outlet
Route 102, Pleasant Street EE1, Lee, MA 01238, USA.
Tel: 413 243 4080 *Fax:* 413 243 4340

Catalogue:	$3
Goods:	Classical CDs & cassettes
Countries sent to:	World
Methods of payment:	Visa, Mastercard, Cheque, Bank Transfer

Berkshire produces a large 186 page black and white catalogue on
newsprint, so it resembles a small fat newspaper. They sell classical
'close-outs and overruns', i.e. recordings which for some reason are
being sold off cheap. The thousands of recordings are divided into

sections for LPs, cassettes and CDs and within this are listed by record company.

Prices are very competitive, with CDs starting at $6, cassettes at $3 and LPs $2. Hunting through the listings can take time but is worth it. For delivery by DHL (3–9 days worldwide), the charge is $12 for the first item and $1.20 for each additional one. Surface post is cheaper, at $7 and $1.10 respectively, but takes 2–4 months.

Bose Express Music
International Music Company, TAT-Mountain, Framingham, MA 01701, USA. *Tel:* 508 879 7330 *Fax:* 508 875 0604

Catalogue:	$14
Goods:	CDs, cassettes
Countries sent to:	World
Methods of payment:	Visa, Mastercard, Diners Club, Cheque, Bank Transfer

Bose, in that typically American way, claim to be 'the world's most complete music source'. Whether or not this is true, their 288 page catalogue is certainly extensive and lists over 75,000 titles covering virtually every label and taste. The entry on each item is kept brief, just the name, number and price, but otherwise they'd have to issue several volumes. CDs are divided into Rock, Jazz and Nashville in one section and Classical in the other. Within that albums are listed alphabetically.

CDs can be as low as $8 but between $12 and $16 seems average. International orders must be paid for by credit card. In addition there is a $6 handling charge plus $2 per item for postage overseas. This does not make Bose the cheapest source of CDs in the US but they may well stock items you cannot get elsewhere.

CDX Classical

The Olde Coach House, Windsor Crescent, Radyr, South Glamorgan CF4 8AE, United Kingdom. *Tel:* 0222 844443 *Fax:* 0222 842878

Catalogue:	Free
Goods:	CDs
Countries sent to:	World
Methods of payment:	Visa, Mastercard, Amex, Diners Club, Cheque, Bank Transfer

CDX can order any CD but specialize in the classical labels. They publish a periodical price list with details of new releases and can quote for older issues. They also sell laserdiscs, CDV, DAT, Digital Compact Cassettes, Mini Discs, LPs and standard cassettes.

Postage is free on all goods within UK, £1 per item to Europe, £2 elsewhere.

C.S.M.T. Mail Order Service

#510, 1701 Centre Street N.W., Calgary, AB T2E 8A4, Canada. *Tel:* 403 277 6688 *Fax:* 403 277 6687

Catalogue:	$2
Goods:	CDs, cassettes, books, sheet music
Countries sent to:	World
Methods of payment:	Visa, Cheque, Bank Transfer

C.S.M.T. stands for the Canadian Society for Musical Tradition, which was set up to conserve and promote Canadian folk music. A non-profit making corporation, it produces a 68 page black and white catalogue listing folk music recordings on CD, vinyl and cassette.

It costs Canadian $20 to join the society, which provides a copy of the catalogue and $2 off every item. Alternatively you can order the catalogue without joining for $2. CDs are $21 ($19 for members), cassettes from $10.

Elderly Instruments

1100 North Washington, PO Box 14210, Lansing, MI 4890, USA.
Tel: 517 372 7890 *Fax:* 517 372 5155

Catalogue:	$2
Goods:	CDs, records, cassettes & instruments
Countries sent to:	World
Methods of payment:	Visa, Mastercard, Diners Club, Bank Transfer

Elderly Instruments, despite its name, sells not only new instruments but also CDs, cassettes, videos and books – in fact anything connected to music. They have excellent instructional books, videos and cassettes as well as music simply for listening to. There are five different catalogues: Books & Videos; Records, Cassettes & CDs; Acoustic Instruments & Accessories; Electric Instruments & Accessories and finally a monthly Used Instrument List.

The main catalogues are around 84 pages, well laid out and comprehensive. When requesting one, be sure to ask for the special international order form. Instructional cassettes start around $5.50 and are available for just about every instrument imaginable. Videos start at $16.50, but are of course in US format (see COMPATIBILITY, above, for details). CDs start at around $12. There is a $2.50 handling charge per order; surface mail is $6.55 for up to 2lb while air mail is $9.25 for 1lb (to UK, other destinations may vary).

Laser Library Ltd

PO Box 145, Ipswich, Suffolk IP8 4LQ, United Kingdom.
Tel: 0473 658155 *Fax:* 0473 658155

Catalogue:	Free
Goods:	Laserdiscs, videodiscs
Countries sent to:	World
Methods of payment:	Visa, Mastercard, Cheque, Bank Transfer

The Laser Library is an invaluable source for the increasingly popular laserdiscs. They carry a wide range of discs which start at around £16, including classical titles. They also stock CDV albums. Their catalogue is essentially a simple price list, but with many discs discounted it seems well worth investigating. It is not necessary to join the library to order.

Macfarland-Baliverne Ltd

Box 57202, Jackson Station, Hamilton, ON L8P 4X1, Canada.

Catalogue:	Free
Goods:	Classical CDs & cassettes
Countries sent to:	World
Methods of payment:	Cheque, Bank Transfer

A specialist mail order company, Macfarland-Baliverne produces a monthly (actually 17 times a year) catalogue-cum-newsletter 'Oversampling'. This 20 page booklet contains descriptions of their latest stock of classical CDs.

Prices vary, starting at around Canadian $20 for a single CD up to $60 for a boxed set. They will also track down hard-to-find albums and are small enough to have a personal relationship with their customers.

MDT Classics Ltd

6 Old Blacksmiths Yard, Sadlergate, Derby, Derbyshire DE1 3PD, United Kingdom. *Tel:* 0332 368251 *Fax:* 0332 383594

Catalogue:	Free
Goods:	Classical CDs
Countries sent to:	World
Methods of payment:	Visa, Mastercard, Diners Club, Cheque

MDT Classics specialize in exporting CDs to the EC, although they will ship anywhere. Their simple 12 page black and white catalogue is really no more than a price list of labels – virtually every one in existence. Prices start as low as £4.50 for budget editions, with postage free within the UK and £1 per disc to the rest of the EC. Interested readers therefore need to know the label and number of any recording they wish to order.

Music Hunter
60 East 42 Street, Suite 311o, New York, NY 10165, USA.
Tel: 212 687 5039 *Fax:* 212 687 5041

Catalogue:	n/a, see below
Goods:	CDs, laserdiscs, cassettes etc.
Countries sent to:	World
Methods of payment:	Visa, Mastercard, Amex, Cheque, Bank Transfer

Music Hunter does not issue its own catalogue but offers a service to find virtually any recording from anywhere in the world. They have over 100,000 titles on their database and pride themselves on a fast efficient service. This is not restricted to any one type of music but covers classical, rock, dance, independent labels and so on. They also stock videos (VHS American format) and laserdiscs.

They recommend using the Schwann catalogues of current recordings, which they will ship overseas at $13.99 for the Schwann Spectrum (non-classical) and $19.99 for the Schwann Opus (classical). No information was available on prices of CDs.

The Music Shop
West Haddon NN6 7AA, United Kingdom. *Tel:* 0788 510693
Fax: 0788 510693

Catalogue:	Free
Goods:	Classical CDs & laserdiscs
Countries sent to:	World
Methods of payment:	Visa, Mastercard, Cheque, Bank Transfer

The Music Shop advertises regularly in *Gramophone* magazine but does not produce a separate catalogue. However, they will send out a simple price list divided up by label. Apart from CDs they also sell videos (VHS PAL) and laserdiscs.

The 'Original' Kids' Video Store
PO Box 609, Station K, Toronto, ON M4P 2H1, Canada.
Tel: 416 483 4104

Catalogue:	$2
Goods:	Pre-recorded children's videos
Countries sent to:	World
Methods of payment:	Visa, Mastercard, Bank Draft

This is said to be the biggest outlet for children's videos in Canada. The A4 format 36 page directory lists hundreds of titles divided up into different subjects. Prices are around Canadian $18 but remember that these are American, not British, format.

Records International
PO Box 1140, Goleta, CA 93116, USA. *Tel:* 805 687 0327
Fax: 805 687 0327

Catalogue:	Free
Goods:	CDs
Countries sent to:	World
Methods of payment:	Visa, Mastercard, Cheque, Bank Draft

Records International issue their catalogue monthly with details of rare classical recordings from around the world. They also produce their own recordings. The 16 page catalogues contain long, knowledgeable descriptions of each work. Prices vary, starting at around $12.

Roots & Rhythm
6921 Stockton Avenue, El Cerrito, CA 94530, USA.
Tel: 510 525 1494 *Fax:* 510 525 2904

Catalogue:	Free
Goods:	CDs, cassettes, LPs, videos
Countries sent to:	World
Methods of payment:	Visa, Mastercard, Cheque, Bank Draft

Roots & Rhythm publish a wonderful 40 page newsletter-cum-catalogue, issued every two months or so, and featuring in-depth reviews of their latest stock of recordings. They also publish 14 separate catalogues specializing in different areas, for which there is a small charge. They cover an enormous range of popular music from all kinds of labels, including Blues, Gospel, Rhythm & Blues, Soul, Doo-Wop, vintage Rock'n'Roll, Country, Folk, World Music, Blue Grass, Rockabilly, Old Timey and Jazz. The company is run by enthusiasts and this shows in the straightforward and honest reviews of the recordings. Recommended.

Roundup Records
1 Camp Street, Cambridge, MA 02141–1194, USA.
Tel: 617 661 6308 *Fax:* 617 868 8769

Catalogue:	See below
Goods:	Recorded music & videos
Countries sent to:	World
Methods of payment:	Visa, Mastercard, Bank Transfer

Roundup produce a master catalogue with over 15,000 recordings and send out six supplementary catalogues a year. Subscriptions for overseas customers are $21 for both and $15 for just the supplementary catalogues.

As well as CDs they sell cassettes, LPs, music videos, books and T-shirts. The range of music, although non-classical, is wide: Blues, Gospel, Blue Grass, Folk, Cajun, Country, World, Jazz, Reggae and Rock and Roll. The catalogues are not simply listings but provide a good deal of background information on each recording.

Cassettes start at around $8 and CDs $12. Roundup have a well-organized international department and are used to sending goods worldwide. For the UK postage is $15 for the first three CDs, $20 for up to five then $3 for each over five.

Scorpio Discount Records, Tapes & CDs

Scorpio Music Inc., 2500 East State Street, Hamilton, NJ 08619, USA.
Tel: 609 890 6000 *Fax:* 609 890 0247

Catalogue:	Free
Goods:	Discount CDs, cassettes, LPs
Countries sent to:	World
Methods of payment:	Visa, Mastercard, Cheque, Bank Transfer

Scorpio sell a huge range of CDs, cassettes and LPs at extraordinarily cheap prices – cassettes start at 50c, CDs at $1.75. However, most of these are the equivalent of 'remainders', i.e. not the latest releases. You may also have to buy lots of 25 at a time. The company publishes a number of price lists for different formats, giving brief descriptions of the label, number, artist and title. They also sell a selection of stereo headphones and blank cassettes.

Silver Service CD

24 Touch Wards, Dunfermline, Fife KY12 7TG, Scotland, United Kingdom. *Tel:* 0383 738159 *Fax:* 0383 726083

Catalogue:	n/a
Goods:	CDs, cassettes, videos
Countries sent to:	World
Methods of payment:	Visa, Mastercard, Amex, Diners Club, Cheque, Bank Transfer

Silver Service do not publish a catalogue but stock a good range of CDs, cassettes and videos (VHS PAL), which they will send anywhere in the world. Readers should contact them direct with their requirements.

Sugar Hill Records

PO Box 55300, Durham NC 27717–5300, USA. *Tel:* 919 489 4349
Fax: 919 489 6080

Catalogue:	Free
Goods:	Blue Grass, folk, singer-songwriters
Countries sent to:	World
Methods of payment:	Visa, Mastercard, Bank Transfer

Sugar Hill sell CDs and cassettes of mainly Blue Grass music. Their
12 page catalogue gives brief details of many recordings, available on
CD, cassette and LP. Shipping is always via surface mail unless
otherwise requested. CDs sell for $15, cassettes and LPs $10–18.

Tandy Records Ltd

24 Islington Row, Five Ways, Birmingham B15 1LJ, United Kingdom.
Tel: 021 455 8866 *Fax:* 021 454 3389

Catalogue:	Free
Goods:	Classical CDs
Countries sent to:	World
Methods of payment:	Visa, Mastercard, Cheque

Tandy issue a packed, closely printed 64 page black and white
catalogue. The huge range of classical CDs are listed by label and
within price bands. These start at around £6 and go up to £14. They
also have a sale selection of CDs and LPs with some genuine bargains.

The descriptions are very brief – not much more than label reference
numbers and title – but Tandy also sell the bible of classical recordings,
'The New Classical Catalogue', published by *Gramophone* magazine
and available for £28 in the UK, £30 to Europe and £33 elsewhere.

SMOKING

Birchall's of Blackpool Ltd
14 Talbot Road, Blackpool, Lancs FY1 1LF, United Kingdom.
Tel: 0253 24218 *Fax:* 0253 291659

Catalogue:	£0.25
Goods:	Cigars, pipes & tobacco
Countries sent to:	World
Methods of payment:	Visa, Mastercard, Cheque, Bank Transfer

A specialist tobacconist, Birchall's was founded in 1834, making it one of the oldest in Britain. They continue to run a retail shop but also have a thriving international mail order business.

The 16 page catalogue describes their wide selection of pipes, cigars and blended tobaccos from around the world. It also includes a range of walking sticks along with coffee to complement the tobacco and snuff. Birchall's has even produced a video 'At Peace with your Pipe', which tells you all you will ever need to know about pipe smoking (VHS, PAL format). Finally, there is a postal pipe repair service and a selection of smoker's accessories.

Pipes start at £16.95 and go up to £80 for handmade Ferndown briar pipes. Cigars, including Havana cigars, are priced from £3 to £30. Bear in mind that tobacco products are likely to incur heavy extra duty.

Georgetown Tobacco & Pipe Stores
3144 M Street, Washington, DC 20007, USA. *Tel:* 202 338 5101
Fax: 202 338 0008

Catalogue:	$2
Goods:	Cigars & tobaccos
Countries sent to:	Europe, Asia, USA, Australasia
Methods of payment:	Visa, Mastercard, Amex, Bank Draft

Georgetown produce two catalogues, one for pipe tobaccos the other featuring cigars and accessories. The first, an attractive 20 page publication, has around 34 different blends of tobacco unique to this company with delightful names such as Jaberwock, Rappahannock and Shenandoah. Each one is given a brief description and most are around $5 for 4oz.

The other catalogue is printed like a glossy newspaper and carries a good selection of pipes, smoking accessories and cigars from a variety of manufacturers. It also sells a few gifts and a line of beautiful pens by Omas (an Italian company). It may be imagination, but both catalogues seem to give off a rather pleasant tobacco aroma.

Irwan Ries and Co.
17 South Wabash Avenue, Chicago, IL 60603 USA.
Tel: 312 372 1306 *Fax:* 312 372 1416

Catalogue:	Free
Goods:	Cigars, pipes, tobacco
Countries sent to:	World
Methods of payment:	Visa, Mastercard, Amex, Bank Draft

Irwan Ries has been selling tobacco, cigars and pipes for 136 years. Unfortunately their catalogue was out of print when we went to press.

W.O. Larsen

9 Amagertorv, DK 1160 Copenhagen K, Denmark. *Tel:* 45 33 122050
Fax: 45 33 156322

Catalogue:	Free
Goods:	Handmade pipes
Countries sent to:	World
Methods of payment:	Visa, Mastercard, Amex, Diners Club, Cheque

This company, founded in 1864, holds a Royal Warrant from the Danish court. Their 4 page catalogue is written in English and features colour photographs of many different types of pipe. All are hand-crafted with a beautiful finish. Prices are available on request.

Andrew Marks, Pipemaker

RDZ Box 1916, Middlebury, VT 05753, USA. *Tel:* 802 462 2112

Catalogue:	Free
Goods:	Briar pipes
Countries sent to:	World
Methods of payment:	Cheque

No catalogue or price list, just a large card with this pipemaker's name and address. Andrew Marks has been handmaking briar pipes since 1969 and will discuss an individual's needs by mail or phone.

SPORTS

Akers Ski
Box 2806, Andover, ME 04216, USA. *Tel:* 207 392 4582
Fax: 207 392 1225

Catalogue:	$3
Goods:	Cross-country ski equipment
Countries sent to:	World
Methods of payment:	Visa, Mastercard, Cheque, Bank Transfer

A very small company, Akers specialize in cross-country ski equipment and they do not sell downhill skis. Strictly for the enthusiast, their 40 page, black and white catalogue describes skis, boots, poles, books, videos, some clothes and gloves. Postage on some items can be expensive.

A pair of Asnes Tur-Langren wooden skis cost $140, a pair of Alpina NN2 102 boots $65 and a pair of Fischer RCS Skating racing skis $375.

Barts Waterskier Catalog
Barts, PO Box 294, North Webster, IN 46555, USA.
Tel: 219 834 7666 *Fax:* 219 834 4246

Catalogue:	$5
Goods:	Watersports equipment
Countries sent to:	World
Methods of payment:	Visa, Mastercard, Amex, Cheque, Bank Draft

This colourful 52 page catalogue is full of all sorts of watersports equipment. This includes waterskis, wet-suits, tow ropes, lifejackets, boat launches, marine electronics and toys. They have an interesting range of swimsuits which allow you to tan all over as well as accessories for boats and a number of lilos and other inflatables.

Berry Scuba Company

6674 Northwest Highway, Chicago, IL 60631, USA.
Tel: 312 763 1626 *Fax:* 312 775 1815

Catalogue:	Free
Goods:	Scuba equipment
Countries sent to:	World
Methods of payment:	Visa, Mastercard, Amex, Cheque, Bank Transfer

This company has been in the business of supplying all sorts of scuba equipment for 35 years and can truly be said to be experts in the field. However, their catalogue did not arrive in time so we are unable to comment on the range or prices of goods.

The Boomerang Man

1806 North 3rd Street, Monroe, LA 71201, USA. *Tel:* 318 325 8157
Fax: 318 323 9238

Catalogue:	Free
Goods:	Boomerangs
Countries sent to:	World
Methods of payment:	Visa, Mastercard, Bank Transfer

Rich Harrison is a boomerang nut and his delightful 'catalogue' – 4 pages with mono illustrations – is full of every conceivable variation. Interestingly, boomerangs now come from all round the world – there are even several from Britain – and Harrison gives useful descriptions of each one. Prices are very reasonable, with most selling between $15 and $20, though some go as low as $3. And most important – they come back! As Harrison notes: 'A boomerang is not a boomerang unless it boomerangs'. Profound.

Cabela's
812 13th Avenue, Sidney, NE 69160, USA. *Tel:* 308 254 5505
Fax: 308 254 6102

Catalogue:	Free
Goods:	Sports equipment
Countries sent to:	World
Methods of payment:	Visa, Mastercard, Amex, Diners Club, Cheque, Bank Transfer, International Money Order

No catalogue at the time of going to press, but Cabela's tell us they sell a wide range of sports equipment.

Century Martial Arts
Dept SOF, 1705 National Boulevard, Oklahoma City, OK 73110, USA.
Tel: 405 732 2226 *Fax:* 405 737 8954

Catalogue:	Free
Goods:	Martial arts equipment
Countries sent to:	Asia, Europe, USA, Australasia
Methods of payment:	Visa, Mastercard, Cheque, Bank Draft

'The World's Largest brings you the World's Best', so boasts the front cover of this 86 page colour catalogue for the martial arts. The stock covers uniforms and belts, training equipment and accessories, sparring gear and weapons, along with books and videos. Apparently Chuck Norris shops here and has written an endearing recommendation at the front of the catalogue.

Cycle Goods
2801 Hennepin Avenue South, Minneapolis, MN 55408, USA.
Tel: 612 872 7600 *Fax:* 612 872 0926

Catalogue:	$5
Goods:	Bicycle accessories & parts & also see below
Countries sent to:	World
Methods of payment:	Visa, Mastercard, Amex, Diners Club, Bank Draft

Unfortunately this catalogue was out of print as we went to press but should be re-issued in 1994. It will feature all types of bicycling goods and accessories as well as ice skates, cross-country skis, clothing and rollerblades.

Don's Discount Golf & Tennis
10880 Biscayne Boulevard, Miami, FL 33161, USA.
Tel: 305 895 0121 *Fax:* 305 895 0292

Catalogue:	n/a
Goods:	Golf & tennis equipment
Countries sent to:	World
Methods of payment:	Visa, Mastercard, Amex, Diners Club

Don's do not produce a catalogue but will send goods overseas. As their name suggests, they sell golf and tennis gear and interested readers should contact them direct with details of their requirements.

Greaves Sports
23 Gordon Street, Glasgow, Scotland G1 3PW, United Kingdom.
Tel: 041 222 3322 *Fax:* 041 221 9200

Catalogue:	Free
Goods:	Sports equipment & clothing
Countries sent to:	World
Methods of payment:	Visa, Mastercard, Amex, Diners Club, Cheque

Greaves sell equipment for virtually every sport except fishing. However, their catalogue was not available as we went to press – we are told it will be available from Christmas 1993.

Holabird Sports Discounters
Rossville Industrial Park, 9008 Yellow Brick Road, Baltimore, USA.
Tel: 410 687 6400 *Fax:* 410 687 7311

Catalogue:	Free
Goods:	Tennis & squash racquets
Countries sent to:	World
Methods of payment:	Visa, Mastercard, Cheque

Holabird issue a tightly printed 8 page catalogue/price list featuring tennis racquets from many different manufacturers including Prince, Head, Rossignol, Slazenger, Wilson, Dunlop, Yonex, Mizuno, Fox, Yamaha, Wimbledon and others. They also stock squash racquets, sports bags, some clothing and an excellent range of shoes for tennis, squash, running, aerobics and walking (including Timberland).

The company prides itself on keeping prices low and seems to live up to its promise of 'the lowest prices anywhere'. A Prince CTS Thunderstick tennis racquet is $116, a Slazenger Mystique $144, a Yonex RD-3 Midplus $92. A pair of Addidas Advantage tennis shoes are $45, New Balance CT 500's $37, Reebok Aerobic Lite $50, Timberland 8" $80.

Northwest River Supplies
2009 S. Main, Moscow, ID 83843, USA. *Tel:* 208 882 2382
Fax: 208 883 4787

Catalogue:	Free
Goods:	Watersports equipment
Countries sent to:	World
Methods of payment:	Visa, Mastercard, International Money Order

Self-styled 'Paddlesports Supplier to the World', this company does indeed issue a comprehensive catalogue. Fifty-two colour pages display clothes, inflatable boats, oars, canoes, helmets and accessories. All are high quality, clearly described and illustrated with excellent photographs.

PMC Discounts

2851 John Street, Markham, ON L3R 5R7, Canada.
Tel: 416 474 0404 *Fax:* 416 474 0407

Catalogue:	Free
Goods:	Flying Discs
Countries sent to:	World
Methods of payment:	Visa, Cheque, Amex, Bank Transfer

This is 'Canada's largest sportsdisc source', although how hard that would be to achieve can only be guessed at. More well known as Frisbees, they come in a bewildering variety along with books, videos and even kits for playing 'disc golf'. The 20 page catalogue has clear descriptions, advice on throwing and other information for enthusiasts.

Discs are all around Canadian $12 with reductions for large orders.

Rayco Tennis Products

1434 University Avenue, San Diego, CA 92103, USA.
Tel: 619 295 0325 *Fax:* 619 295 2829

Catalogue:	Free
Goods:	Tennis racquets
Countries sent to:	World
Methods of payment:	Visa, Mastercard, Cheque, Bank Transfer

This specialist company just sells tennis equipment, with an emphasis on racquets. They publish a simple brochure and price list. You can choose the frame and then have it strung with any one of a wide variety of strings. They also stock grips, socks and a small range of shoes and clothes. The owner, Bob Ray, has also invented a series of extra-long racquets, up to the legal limit of 32". He claims these are easier to use and promote greater accuracy.

A Head graphite frame comes in at $70, a Yonex at $50 and a Prince Synergy $100 (all need stringing). A pair of Nike Air Tech III shoes is $55, while the extra-long 'Longfeather' racquets start at $40 rising to $100.

Reliable Racing Supply

630 Glen Street, Queensbury, NY 12804, USA. *Tel:* 518 793 5677
Fax: 518 793 6491

Catalogue:	$1
Goods:	Ski equipment & clothes
Countries sent to:	Asia, Europe, Australasia
Methods of payment:	Visa, Mastercard, Amex, Diners Club, Cheque

This 32 page colour catalogue is a must for any serious skier. Packed
with all sorts of accessories, tools, clothes and of course skis, it has a
number of items which never seem to make it across the Atlantic.
These include various training aids, such as the 'Techni-ski', which
enables one to practise on a road or pavement. However, there is only
a limited line of boots and the emphasis is on the proficient skier.

Ski Limited

7825 South Avenue, Youngstown, OH 44512, USA.
Tel: 216 758 5214 *Fax:* 216 758 8652

Catalogue:	$2.50
Goods:	Water skiing equipment
Countries sent to:	World
Methods of payment:	Visa, Mastercard, Amex, Cheque

We did not receive this catalogue but gather it covers water skiing
equipment, including the skis themselves, and associated boat supplies.

Skin Diver

1632 South 250th Street, Des Moines, WA 98198, USA.
Tel: 206 878 1613 *Fax:* 206 824 3323

Catalogue:	n/a
Goods:	Wet suits
Countries sent to:	World
Methods of payment:	Visa, Mastercard

Skin Diver have been making custom wet suits for over 25 years and
provide an excellent service for customers the world over. They do not
publish a catalogue but send out a small brochure with details of their

products, instructions on how to measure yourself and an order form.

A basic one-piece suit for a man is around $90, a two-piece just over $100. You can then add various other options, such as boots, gloves, face mask and so on. There are different versions for skin diving and water skiing.

Tecfen Corporation
58 60 C Hollister Avenue, Santa Barbara, CA 93117, USA.
Tel: 805 967 1153 *Fax:* 805 967 1295

Catalogue:	Free
Goods:	Mountaineering equipment
Countries sent to:	World
Methods of payment:	Visa, Mastercard, Bank Transfer

Tecfen is a manufacturer and supplier of equipment to search and rescue teams. Customers include police forces and emergency services.

The 51 page glossy catalogue is printed in full colour with very detailed descriptions of the items on offer. This is important as the strength and durability of all the equipment is paramount. The range covers ropes, pulleys, harnesses, webbing, and lights and signalling equipment. There are good sections on medical products and water rescue equipment.

There is also a useful section of books and catalogues including High Angle Rescue Techniques, Search and Rescue Fundamentals and the CMC Rope Rescue Manual.

TECHNOLOGY

Comcor

7 Doell Plaza, Yonkers, NY 10704, USA. *Tel:* 914 968 2100
Fax: 914 968 2155

Catalogue:	Free
Goods:	Phone equipment
Countries sent to:	World
Methods of payment:	Visa, Mastercard, Amex, Diners Club, Cheque, Bank Draft

No catalogue as we went to press but they sell a selection of telephones and accessories.

Darentek Corporation

Box 58, 325 Jack Street, Kemptville, Ontario, ON K0G 1J0, Canada.
Tel: 613 258 6106 *Fax:* 613 258 7962

Catalogue:	Free
Goods:	Solar power equipment
Countries sent to:	World
Methods of payment:	Mastercard, Cheque, Bank Transfer

Darentek is one of Canada's leading suppliers and manufacturers of photoelectric technology. They sell a range of solar equipment to generate electricity and purify water.

There is no catalogue but rather a number of fact sheets describing each product. These are not cheap and only really suitable for people seriously considering this form of renewable energy. However, for some users this may well be worth while. For example, one product pumps water for cattle and is powered entirely by the sun.

El-Fence Ltd
Moose Harbour, RR #1, Liverpool, NS B0T 1K0, Canada.
Tel: 902 354 2889 *Fax:* 902 354 3255

Catalogue:	$2, refundable
Goods:	Fences & waterpumps
Countries sent to:	Europe, USA
Methods of payment:	Cheque, Bank Transfer

El-Fence are so called because of their main product range, electric
fences. These are designed to keep animals out of certain areas. They
specify bears from beehives and coons from gardens. Strangely, they
only export to the UK in Europe so may not have a large customer
base. However, they also sell an ingenious waterpump which requires
no power source other than the river itself and a range of other goods
for the farm.

Energy Alternatives
Morewater Road, RR #1, Lasqueti Island, BC V0R 2J0, Canada.
Tel: 604 333 8898 *Fax:* 604 333 8898

Catalogue:	$10
Goods:	Renewable energy equipment
Countries sent to:	World
Methods of payment:	Visa, Mastercard, Cheque, Bank Draft

The 72 page catalogue isn't just a list of goods but a complete guide to
renewable energy. With its many helpful articles on all aspects of this
technology it is the perfect introduction to the subject. They sell
photovoltaics, chargers, solar hot water systems, wind generators,
complete systems and just about everything needed to lessen your
reliance on traditional energy sources. An excellent publication.

LFI/Bestek Group Inc.
19–2485 Lancaster Road, Ottawa, ON K1B 5L1, Canada.
Tel: 613 523 5211 *Fax:* 613 523 5211

Catalogue:	Free
Goods:	Solar power products
Countries sent to:	World
Methods of payment:	Cheque, Bank Transfer

No catalogue but rather some fact sheets describing LFI's products. These are advanced solar lighting systems. They are also a security consultancy, offering high-tech protection solutions, though obviously this is not something available through the mail!

Matrix Energy Inc.
64 Heritage Way, Kirkland, PQ H9J 2N2, Canada.
Tel: 514 630 5630 *Fax:* 514 426 9123

Catalogue:	Free
Goods:	Solar products & wind turbines
Countries sent to:	World
Methods of payment:	Visa, Bank Transfer

This comprehensive and informative 76 page catalogue tells you all you need to know about solar power for the home. With complete home power systems as well as individual components such as solar modules, batteries, pumps and mounting frames, it makes the prospect of 'free' electricity a real possibility. They also sell wind turbines, hydroelectric power systems and hot water solar panels. On a smaller scale are solar powered fans, torches, bike lights, battery rechargers and – my favourite – a solar powered hat with built-in fan!

Prometheus Energy
400 Creditstone Road, Unit 33, Concord, ON L4K 3Z3, Canada.
Tel: 416 660 7868 *Fax:* 416 660 7868

Catalogue:	Free
Goods:	Renewable energy products
Countries sent to:	World
Methods of payment:	Mastercard, Bank Transfer

This informative 68 page catalogue does not simply detail products for sale but is a comprehensive introduction to solar powered energy – it even includes a brief synopsis of the Promethean myth. The company specializes in solar electricity, wind energy, hydroelectric units and all the equipment you need to make use of these renewable resources. For anyone seriously interested in the subject, this is a must.

TOOLS

Furnima Industrial Carbide Inc.
Biernacki Road, Box 308, Barry's Bay, ON K0J 1B0, Canada.
Tel: 613 756 3657 *Fax:* 613 756 1400

Catalogue:	Free
Goods:	Carbide tooling
Countries sent to:	World
Methods of payment:	Visa, Mastercard, Cheque, Bank Draft

Furnima produce and sell carbide tooling for woodworkers. These include router bits, shaper cutters and saw blades. They specialize in unique and unusual profiles, many of which are difficult to get from other sources.

Garrett Wade
161 Avenue of the Americas, New York, NY 100013–1299, USA.
Tel: 212 807 1155 *Fax:* 212 255 8552

Catalogue:	$4
Goods:	Woodworking tools & supplies
Countries sent to:	World
Methods of payment:	Visa, Mastercard, Amex, Cheque, Bank Transfer

Garrett Wade produce a marvellous 228 page colour catalogue full of every conceivable woodworking tool as well as a selection of books. Beautifully illustrated with helpful descriptions they sell only the best and do it brilliantly.

House of Tools
100 Mayfield Common, Edmonton, AB T5P 4K9, Canada.
Tel: 403 486 0123 *Fax:* 403 486 2275

Catalogue:	Free
Goods:	Woodworking tools
Countries sent to:	World
Methods of payment:	Visa, Mastercard, Cheque, Bank Transfer

House of Tools produce a wonderful 75 page colour catalogue packed with all sorts of woodworking tools. These include a good range of power tools, from drills and sanders to bandsaws and routers as well as clamps, safety wear, hammers, drill bits, chisels, squares and so on. Prices are guaranteed to be the lowest in Canada and the company will ship anywhere. They also carry a good number of books on woodworking.

A DeWalt circular saw is Canadian $230, a power screwdriver $140, a set of 6 Record chisels in a case $67, a Marples square $20.

Lee Valley Tools Ltd
PO Box 6295 Stn J, 1080 Morrison Drive, Ottawa, ON K2A 1T4, Canada. *Tel:* 613 596 0350 *Fax:* 613 596 3073

Catalogue:	Free
Goods:	Speciality woodworking tools
Countries sent to:	World
Methods of payment:	Visa, Mastercard, Cheque, Bank Transfer

An 80 page colour catalogue selling high-class woodworking tools. These range from traditional items such as brass and wood marking gauges, up to the latest hi-tech tools (though there is only a limited range of power tools). For serious woodworkers, this is a terrific catalogue, with pages of chisels, turning tools, books, vices and benches.

A set of 5 L.V. chisels is Canadian $40 a 9" Record bench plane $60, a Sandvik 26" crosscut saw $30.

McFeely's
712 12th Street, PO Box 3, Lynchburg, VA 24505–0003, USA.
Tel: 804 846 2729 *Fax:* 804 847 7136

Catalogue:	$2
Goods:	Woodworking tools
Countries sent to:	World
Methods of payment:	Visa, Mastercard, Bank Transfer

Although we did not have a chance to see this catalogue before going to press, we understand it features an extensive range of woodworking tools.

Wood Carvers Supply Inc.
PO Box 7500, Englewood, FL 34295–7500, USA. *Tel:* 813 698 0222
Fax: 813 698 0329

Catalogue:	$3
Goods:	Wood carving tools
Countries sent to:	World
Methods of payment:	Visa, Mastercard, Amex, Cheque, Bank Transfer

Founded in 1955, this company stocks all kinds of supplies for carving, from chisels through sharpeners to power tools, books and plans – in all over 2000 items. The 78 page colour catalogue is well designed with plenty of informative text written by enthusiasts. One particular product struck me – a pair of gloves made out of the same material as bullet-proof vests, to prevent cuts when carving.

Woodchips Carving Supplies
8521 Eastlake Drive, Burnaby, B.C., V5A 4T7 V5M 1M2, Canada.
Tel: 604 421 1101 *Fax:* 604 421 1052

Catalogue:	Free
Goods:	Wood carving tools
Countries sent to:	World
Methods of payment:	Visa, Mastercard, Cheque, Bank Transfer

Woodchips is THE source for wood carving supplies. Their 70 page catalogue features power tools by Foredom, NSK and Dremmel, has dozens of wood carving chisels and knives along with sharpening equipment, rasps, sanding drums, drill bits and so on. They also stock a large range of books and videos on carving and woodwork.

Woodline the Japan Woodworker
1731 Clement Avenue, Alameda, CA 94501, USA. *Tel:* 510 521 1810
Fax: 510 521 1864

Catalogue:	$1.50
Goods:	Japanese woodworking tools
Countries sent to:	World
Methods of payment:	Visa, Mastercard

This fascinating 72 page black and white catalogue features an excellent range of traditional Japanese woodworking tools. For example, there are the Noko Giri, or saws, which cut on the pull rather than push stroke, thus allowing for delicate, accurate work. There are also carving chisels, hammers, planes and knives. In addition the catalogue carries a selection of Western tools, including power saws and sanders, along with books on woodworking.

TOYS

B.C. Playthings
1065 Marine Drive, North Vancouver, BC V7P 1S6, Canada.
Tel: 604 986 4111

Catalogue:	Free
Goods:	Pre-school, educational toys
Countries sent to:	World
Methods of payment:	Visa, Mastercard, Cheque, Bank Transfer

A 36 page black and white catalogue specializing in educational toys. The founder, Pat Gallaher, was dissatisfied with the range of toys for his children so started a business dedicated to items that both stretched and entertained children. Despite the slightly worthy feel of this enterprise, the catalogue is full of interesting products suitable for toddlers upwards.

There are games, puzzles, construction kits, science sets, art supplies, books and cassettes, all professionally chosen to help children develop. Wooden puzzles start at Canadian $9, Bio wooden train sets sell for $50 upwards and all cassettes are $14.

Ron Fuller Toys
Laxfield, Woodbridge, Suffolk, United Kingdom. *Tel:* 0986 798 317

Catalogue:	Free
Goods:	Handmade toys
Countries sent to:	World
Methods of payment:	Cheque, Bank Draft

Ron Fuller has been making his unique toys and automata since the 1960s. They are beautifully made, somewhat bizarre creations, with lots of moving parts. He does not issue a catalogue but sends out a number of sheets showing past work. This includes a set of three circus lions who automatically open their mouths, an angry couple one of whom keeps putting his fingers in his ears and a Doctor who actually writes out a prescription – illegible of course!

Hamleys
188–196 Regent Street, London W1R 6BT, United Kingdom.
Tel: 071 734 3161 *Fax:* 071 434 2655

Catalogue:	n/a
Goods:	Toys & games
Countries sent to:	World
Methods of payment:	Visa, Mastercard

Hamleys is perhaps the world's most famous toy shop, situated on Regent Street in London and a Mecca for all children. They carry an enormous range of toys and games (over 35,000 items) and used to issue a catalogue. However, they no longer do this but do continue to operate an international mail order business. Interested readers should contact them directly with their requirements. This is not ideal but if you do know what you want the service works well.

Michael Lazarus Associates
242/244 St John Street, London EC1V 4PH, United Kingdom.
Tel: 071 250 3988 *Fax:* 071 608 0370

Catalogue:	Free
Goods:	Kites & dog raincoats
Countries sent to:	World
Methods of payment:	Visa, Mastercard, Cheque, Bank Transfer

This company sells the famous Ferrari kites which are claimed to be the easiest kites to fly in the world. Their Sky Ram model has no struts or frame but works on the same principle as a paraglider, namely air filling a series of cells. This means they can be flown in very light winds, cannot break and fold up small enough to stuff into a pocket. The single page leaflet gives further information on this and also a stunt kite – however, it does not mention the fascinating dog raincoat which also appeared on our returned questionnaire!

Sky Ram kites start at £18.95 and go up to £48 for the largest size. The stunt kites are £39 rising to £58.

Part 3
APPENDICES

Appendix I

SHIPPING COSTS

These vary from company to company and from country to country.
The tables only offer a rough guide. Check with individual suppliers
for full details on specific items.

US to Europe Shipping Costs in US $

Weight *lb*	Federal Express *(1–2 weeks)*	Airmail *(2–3 weeks)*	Surface *(2–3 months)*
0 – 1	35	9.25	6.55
1 – 2	35	14.25	6.55
2 – 3	35	19.25	8.65
3 – 4	35	24.25	10.75
4 – 5	50	29.25	12.85
5 – 6	50	33.25	14.95
6 – 7	50	37.25	17.05
7 – 8	50	41.25	19.15
8 – 9	50	45.25	21.25
9 – 10	50	49.25	23.35
10 – 11	65	53.25	25.45
11 – 12	65	57.25	27.55
12 – 13	65	61.25	29.65
13 – 14	65	65.25	31.75
14 – 15	65	69.25	33.85
15 – 16	85	73.25	35.95
16 – 17	85	77.25	38.05

17 – 18	85	81.25	40.15
18 – 19	85	85.25	42.25
19 – 20	85	89.25	44.35
20 – 21	85+	93.25	46.45
21 – 22	85+	97.25	48.55

Additional lb: Federal Express: $1.92, Airmail: $4 up to maximum of 66lb, Surface: $2.10

UK Postal Charges

ParcelForce, the part of the Royal Mail which handles parcels, offers three international services:

Datapost: Express delivery, includes insurance. Europe 1 day, USA 1 day, Australia 3 days

Standard: Europe 6 days, USA 8 days, Australia 9 days

Economy: Europe 10 days, USA 28 days, Australia 46 days

The following table gives some idea of costs, in pounds sterling. Full details can be found at any Post Office or toll free on 0800 22 44 66

Service	Weight Kg	EC	Europe	Zone 3	Zone 4	Zone 5	Zone 6
Data	.5	25.00	27.00	26.00	29.00	33.00	36.00
Stand	.5	11.00	12.00	10.00	13.00	13.00	13.00
Ec	.5	9.50	9.50	10.00	13.00	9.00	9.00
Data	1.0	26.50	28.70	28.50	32.30	38.00	41.00
Stand	1.0	11.90	13.50	12.50	15.20	16.30	16.30
Ec	1.0	10.50	10.50	11.60	15.00	10.50	10.50
Data	1.5	28.00	30.40	31.00	35.60	43.00	46.00
Stand	1.5	12.80	15.00	15.00	17.40	19.60	19.60
Ec	1.5	11.50	11.50	13.20	17.00	12.00	12.00
Data	2.0	29.50	32.10	33.50	38.90	48.00	51.00
Stand	2.0	13.70	16.50	17.50	19.60	22.90	22.90
Ec	2.0	12.50	12.50	14.80	19.00	13.50	13.50

Zone 3:   USA & Canada
Zone 4:   Far East & Australasia
Zone 5/6:   Rest of world

Typical Weights of Selected Items

Obviously exact weight varies with each product but this table gives a
rough guide. Small items, such as a tie, still count as the minimum of
1lb so it may be worth ordering several things at once.

Item	Weight in lb	Weight in g/kg
Belt	1	450g
Blouse	1	450g
Briefcase	5	2.26kg
Coat	5	2.26kg
Dress	2	900g
Gloves	1	450g
Jeans	2	900g
Luggage	2	900g
Shirt	1	450g
Shoes (m)	5	2.26kg
Shoes (f)	3	1.36kg
Skirt	1	450g
Suit	4	1.8kg
Sweater	1	450g
Tie	1	450g
Trousers	2	900g

In addition to the weight of the product you have to include the weight
of the packaging. Again, this varies from company to company but
these give some idea:

Weight of goods	Weight of packaging
Under 5lb	1lb
5 –7lb	2lb
Over 7lb	3lb

Insurance

Federal Express includes insurance. For insurance arranged through
Post Offices, see below.

US Mail Service
in US $

Value	Insurance
1 – 50	1.60
50 – 100	2.40
100 – 200	3.50
200 – 300	4.60
300 – 400	5.40
400 – 500	6.20
500 – 600	6.60
600 – 700	6.90
700 – 800	7.20
800 – 900	7.50
900 – 1000	7.80

UK Royal Mail Insurance
in UK £

Value	Insurance
150	1.90
300	2.15
450	2.40
600	2.65
750	2.90
900	3.15
1050	3.40
1200	3.65
1500	3.90

Appendix II

US States & Time Zones

Abbreviation	State	Time zone	GMT difference
AL	Alabama	Central	–6 hours
AR	Arkansas	Central	–6
AZ	Arizona	Mountain	–7
CA	California	Pacific	–8
CO	Colorado	Mountain	–7
CT	Connecticut	Eastern	–5
DC	Washington DC	Eastern	–5
DE	Delaware	Eastern	–5
FL	Florida	Eastern	–5
GA	Georgia	Eastern	–5
IA	Iowa	Central	–6
ID	Idaho	Mountain	–7
IL	Illinois	Central	–6
IN	Indiana	Central	–6
KS	Kansas	Central	–6
KY	Kentucky	Eastern/Central	–5/–6*
LA	Louisiana	Central	–6
MA	Massachusetts	Eastern	–5
MD	Maryland	Eastern	–5
ME	Maine	Eastern	–5
MI	Michigan	Eastern	–5
MN	Minnesota	Central	–6
MO	Missouri	Central	–6
MS	Mississippi	Central	–6
MT	Montana	Mountain	–7

NC	North Carolina	Eastern	−5
ND	North Dakota	Central/Mountain	−6/−7*
NE	Nebraska	Central/Mountain	−6/−7*
NH	New Hampshire	Eastern	−6
NJ	New Jersey	Eastern	−6
NM	New Mexico	Mountain	−7
NV	Nevada	Pacific	−8
NY	New York	Eastern	−5
OH	Ohio	Eastern	−5
OK	Oklahoma	Central	−6
OR	Oregon	Pacific	−8
PA	Pennsylvania	Eastern	−5
RI	Rhode Island	Eastern	−5
SC	South Carolina	Eastern	−5
SD	South Dakota	Central/Mountain	−6/−7*
TN	Tennessee	Central	−6
TX	Texas	Central	−6
UT	Utah	Mountain	−7
VA	Virginia	Eastern	−5
VT	Vermont	Eastern	−5
WA	Washington	Pacific	−8
WI	Wisconsin	Central	−6
WV	West Virginia	Eastern	−5
WY	Wyoming	Mountain	−7

*Time line runs through State.

Appendix III

EC Import Tariff Rates

The list of goods and their rates of duty fills four large volumes. Here we reproduce details of the most common products. Full details are contained in *Customs Tariffs*, published by H.M. Customs and Excise (see under *Further Information*).

Duty on Selected Goods (as % of value)

Carpets	4–14
Footwear	4.6–20
Electrical	4–8.9
Chainsaws	4.5
Vacuum cleaners	4
Mixers	5.1
Shavers	4.6
Hair dryers	6
Hair curlers	6
Microwaves	5.1
Toasters	5.1
Telephones	7.5
Faxes	7.5
Headphones	7
Amplifiers	4.9
Loudspeakers	4.9
Record decks	9.5
Cassette deck (car)	9.5
CD players	9.5
Answering machines	7
Cassette decks	7

Video recorders	14
Tapes	4.9
Records	4.9
CDs	4.9
Transmitters	
(i.e. cordless phones)	4.9
Video cameras	4.9
Radar detectors	6.2
Hi-fi equipment	14
Pagers	12
TVs	14
Burglar alarms	4.4
Lamps	6
Computers	14
Contact lenses	7.5
Sunglasses	7.5
Lenses	7.5
Camera lenses	10
Spectacle frames	5.1
Cameras	7.2
Photocopiers	7.2
Watches	5.1
Clocks	5.8–6.2
Musical instruments	5.8–7.5
Furniture	5.6
Toys	8
Sports equipment	6
Pens	7.2
Silk	3–7.2
Wool	0–17
Cotton	0–10
Denim	10

♦ **WARNING** Some goods originating in South East Asia (including Japan) have different tariffs. These are worked out by the individual company. For example, while CD players made by Sony attract 10% duty, those by Onkyo pay only 8.3%. VHS tapes manufactured in Hong Kong pay 21.9% while those from Korea only 3.8%.

It is therefore worth checking the country and company of origin and working out which attract least duty. See *Further Information*, below.

Prohibited Goods

Certain products are prohibited from being imported and Customs officials will enforce these regulations. Some of the items are clearly undesirable (fire-arms and explosives being obvious examples), others are more arcane.

Goods and Products Prohibited from Import (EC)

Animals
Anglers lead weights (some, not all)
Bees (?!)
Citizen Band Radios
Cordless phones on frequencies not more than 853 MHz*
Counterfeit goods
Explosives
Flick knives
Horror comics (!)
Peat moss
Prison made goods
Radio transmitters which transmit in the 26.1–28MHz band*
Semen of animals (a very popular item, I'm sure)
Whales (too difficult to fit through the letter box)

*For further information on the UK restrictions request the Cordless Telephone Information Sheet (RA 193) from:

Radio Communications Agency
Waterloo Bridge House
Waterloo Road
London
SE1 8AU
Tel: 071 215 2297

In addition, the Royal Mail has some regulations, most of which are shared with postal systems in other countries.

Goods Prohibited From Being Sent by Royal Mail

Pathological specimens – e.g. blood, urine, semen etc., unless by authorised person (doctor, vet etc.)
Illegal drugs
Poisons – any substance which could harm an employee
Living creatures – with certain exceptions
Radioactive materials
Compressed gases
Oxidising material
Corrosives
Asbestos
Flammable liquids
Flammable solids
Paints, varnishes, enamels etc.
Matches
Obscene materials
Counterfeit currency & stamps
Perishable goods

Aerosols and lighters are allowed in certain circumstances. For a copy of the full regulations contact your local Customer Service Centre (see telephone book) or pick up a copy of 'Prohibited & Restricted Goods' from any Post Office.

Protected Species

While not wishing to import a Paraguayan yacari alligator as a pet you might find stores making boots and clothing out of its skin. It is illegal to import the skins of CITES protected animals into countries which are signatories to this UN agreement. These include the US, Canada and the EC. The companies listed in the directory are aware of the legislation and identify in their catalogues which products may be exported to which countries, but if in doubt contact your local Customs office.

Further Information

The four-volume set *H.M. Custom and Excise Tariffs* is carried by most major reference libraries or can be consulted at local Customs and Excise offices (see phone book).

For duty rates on S.E. Asian companies see Volume II, Part II, Chapter 85.

Appendix IV

CONVERSION TABLES

Clothing

MEN'S CLOTHES
Suits & Coats (chest measurements)

UK in	Europe size	USA in	Japan cm
36	46	36	92
38	48	38	96
40	50	40	102
42	54	42	108
44	56	44	112
46	58	46	117
48	60	48	122
50	64	50	127

Shirts

14	36	14	36
14.5	37	14.5	37
15	38	15	38
15.5	39	15.5	39
16	40	16	40
16.5	41	16.5	41
17	42	17	42

Shoes

7	41	8	26
7.5	42	8.5	26.5
8	42	9	27
8.5	43	9.5	27.5
9	43	10	28
9.5	44	10.5	28.5
10	44	11	29
10.5	45	11.5	29.5
11	46	12	30

WOMEN'S CLOTHING SIZES

UK	France/Spain	Italy	Rest Europe	USA	Japan	Canada
8	36	38	34	2/4	7/9	6
10	38	40	36	6	11	8
12	40	42	38	8	13	10
14	42	44	40	10	13/15	12
16	44	46	42	12/14	15/17	14
18	46	48	44	16	19	16

Hosiery

UK	Europe	USA
8	0	8
8.5	1	8.5
9	2	9
9.5	3	9.5
10	4	10
10.5	5	10.5

Shoes

4.5	38	6
5	38	6.5
5.5	39	7
6	39	7.5
6.5	40	8
7	41	8.5

CHILDREN'S CLOTHES

	UK	Europe	USA
Height	43 in	125 cm	
Age	4–5	7	4
	48	135	
	6–7	9	6
	55	150	
	9–10	12	8
	58	155	
	11	13	10
	60	160	
	12	14	12
	62	165	
	13	15	14

Remember – in the UK children's clothes do not attract VAT and so can be a particularly good bargain.

CHILDREN'S SHOES

UK	Europe	USA
2	18	3.5
3	19	4.5
3.5	20	5
4.5	21	6
5.5	22	7
6	23	7.5
7	24	8.5
7.5	25	9
8.5	26	10
9.5	27	11
10	28	11.5
11	29	12.5
11.5	30	13
12.5	31	1
13	32	1.5

Clothing Size Tips

Most catalogues include detailed instructions on how to measure yourself for various items. They also offer your money back or replacement articles if they do not fit properly.

One way of making sure something will be the right size is to take measurements from an item of clothing you already have and you know to fit. You can do this for shoes as well.

MEASUREMENTS

The US still uses inches and feet, yards and miles. The UK, while officially changing to the metric system, has not entirely done so. Europe and Canada are metric while South East Asia uses both systems.

Length

1 centimetre	0.3937 inch	1 inch	2.54 centimetres
1 metre	1.0936 yard	1 foot	30.48 centimetres
1 kilometre	0.6214 mile	1 yard	0.9144 centimetres
		1 mile	1.6093 kilometres

TO CONVERT

Metres to feet	x 3.2810	Inches to centimetres	x 2.5400
Metres to yards	x 1.0936	Feet to centimetres	x 0.3048
Kilometres to miles	x 0.6214	Miles to kilometres	x 1.6214

Weight

1 gram	0.0353 ounces	1 ounce	28.35 grams
1 kilogram	2.2046 pounds	1 pound	0.4536 kilogram

TO CONVERT

Grams to ounces	x 0.0353	Ounces to grams	28.35
Grams to pounds	x 0.0022	Pounds to grams	x 453.60

Appendix V

Electronic Shopping

Electronic shopping is the future. While it is not yet that common the infrastructure is being laid and within a few years we will all be as familiar with it as we now are with cash machines or remote controls.

Put simply it is shopping via your computer screen. A personal computer is hooked up to the service through the phone line. You can then tap into a number of shops on screen. These display their goods and prices rather like a printed catalogue. The main difference is that searching for items is much easier. You simply type in details of the product you are after, say a washing machine or camera, and in a few seconds the screen fills with information on models available. Ordering is equally simple. Just type in your name, address and credit card number along with the reference number of the product. Within a few days the package will be on the doorstep.

Electronic shopping has yet to take off in the UK but is already big business in the USA, with an increasing number of mail order houses adding it to their services. Most of these on-line malls can only be accessed by calling the US direct, which of course can become very expensive. However, there is one which can be used through a local number. This means you pay only for the local phone call and connect charges (around $12 an hour). This system, called CompuServe is a very cheap way of accessing a huge network of electronic shops (and a good many other services besides).

To use it you need a computer and a modem. A one-off fee of around £25 provides software and phone back-up. Charges are then by the hour, but these are very reasonable off peak.

Purchasing aeroplane tickets this way is particularly attractive because the official source (i.e. CompuServe) is based in the USA.

This enables one to benefit from some very cheap offers simply not available in this country (even on flights either to or within the States).

COMPUSERVE PHONE NUMBERS

Country	Toll Free	Direct
Argentina		(54) 1 372 7883
Australia	008 023	(61) 2 410 4555
Canada		(1) 614 457 8650
Chile		(56) 2 696 8807
Germany	0130 4643	(49) 8966 550 222
Japan	0120 22 1200	(81) 3 5471 5806
Korea	080 022 7400	(82) 2 569 5400
New Zealand	0800 441 082	
South Africa		(27) 12 841 2530
Switzerland	155 31 79	
Taiwan		(886) 2 515 7035
UK	0800 289 458	0272 255 111
US	800 848 8990	614 457 8650
Venezuela		(58) 2 793 2984
Elsewhere		(1) 614 457 8650

For a considerable discount on your CompuServe account, quote this ID number: 1000 10 2411.

Appendix VI

USEFUL ADDRESSES

Customs Authorities

Australia
Bureau of Customs,
Department of Business & Consumer Affairs, Canberra, ACT

Belgium
Ministère des Finances
Administration des Douanes et Accises, Cité administrative de l'Etat,
Tour Finances – Boite 37, Boulevard du Jardin Botanique 50,
1010 Bruxelles

Canada
Canadian Chamber of Commerce
55 Metcalfe Street, Suite 1160, Ottawa, K1P 6N4

Denmark
Ministry of Taxation
Central Customs & Tax Administration, Amaliegada 44, DK-1256,
Kobenhavn K

France
Direction Générale de Douanes et Droits Indirects
Ministère de l'Economie, des Finances et du Budget,
23 bis rue de l'Universite, 75700 Paris

Germany
Bundesministeriums der Finanzen
Postfach 13 08, 5300 Bonn 1

Greece
Ministry of Finance
General Directorate of Taxation & Public Property,
Division 14 VAT & Special Taxes, Sina 2–4, 104 72 Athens

Ireland
Office of the Revenue Commissioners
Dublin Castle, Dublin 2

Italy
Ministero delle Finanze
Dipartmento delle Dogane e delle Imposte Indirette,
11 Capo delle Circoscrizione reggente, Roma

Luxembourg
Administration des Douanes
L-2010 Luxembourg

Netherlands
Directoraat-Generaal der Belastingen
Korte Voorhout 7, Postadres Postbu 20201, 2500 EE S-Gravenhage

New Zealand
Ministry of Commerce
PO Box 1473, Bowen State Building, Bowen Street, Wellington 1

Portugal
Ministerio dos Financas
Direccao de Servicos de Administracao dos Impostos Internos,
Rua da Alfandegas 5, 1194 Lisboa

Spain
Direccion General de Aduanas e Impuestos Especiales
Ministerio de Economica y Hacienda, Guzman El Bueno 137, 28003
Madrid

United Kingdom
HM Customs & Excise
New Kings Beam House, 22 Upper Ground, London, SE1 9PJ

USA
Office of Information & Publications
Bureau of Customs, Treasury Department, Washington, DC 20026

Trade Associations

Mail order traders' associations
European Mail Order Traders' Association Head Office
Avenue Ed. Lacomble 17, B-1040 Brussels, Tel: 22 736 0348,
Fax: 22 736 0542

Members of the European Mail Order Traders' Association
Austria
Handelsverbrand
Alser Strasse 45, A-1080 Wien, Tel: 732 7809 230, Fax: 732 7809 669

Belgium
Association des Enterprises de Vente a Distance
Avenue Louise 300 B.14, B-Bruxelles, Tel: 2 647 5991, Fax: 2 647 5046

Denmark
Danse Postordreforening
Rosenvaengeis Affe 25, DK-2100 Copenhague 0, Tel: 35 43 40 07,
Fax: 35 43 04 30

Finland
Suomen Suoramarkkinolntiliito Ry
Henry Fordin Katu 5 M, SF-00150, Helsinki, Tel: 358 0 663 744,
Fax: 358 0 663 772

France
Syndicat des Enterprises de Vente par Correspondence et à Distance
BP 438-08, F-75366, Paris, Cedex 08, Tel: 1 42 56 38 86,
Fax: 1 45 63 91 95

Germany
Bundesverband des Deutschen
Versandhandels e.V., Johann-Klotz-Strasse 12, 6000 Frankfurt 71,
Tel: 69 67 50 47, Fax: 69 67 50 98

Italy
Associazione Nazionale fra Aziende di Vendita per Corrispondenza e a
Distanza
Via Melchiorre Gioia 70, I-20125 Milano, Tel: 2 668 2464,
Fax: 2 688 4525

Netherlands
Nederlandse Postorderbond
Postbus 11578, NL-2502 An Den Haag, Tel: 703 6528 37,
Fax:703 6503 93

Norway
Norsk Postordreforening
Postboks 2475 – Solli, N-0202 Oslo 2, Tel: 255 9500, Fax: 255 8225

Portugal
Associacio Portuguesa de Marketing Directo
R. Rodrigo de Fonsaca 204-4 DT, P-1000 Lisboa, Tel: 1 414 0925,
Fax: 1 414 2308

Spain
Associacion Española de Marketing Directo
Aribau 112, 2 la, E-08036 Barcelona, Tel: 3 323 40 61, Fax: 3 451 42 02

Sweden
Svenska Postorder Foreningen
Box 9, S-51054 Bramhult, Tel: 33 13 17 70, Fax: 33 24 89 34

Switzerland
Verband des Schweizerischen Versandhandels
Brandenbergstrasse 30, CH-8304 Wallisellen-Zurich, Tel: 1 830 16 02,
Fax: 1 230 16 08

United Kingdom
The Mail Order Traders' Association of Great Britain
100 Old Hall Street, Liverpool, L3 9TD, Tel: 051 236 7581
Fax: 051 227 2584

Direct marketing associations
Australia
Australian Direct Marketing Association
7th Floor, 22–30 Bridge Street, PO Box 3982, Sydney, NSW 2000

Canada
Canadian Direct Marketing Association
201 Consumers Road, Willowdale, Ontario, M2J 468

Europe
The European Direct Marketing Association
34 rue du Gouvernment Provisoire, B-1000, Brussels, Tel: 22 217 6309
Fax: 22 217 6985

Hong Kong
Hong Kong Direct Mail & Marketing Association
PO Box 7416, Hong Kong

Japan
Nippon Direct Marketing Association
2-2-15 Minami, Aoyama, Wion Aoyama 337, Minato-Ku, Tokyo 107

New Zealand
New Zealand Direct Marketing Association
PO Box 937, Auckland

UK
The British Direct Marketing Association
Grosvenor Gardens House, Grosvenor Gardens, London, SW1W 0BS

USA
The Direct Marketing Association
6 East 43rd Street, New York, NY 10017, Tel: 212 768 7277

Consumer protection offices
Australia
Department of Consumer Affairs, Tel: 2 286 0006

Canada
The Canadian Council of Better Business Bureaux
2180 Steeles Avenue West, Suite 219, Concord, Ontario, L4K 2Z5
Tel: 416 669 1248

Canadian consumer & corporate affairs offices
These divide the country into five areas:

Consumer & Corporate Affairs Office
1489 Hollis Street, Suite 500, Halifax NS, BSJ 3M5, Tel: 902 426 6080

Consumer & Corporate Affairs Office
Complexe Guy-Favreau, 200 ReneLevesque Boulevard West, Suite 502,
East Tower, Montreal, PQ H2Z 1X4, Tel: 514 496 1797

Consumer & Corporate Affairs Office
Federal Building, 4900 Yonge Street, Toronto ON, M2N 6BB,
Tel: 416 224 4031

Consumer & Corporate Affairs Office
202–260 St Mary Avenue, Winnipeg MB, R3C 0M6, Tel: 204 983 2366

Consumer & Corporate Affairs Office
1400–800 Burrard Street, Vancouver BC, V6Z 2HB,
Tel: 604 666 5000

Hong Kong
Consumer Council
19th Floor, China Hong Kong City, Tower 6, 33 Canton Road, Kowloon,
Tel: 736 3322, Fax: 736 7700

United Kingdom
The Office of Fair Trading
Room 310C, Filed House, 14–25 Breams Buildings, London, EC4A 1PS,
Tel: 071 242 2858

USA
The Council of Better Business Bureaux Inc.
4200 Wilson Boulevard, Arlington, VA 22203, Tel: 703 276 0100

US State consumer protection offices
Alabama Office of Attorney General
Consumer Protection Division, 11 South Union Street, Montgomery,
AL 36130, Tel: 205 242 7334

Alaska Consumer Protection Section
Office of Attorney General, 100 Cushman, Suite 400, Fairbanks,
AK 99701

Arizona Complaint and Information
Office of Attorney General, 1275 W. Washington Street, Phoenix,
AZ 85007, Tel: 602 542 5763

Arkansas Consumer Protection Division
Office of Attorney General, 200 Tower Building, 323 Center Street,
Markham Street, Little Rock, AR 72201, Tel: 501 682 2341

California Public Inquiry Unit Office
PO Box 944255, Sacramento, CA 94244-2550, Tel: 916 322 3360

Colorado Consumer Protection Unit
Office of Attorney General, 110 16th Street, 9th Floor Denver,
CO 80202, Tel: 303 620 4581

Connecticut Department of Consumer Protection
State Office Building, 165 Capitol Avenue, Hartford, CT 06106,
Tel: 203 566 4999

Delaware Division of Consumer Affairs
Department of Community Affairs, 820 North French Street,
Wilmington, DE 19801, Tel: 302 577 3250

District of Columbia Department of Consumer and Regulatory Affairs
614 H. Street NW, Washington, DC 20001, Tel: 202 727 7080

Florida Department of Agriculture and Consumer Services
Division of Consumer Services, 209 Mayo Building, 407 S. Calhoun
Street, Tallahassee, FL 32399, Tel: 904 488 2226

Georgia Office of Consumer Affairs
2 Martin Luther King Jr. Drive, Plaza Level, East Tower, Atlanta,
GA 30334, Tel: 404 656 3790

Hawaii Office of Consumer Protection
Department of Commerce and Consumer Affairs, PO Box 3767,
Honolulu, HI 96812, Tel: 808 586 2630

Idaho Office of Consumer Protection
State House, Room 210, Boise, ID 83720, Tel: 208 334 2400

Illinois Consumer Protection Division
Office of Attorney General, 100 W. Randolph Street, 12th Floor,
Chicago, IL 60601, Tel: 312 814 3580

Indiana Consumer Protection Division
Office of Attorney General, 219 State House, Indianapolis, IN 46204,
Tel: 317 232 6330

Iowa Consumer Protection Division
Office of Attorney General, 1300 E. Walnut, Hoover State Office
Building, Des Moines, IA 50319, Tel: 515 281 5926

Kansas Consumer Protection Division
Office of Attorney General, Kansas Judicial Center, 301 W 10th Street,
2nd Floor, Topeka, KS 66612, Tel: 913 296 3751

Kentucky Consumer Protection Division
Office of Attorney General, 209 Saint Clair Street, Frankfort, KY 40601,
Tel: 502 564 2200

Louisiana Attorney General's Consumer Protection Section
Box 94005, Baton Rouge, LA 70804, Tel: 504 342 7013

Maine Bureau of Consumer and Antitrust Division
State House Station #6, Augusta, ME 04333, Tel: 207 289 3661

Maryland Consumer Protection Division
Office of Attorney General, 200 St Paul Place, Baltimore, MD 21202,
Tel: 301 528 8662

Massachusetts Consumer Protection Division
Department of Attorney General, 131 Tremont Street, 1st Floor, Boston,
MA 02111, Tel: 617 727 8400

Michigan Consumer Protection Division
Office of Attorney General, PO Box 30213, Lansing, MI 48919,
Tel: 517 373 1140

Minnesota Consumer Division
Office of Attorney General, 124 Ford Building, St Paul, MN 55155,
Tel: 612 296 2331

Mississippi Consumer Protection
Office of Attorney General, PO Box 22947, Jackson, MS 39225,
Tel: 601 354 6018

Missouri Trade Offence Division
Office of the Attorney General, PO Box 899, Jefferson City, MO 65102,
Tel: 314 751 3630

Montana Consumer Affairs Unit
Department of Commerce, 1424 Ninth Avenue, Helena, MT 59620,
Tel: 406 444 4312

Nebraska Consumer Protection Division
Attorney General's Office, PO Box 94920, Lincoln, NE 68509

Nevada Northern Region
State Mail Room Complex, Las Vegas, NV 89158, Tel: 702 486 7355

New Hampshire Consumer Protection Bureau
Office of Attorney General, State House Annex, Concord, NH 03301,
Tel: 603 271 3641

New Jersey Division of Consumer Affairs
1207 Raymond Boulevard, 7th Floor, Newark, NJ 07102,
Tel: 201 648 4010

New Mexico Consumer Protection Division
Office of Attorney General, PO Drawer 508, Santa Fe, NM 87504,
Tel: 505 827 6060

New York State Consumer Protection Board
99 Washington Avenue, Room 1020, Albany, NY 12210,
Tel: 518 474 8583

North Carolina Consumer Protection Section
Office of Attorney General, Department of Justice Building, PO Box
629, Raleigh, NC 27602, Tel: 919 733 7741

North Dakota Consumer Fraud/Antitrust Division
Office of Attorney General, 600 E. Boulevard Avenue, Bismarck,
ND 58505, Tel: 701 224 3404

Ohio Consumer Complaint Division
Office of Attorney General, 30 East Broad Street, Columbus, OH 43266,
Tel: 614 466 4986

Oklahoma Consumer Unit
Office of Attorney General, State Capitol Building, Room 112,
Oklahoma City, OK 73105, Tel: 405 521 4274

Oregon Financial Fraud Section
Department of Justice, Justice Building, Salem, OR 97310,
Tel: 503 378 4320

Pennsylvania Bureau of Consumer Protection
Office of Attorney General, Strawberry Square, 14th Floor, Harrisburg,
PA 17120, Tel: 717 787 9707

Rhode Island Consumer Protection Division
Department of Attorney General, 72 Pine Street, Providence, RI 02903,
Tel: 401 277 2104

South Carolina Consumer Affairs Office
Office of Attorney General, PO Box 5757, Columbia, SC 29250,
Tel: 803 734 9462

South Dakota Division of Consumer Affairs
Office of Attorney General, State Capitol Building, 500 East Capitol
Avenue, Pierre, SD 57501, Tel: 605 773 4400

Tennessee Antitrust and Consumer Protection Division
Office of Attorney General, 450 James Robertson Parkway, Nashville,
TN 37219, Tel: 615 741 4737

Texas Consumer Protection Division
Office of Attorney General, PO Box 12548, Capitol Station, Austin,
TX 78711, Tel: 512 463 2070

Utah Division of Consumer Protection
Department of Business Regulation, 160 E. 300 South, Salt Lake City,
UT 84111, Tel: 801 530 6601

Vermont Consumer Assistance Program
Perill Hall, UVM, Burlington, VT 05405, Tel: 802 656 3183

Virginia Office of Consumer Affairs
PO Box 1163, Richmond, VA 23209, Tel: 804 786 2042

Washington Attorney General's Office
Consumer Protection and Antitrust Division, 900 4th Avenue, Room
2000, Seattle, WA 98164, Tel: 206 464 7744

West Virginia Consumer Protection Division
Office of Attorney General, 812 Quarrier Street, 6th Floor, Charleston,
WV 25301, Tel: 304348 8986

Wisconsin Office of Consumer Protection
Department of Justice, PO Box 7856, Madison, WI 53707,
Tel: 608 266 1852

Wyoming Consumer Protection
Office of Attorney General, 123 State Capitol Building, Cheyenne,
WY 82002, Tel: 307 777 6286

Mail order preference schemes
Not all countries yet have such services

Belgium
Association des Enterprises de Vente à Distance
Avenue Louise 300 B.14, B-Bruxelles, Tel: 2 647 5991, Fax: 2 647 5046

France
Union Française du Marketing Direct
60 rue la Boetie, 75008 Paris, Tel: 1 42 56 38 86, Fax: 1 45 63 91 95

Germany
Deutscher Direktmarketing Verband (DDV)
Schiersteinstr 29, W-6200 Wiesbaden, Tel: 611 84 3061,
Fax: 611 80 7921

Netherlands
Direkt Marketing Instituut Nederland
Weerdestein 96, 1083 Amsterdam, Tel: 20 42 95 95, Fax: 20 44 01 99

UK
The Mailing Preference Service
Freepost 22, London, W1E 7EZ, Tel: 071 738 1625, Fax: 071 978 4918

This freepost address is only if you are writing from within the UK,
otherwise use address below:

1 Leeward House, Square Rigger Row, Plantation Wharf, London,
SW11 3TX

USA
DMA's Mail Order Preference Service
PO Box 3861, 11 West 42nd Street, New York, NY 10163-3861

Miscellaneous
UK
Advertising Standards Authority
Brook House, 2–16 Torrington Place, London, WC1E 7HN,
Tel: 071 580 5555

Consumers Association
2 Marylebone Road, London, NW1 4DF, Tel: 071 486 5544

Mail Order Protection Scheme
16 Tooks Court, London, EC4A 1LB, Tel: 071 405 6806

Periodical Publishers Association
Imperial House, 15–19 Kingsway, London, WC2B 6UN,
Tel: 071 379 6268

Harp Electronics
237 Tottenham Court Road, London W1, Tel: 071 436 0022,
For telephone adapters

Douglas Electronics Industries Ltd
55 Eastfield Road, Louth, Lincolnshire, LN11 7AL, Tel: 0507 603643,
Fax: 0507 6000502
For transformers to convert US supply to UK

Running Heads
82 East Dulwich Grove, London, SE22 8TW, Tel/Fax: 071 738 4096
Publish **The Deregulated Phone Book**, £12.95 inclusive of p+p in UK,
£14.00 elsewhere.

UPDATES

Information on international suppliers inevitably goes out of date very quickly. Businesses move, change their policy or even go bust. And of course new companies emerge all the time while others decide that it is, after all, worth their while shipping abroad.

Keeping up with these changes is a continual process and we are constantly both monitoring current entries and looking for new ones.

If you would like to be kept informed of future updates, please write to The Global Shopper, Headline Book Publishing, 338 Euston Road, London NW1 3BH.

READERS' REPORTS

Please also write to us to endorse or criticise an existing entry or to nominate companies for inclusion in next year's guide.

Please send your comments to The Global Shopper, Headline Book Publishing, 338 Euston Road, London NW1 3BH.

Indexes

PRODUCT INDEX

This index can only be a rough guide to the huge range of goods available in the catalogues – a comprehensive listing would fill hundreds of pages. Most items from the Major Catalogues are not given individual references as these are too numerous. Such catalogues sell a very large range of products, from clothes through household goods to electronics and in some cases even cars. They are therefore worth looking at if you want general, brand name goods.

Index of Companies